SAGE was founded in 1965 by Sara Miller McCune to support the dissemination of usable knowledge by publishing innovative and high-quality research and teaching content. Today, we publish over 900 journals, including those of more than 400 learned societies, more than 800 new books per year, and a growing range of library products including archives, data, case studies, reports, and video. SAGE remains majority-owned by our founder, and after Sara's lifetime will become owned by a charitable trust that secures our continued independence.

Los Angeles | London | New Delhi | Singapore | Washington DC | Melbourne

INDIA
in the
UNITED NATIONS

INDIA
in the
UNITED NATIONS

Interplay of Interests
and Principles

C. S. R. MURTHY

Los Angeles | London | New Delhi
Singapore | Washington DC | Melbourne

Copyright © C.S.R. Murthy, 2020

All rights reserved. No part of this book may be reproduced or utilized in any form or by any means, electronic or mechanical, including photocopying, recording or by any information storage or retrieval system, without permission in writing from the publisher.

First published in 2020 by

SAGE Publications India Pvt Ltd
B1/I-1 Mohan Cooperative Industrial Area
Mathura Road, New Delhi 110 044, India
www.sagepub.in

SAGE Publications Inc
2455 Teller Road
Thousand Oaks, California 91320, USA

SAGE Publications Ltd
1 Oliver's Yard, 55 City Road
London EC1Y 1SP, United Kingdom

SAGE Publications Asia-Pacific Pte Ltd
18 Cross Street #10-10/11/12
China Square Central
Singapore 048423

Published by Vivek Mehra for SAGE Publications India Pvt Ltd. Typeset in 10.5/13pt Adobe Caslon Pro by Fidus Design Pvt Ltd, Chandigarh.

Library of Congress Cataloging-in-Publication Data

Name: Murthy, C. S. R. (Changavalli Siva Rama), 1955-
Title: India in the United Nations: interplay of interests and principles / C. S. R. Murthy.
Description: New Delhi, India; Thousand Oaks, California: SAGE Publications India Pvt Ltd, [2020] | Includes bibliographical references and index.
Identifiers: LCCN 2020012823 (print) | LCCN 2020012824 (ebook) | ISBN 9789353883522 (hardback) | ISBN 9789353883539 (epub) | ISBN 9789353883546 (ebk)
Subjects: LCSH: United Nations—India—History. | Security, International—India—History. | India—Foreign relations.
Classification: LCC JX1977.2.I47 M86 2020 (print) | LCC JX1977.2.I47 (ebook) | DDC 341.230954—dc23
LC record available at https://lccn.loc.gov/2020012823
LC ebook record available at https://lccn.loc.gov/2020012824

ISBN: 978-93-5388-352-2 (HB)

SAGE Team: Rajesh Dey, Syed Husain Naqvi

*To the memory of my mentors at JNU,
Professors K. P. Saksena and M. S. Rajan*

Thank you for choosing a SAGE product!
If you have any comment, observation or feedback,
I would like to personally hear from you.

Please write to me at **contactceo@sagepub.in**

Vivek Mehra, Managing Director and CEO, SAGE India.

Bulk Sales

SAGE India offers special discounts
for purchase of books in bulk.
We also make available special imprints
and excerpts from our books on demand.

For orders and enquiries, write to us at

Marketing Department
SAGE Publications India Pvt Ltd
B1/I-1, Mohan Cooperative Industrial Area
Mathura Road, Post Bag 7
New Delhi 110044, India

E-mail us at **marketing@sagepub.in**

Subscribe to our mailing list
Write to **marketing@sagepub.in**

This book is also available as an e-book.

Contents

List of Illustrations   ix
List of Abbreviations   xi
Acknowledgements   xv

1. Introduction to India in the United Nations   1
2. Limitations of Consistency, 1945–1989   6
3. Pragmatic Conservatism during the Unipolar 1990s   23
4. Opportunities and Obstacles for India at the UN in the New Century   47
5. India's Aspiration for Permanent Seat in the Security Council   69
6. India's Experiences as Elected Member of the Security Council   89
7. India's Expectations and Experiences in the UN Peacekeeping Operations   115
8. India–Pakistan Conflict: A Test Case for the UN   143
9. India against International Terrorism at the UN   165
10. Contemporary Development Discourse and Diplomacy of India at the UN   189
11. India's Human Rights Record at the UN   207
12. India's Approach to Multilateral Governance of Internet   232
13. Conclusion: Aligning Interests with Principles   249

Bibliography   260
About the Author   288
Index   289

List of Illustrations

Tables

6.1	Overview of India as Non-Permanent Member	93
6.2	India's Abstentions in the Security Council Votes	94
7.1	India's Participation in the UN Peacekeeping Operations, 1956–2019	117
7.2	India's Troop and Police Contributions, 1991–2019	129
10.1	Aid Flows from OECD DAC Countries, 2000–2018 (in Billion US Dollars)	197
10.2	India's Assessed Contributions to the UN Regular Budget, 2001–2019	200
10.3	India's Voluntary Contributions Pledged to UN Funds and Programmes, 2002–2019	202
10.4	India's Grants and Loans to Foreign Countries, 2008–2019 (in ₹Crores)	203
11.1	Status on India and Core Human Rights Instruments	211
11.2	India and UPR Cycles	225
12.1	The Number of IGOs and INGOs during the Years 1981–2018	236

Box

9.1	Salient Features of India's Revised Draft Counter-Terror Convention	172

List of Abbreviations

AU	African Union
ASEAN	Association of Southeast Asian Nations
BRICS	Brazil, Russia, India, China and South Africa
CAT	Convention against Torture and Other Cruel, Inhuman or Degrading Treatment or Punishment
CCIT	Comprehensive Convention on International Terrorism
CD	Conference on Disarmament
CERD	International Convention on the Elimination of All Forms of Racial Discrimination
CIS	Commonwealth of Independent States
CRC	Convention on the Rights of the Child
CRPD	Convention on the Rights of Persons with Disabilities
CTBT	Comprehensive Test Ban Treaty
CTC	Counter-Terrorism Committee
CTED	Counter-Terrorism Executive Directorate
Doc.	Document
ECOSOC	Economic and Social Council
ECOWAS	Economic Community of West African States
EU	European Union
FATF	Financial Action Task Force
FICHL	Forum for International Criminal and Humanitarian Law
G4	Group of 4 on Security Council Reform
G20	Group of 20
GAOR	General Assembly Official Records
GATT	General Agreement on Tariffs and Trade
GCTS	Global Counter-Terrorism Strategy
HIPC	Heavily Indebted Poor Countries
HRC	Human Rights Council

ICANN	Internet Corporation for Assigned Names and Numbers
ICC	International Criminal Court
ICCPR	International Covenant on Civil and Political Rights
ICESR	International Covenant on Economic, Social and Cultural Rights
ICJ	International Court of Justice (World Court)
ICWA	Indian Council of World Affairs
IDA	International Development Association
IGF	Internet Governance Forum
IGO	Inter-Governmental Organization
ILO	International Labour Organization
IMF	International Monetary Fund
INGO	International Non-Governmental Organization
INSTRAW	UN International Research and Training Institute for the Advancement of Women
IORC	Indian Ocean Rim Countries
ISAF	International Security Assistance Force
ITR	International Telecommunication Regulations
ITU	International Telecommunication Union
MDG	Millennium Development Goals
MEA	Ministry of External Affairs
MONUSCO	UN Organization Stabilization Mission in Democratic Republic of the Congo
NAM	Non-Aligned Movement
NATO	North Atlantic Treaty Organization
NHRC	National Human Rights Commission
NHRIs	National Human Rights Institutions
NIEO	New International Economic Order
NPT	Nuclear Non-Proliferation Treaty
OAS	Organization of American States
ODA	Official Development Assistance
OECD	Organization for Economic Co-operation and Development
OHCHR	Office of High Commissioner for Human Rights
ONUC	UN Operation in Congo
P5	Five Permanent Members of the UNSC

PBC	Peace-Building Commission
PMIUN	Permanent Mission of India to UN, New York/ Geneva
PRST	UN Security Council Presidential Statement
PV	Plenary Verbatim
RES	Resolution
SCO	Shanghai Cooperation Organization
SCOR	Security Council Official Records
SDG	Sustainable Development Goals
SR	Summary Record
UDHR	Universal Declaration of Human Rights
UfC	Uniting for Consensus
UN	United Nations
UNAMA	UN Assistance Mission in Afghanistan
UNAMIR	UN Assistance Mission in Rwanda
UNAMSIL	UN Mission in Sierra Leone
UNCHR	UN Commission on Human Rights
UNCIP	UN Commission on India and Pakistan
UNCIRP	UN Committee on Internet-Related Policies
UNCTAD	UN Conference on Trade and Development
UNDOF	UN Disengagement Observer Force
UNDP	UN Development Programme
UNEF	UN Emergency Force
UNEP	UN Environment Programme
UNFCCC	UN Framework Convention on Climate Change
UNFICYP	UN Force in Cyprus
UNFPA	UN Fund for Population Activities
UNGA	UN General Assembly
UNHCR	UN High Commissioner for Refugees
UNICEF	UN Children's Fund
UNIFEM	UN Development Fund for Women
UNIFIL	UN Interim Force in Lebanon
UNIPOM	UN India-Pakistan Observer Mission
UNMEE	UN Mission in Ethiopia and Eritrea
UNMIL	UN Mission in Liberia
UNMISS	UN Mission in South Sudan
UNMOGIP	UN Military Observer Group in India and Pakistan

UNODC	UN Office on Drugs and Crime
UNOSOM	UN Operation in Somalia
UNRWA	UN Relief and Works Agency
UNSC	UN Security Council
UNSG	UN Secretary-General
UNPROFOR	UN Protection Force
UNTAG	UN Transition Assistance Group in Namibia
UNTSO	UN Truce Supervision Organization
UNV	UN Volunteers
UPR	Universal Periodic Review
WCIT	World Conference on International Telecommunications
WFP	World Food Programme
WIPO	World Intellectual Property Organization
WMDs	Weapons of mass destruction
WSIS	World Summit on the Information Society
WTO	World Trade Organization

Acknowledgements

I wish to recall the encouragement and support I received from several sources while working on this book. Foremost, I would like to pay my respectful tributes to Late Professor K. P. Saksena and Late Professor M. S. Rajan, who had unfailing faith in my potential and imbued in me enduring values which guide me professionally and personally even today. Although this book is a reflection of ideas and thoughts accumulated during the past nearly three and a half decades of my teaching and research experience principally at Jawaharlal Nehru University (JNU), the writing of the book was partly undertaken during the period of my sabbatical leave in the academic year 2018–2019. I wish to record my appreciation to my university for this reason. At the same time, my colleagues in the Centre for International Politics, Organization and Disarmament had willingly shouldered duties on my behalf in my absence. Besides, many of them have shown great interest in the progress of this work. I am thankful to them too. Again, I wish to acknowledge the encouragement and inspiration I received constantly from my dear friend and colleague, Professor B. S. Chimni.

The original versions of four chapters in the present book were previously published. In this connection, I wish to express my sincere thanks to *International Studies*, a journal of the School of International Studies, JNU, for readily permitting to include in this book an updated version of my articles previously published there. Similarly, sincere thanks are due to Professor P. Sahadevan and Professor Ankush Sawant in whose edited volumes of 2001 and 2010 respectively, the original versions of Chapters 8 and 6 appeared. They generously gave me the required permission. Likewise, Chapter 3 is the modified version of the chapter written for a volume edited by late Professor Nalini Kant Jha in 2000. Needless to say, they all have been thoroughly modified and updated.

I am thankful to the anonymous reviewer for the very positive and constructive feedback, which helped me to strengthen parts of my arguments in the book. I owe a word of hearty thanks to SAGE as well for their active professional assistance through all stages of the present publication.

On a personal note, my family—Annapurna, Aditya and Ashish—showed admirable understanding and patience while I was busy with the writing part. Finally, on this occasion, I cannot help but fondly remember my mother (who passed away in early 2019) for her eternal affection and love.

CHAPTER 1

Introduction to India in the United Nations

India's enmeshment in international organizations is remarkable. India is associated with nearly 3,700 international organizations including 200 intergovernmental ones, as per the latest statistics compiled by the Brussels-based Union of International Associations. Further, secretariats of 169 organizations are located in India. India enjoys the 26th position overall. Notably, it is the most international organizations-entangled country, next only to Brazil from Global South leaving China behind. This should not in any way brush aside the cautious approach India adopts to the civil society actors in relation to the sovereignty principle.

By virtue of its growing profile in the recent decades, India's role in world politics naturally generates a good deal of interest in India and outside. But the nature and nuances of the country's participation in the political processes at the United Nations (UN) are limited to momentary, if superficial, attention in scholarly and opinion-making circles. Numerous former practitioners have published their accounts pertaining to their period of service, mostly dwelling on security aspects. This limitation in general applies to book-length studies by scholars also, although in the recent one or two decades even such scholarly publications are found to be scarce. This book is an attempt to address the perceived gap to provide a holistic and systematic understanding of India's long and rich association with the UN ever since it was established 75 years ago. Notably, publication of this book coincides with the special occasion of completion of 75 years of UN activities with which India's association predates its independence.

The basic thrust of the analysis in the book is to argue that India's commitment to the larger principles of the international community as represented by the UN has not been, and cannot realistically be, either complete or consistent. Rather, India's diplomatic effort has always been to better align the UN principles to suit its interests and, if necessary, to privilege its interests over principles. On the whole, the interplay between interests and principles in India's role provides a window view to the successes and setbacks in the country's foreign policy conduct at the UN forums. And surely, the book is not about ranking the performance of one government over others, but to portray a continuing interplay between India's interests and international norms.

Among the leading mainstream international relations theories, Realist and Liberal schools offer contrasting perspectives on the understanding of why states need international organizations like the UN. While the realist perspective perceives international organizations as entirely dependent on the power of dominant states and help the sustenance of existing systemic balance, the liberal scholarship would explain why states bestow a measure of authority to international organizations to optimize their interests in a cooperative mode for framing and monitoring rules of compliance effectively in a given issue area. On the other hand, the constructivist theory emphasizes ideational and non-material aspects and allows agency to international organizations facilitating social communication among actors for framing and reframing identities, values and interests of states. Broadly, it is the liberal and constructivist lenses that the author would like to use for analysing the priorities, policies and outcomes of India's performance in the UN.

The precise details of the elements of the book have progressively evolved differently from what was intended at the initial planning stage.

The discussion presently is organized in the form of 11 substantive chapters, besides Introduction and Concluding Observations. These 11 chapters broadly belong to three strands that encompass historical, institutional and substantive issue areas of contemporary relevance and concern to India's role at the UN. Chapters 2 and 3 respectively dwell on the general directions of India's participation in the Cold War era and in the early years of the post-Cold War UN. Notably, Chapter 2 tries to capture the purposes and priorities pursued by the governments headed by Jawaharlal Nehru and his familial successors, viz. Indira Gandhi and Rajiv Gandhi. Chapter 3 takes up major dilemmas of post-Cold War India evident in its encounters at the world body in the shadow of American unipolarity, particularly in the 1990s. Chapter 4 extensively discusses the breadth of issue areas India has addressed at the UN bodies in the 21st century with reference to major inter- and intrastate armed conflicts, non-traditional threats to security, aspects of nuclear disarmament, environment protection and sustainable development in the era of globalization, and the question of strengthening the role of the UN to deliver better on the growing needs of the member countries.

The second set of chapters focuses on India's experiences in the UN Security Council (UNSC) and its aspirations to be a permanent member of that body when enlarged. Chapter 5 attempts a critical evaluation of the structural design of the Council as a context for the case to make the Council more democratic and representative in its composition and functioning. The thrust of the chapter is to discuss the criteria India suggests for expansion of both the permanent and non-permanent member category seats by virtue of which its claim would become quite obvious, the bilateral and multilateral strategies launched in pursuance of the aspiration ever since it was publicly articulated some 25 years ago, and the major factors that account for lack of breakthrough on this question so far. The next chapter is a related one: India's role as a non-permanent member of the Security Council, ever since it was first elected for a two-year term beginning in 1950. The seven times it served so far yield interesting, if not important, trends and patterns of India's approaches to the role of principles in resolving peace and security problems, the extent of pragmatism it brought in relation to various questions and the tool kit it had put to use. By and large, India emerges as a bridge builder not as an outlier.

The third set comprises six chapters addressing specific issue areas of contemporary and historical significance to India's role at the UN. They range from India–Pakistan conflict, international peacekeeping, the problem of international terrorism, protection of human rights, the issue of Internet governance, and economic and sustainable development. Chapter 7 examines India's policy choices regarding participation in the UN peacekeeping operations, the trends in the contemporary phase of its troop and civilian police contributions, and the grievances India has regarding planning and management of those operations. Chapter 8 looks at the India–Pakistan long-standing conflict from the UN perspective to discern how and why the UN responded to complicated issues involved by eschewing blame game against either country and by taking up field-based and political conciliation work based on common points in the claims made by each side mainly on the Kashmir question, followed by a deeply disappointed India's deliberate policy to keep the UN away from its problems with neighbouring countries. Chapter 9 touches upon India's attempts to prioritize action against international terrorism through the UN instrumentality, and the extent to which its strategy to delegitimize terrorism as an instrument of state policy has played out while the problems its initiative on comprehensive convention against international terrorism continue to persist.

Chapter 10 focuses on India's development diplomacy at the UN, with particular reference to its efforts to speak for the needs of the small developing and island countries, its criticism of the failure of advanced countries to meet the agreed levels of official development assistance (ODA) or the persistent denial of access to the markets of developed countries for products of developing countries, and India's growing profile as provider of financial support to the development and humanitarian activities of numerous UN agencies. Chapter 11 deals with the touchy issue of human rights and India's perspectives on institutional and substantive questions concerning the functioning of the newly created Human Rights Council. The chapter specifically dwells on the three cycles of Universal Periodic Review (UPR) on India's human rights record in the Council. Chapter 12 takes up for discussion the phenomenon of global governance, particularly the much contested area of Internet governance, and the positions India has adopted in the recent years to balance its security concerns with the legitimate interests of user groups.

Chapter 13 offers a set of concluding observations on how India's participation has sought to aim at beneficial interplay between its interests and larger principles of interstate conduct in the wide range of questions. Finally, a word of clarification is in order. While most chapters are written for the book, Chapters 2, 6 and 8 represent extensively modified and updated versions of previously published chapters in edited volumes. And Chapter 12 is updated version of an article published in *International Studies*.

CHAPTER 2

Limitations of Consistency, 1945–1989

The activities of the UN during the first 45 years of existence were coloured in many ways by the system-wide tumult dominated by the military and ideological rivalry between the United States and the former Soviet Union. Given this constraining systemic feature, India as a newly independent country had experienced the dilemma of making a choice between two alternative options, viz. seizing opportunities to claim a role in world politics by strongly supporting the UN or getting deeply dissatisfied with the organization's inability or unwillingness to do things as per its preferences. Therefore, it would be inaccurate to say that the Cold War phase of India's approach to, and engagement with, the UN is devoid of any inconsistency.

In these years, India has stabilized as a mature democracy with leadership provided by certain strong personalities as prime ministers in the execution of country's policy towards the UN. This policy is guided principally by two factors, viz. the changing geopolitical conditions in the neighbourhood and the personality of the incumbent prime ministers (Mathur 1995: 71–73). These 45 years in Indian politics were dominated by three prime ministers belonging to what is commonly dubbed as Nehru–Gandhi era. While Prime Minister Jawaharlal Nehru held the external affairs portfolio also, his successors assigned the job to senior colleagues. But, as it turned out, both the familial political heirs of Nehru—whether it was Indira Gandhi or Rajiv Gandhi—took more than ordinary interest in foreign policy matters.

Since the UN was born roughly two years before India's independence, a reference to this initial transitional period would be instructive. India was a participant in the San Francisco Conference that negotiated and approved the UN Charter during April–June 1945. Although it was a colony, India was granted original membership of the organization, presumably in recognition of the notable contribution to the effort to win the World War. Surely the British colonial masters expected India to serve solely the British imperial interests during deliberations in respect of critical questions concerning the organizational design at the conference. The official delegation named by Britain limited itself to raising relatively minor issues, but essentially supporting the positions taken by the four sponsoring Powers. Mahatma Gandhi had strong views on the nature of the official delegation. He is quoted to have said: 'Either India at San Francisco is represented by an elected representative, or not at all' (Rajan 1973: 434). It is of course true that an unofficial delegation was sent by the Indian National Congress, but it did not get direct access to the official proceedings whereas it succeeded in garnering support to the freedom movement. The Indian nationalist opinion was convinced that the Anglo-American design of the UN in San Francisco 'would simply retain old imperial systems and race-based politics' (Bhagavan 2013: 2). Further point of critical appraisal related to the trusteeship concept, which only aimed to maintain the status quo through a new technique of administration, rather than widening the system of freedom of dependent peoples (ICWA 1957: 24). In short, the UN normative and institutional framework is an inheritance from the colonial era. From the nationalist perspective, the official India's performance in the making of the Charter was quite blunt. For instance, a leading national daily, *The Hindu*, bemoaned that

> India has been a good little boy among the 45 delegates never saying an improper thing likely to offend Britain and the other Big Four, meek and content to stand and wait, because that too is service. She has lost an opportunity which will never come again. To put it

mildly, India's role during the initial months of the United Nations was an unfair legacy inherited by independent India. (Rajan 1973: 456)

Then, by the time the first session of the General Assembly was half way through, Jawaharlal Nehru took over first as the vice president in the interim government in 1946, and later as the country's first Prime Minister, with the longest ever innings until his death in 1964.

The Nehru Years: Coupling Commitment to the UN and the Compulsion of Safeguarding Interests

A perspective on India's participation in the UN in the early years needs to be traced to the Nehruvian ideas and inclinations, which essentially emanate from his eloquent articulation of non-aligned or independent foreign policy, the pursuit of which made the UN an invaluable tool. In his radio address after assuming office, Nehru laid out the path ahead for the country in foreign affairs (Nehru 1961: 2):

> We shall take full part in international conferences as a free nation with our own policy and not merely as a satellite of another nation. We hope to develop close and direct contacts with other nations and to cooperate with them in the furtherance of world peace and freedom.... We believe that peace and freedom are indivisible and the denial of freedom anywhere must endanger freedom elsewhere and lead to conflict and war. We are particularly interested in the emancipation of colonial and dependent countries and peoples, and in the recognition in theory and practice of equal opportunities for all races. We repudiate the Nazi doctrine or racialism wherever and in whatever manner it may be practiced. We propose, as far as possible, to keep away from the power politics of groups, aligned against one another which have led in the past to world wars and which may again lead to disasters of even vaster scale.

Nehru's India began with a conscious effort to synchronize national policy principles with the collective goals of the world community as enshrined in the UN Charter. Therefore, working towards realization of the purposes of the UN implied implementation of India's foreign policy goals. In other words, a strong and effective UN was in harmony with India's national and larger interests. Nehru shared his vision about the country's role in the UN, during his speech at the Columbia University, New York, in 1949 thus:

> Towards the United Nations, India's attitude is that of wholehearted cooperation and unreserved adherence, in both spirit and letter, to the Charter governing it. To that end India will participate fully in its various activities and endeavour to play that role in its councils to which her geographical position, and contribution towards peaceful progress entitle her. (quoted in ICWA 1957: 27–28)

India was conscious of the iniquitous and undesirable structural features of the international system, which may be beyond the capability of the UN to swiftly alter. The UN could only be an instrument of peaceful change howsoever piecemeal that change might be. The UN has the potential of playing a helpful role in such basic objectives as protection of human rights, liberation of dependent peoples and development of economically disadvantaged countries. However, India's shortcomings in terms of military/economic power were too glaring to enable it to aspire for a major say in the management of world affairs; hence, India perceived the UN as an 'incomparable vehicle of communication' to bank upon its long historical, cultural heritage for projecting moral leadership (Berkes and Bedi 1958: 33). The need to achieve India's high visibility necessitated what was called 'airy idolization' (Rana 1970: 52) of the UN. Nehru, in an address to the General Assembly in November 1948, said: 'Let no one think that any nation, any community can misbehave. The United Nations is here to prevent any fear or hurt' (Nehru 1948).

In regard to the maintenance of international peace and security, India believed that the UN should emphasize peaceful methods of mutual accommodation and understanding through negotiations directly or with the help of third party. This belief prompted Indian leaders to flag the problem of ill-treatment of people of Indian origin in South Africa on racial grounds, in the very first session of the

General Assembly. As history bears out, this initiative became the stepping stone for waging a long struggle against apartheid with the active UN endorsement till the racist regime collapsed decades later. Similarly, India lost no time to bring to the fore the economic development needs of the poor countries in the Economic and Social Council when it was elected as the organ's first president. Indian economists proposed inception of the UN Economic Development Administration in 1949 to finance growth in less developed countries; the idea resulted finally in the inception of technical assistance window within the UN and a soft lending agency outside. The reference here is to the UN Development Programme (UNDP) and the International Development Association. Besides, Nehru's sister, Vijaya Lakshmi Pandit, a familiar personality as a leader of Indian delegation, was elected as the president of the 1953 General Assembly session. In the area of disarmament, nuclear arms race was sought to be arrested by an out-of-box suggestion in 1954 for halting all types of nuclear tests. This led a decade later to the signing of the Partial Test Ban Treaty to outlaw nuclear tests in under water, outer space and in the atmosphere in 1963. India was among the first to ratify the treaty (Jaipal 1986).

At the height of the Cold War, India under Nehru's leadership carved out a special place for advocacy of moderation in maintaining international peace and security. The Indian perspectives mattered much not only in bringing a ring of moral authority, but also in seeking to expand the influence of the UN on ground. The Korean conflict during 1950–1953 presented India the first opportunity to advocate a non-confrontationist approach to easing problems between the competing camps of the West and the East. India expressed reservations on the 'Uniting for Peace' move to substitute the Security Council with the General Assembly to take necessary measures on matters unresolved in the Council owing to the veto exercised by the Soviet Union. India recommended reconciliation with Communist China to find a way out of the military deadlock in Korea. On the other hand, India mobilized the Afro-Asian countries into a single coalition to give vent to their collective voice. The respect India has come to earn is represented by the fact that India was named chairman of the Neutral Nations Repatriation Commission in 1953 to facilitate smooth exchange of prisoners. Hence, the Korea episode showed to India the potential of the non-aligned approach to making the world safe for peace.

An extension of this approach happened in the wake of the Suez crisis in 1956. India firmly held that Egypt's territorial sovereignty was inviolable and hence the invading foreign troops must withdraw. The modus operandi to achieve the objective was the establishment of a non-fighting, non-partisan UN force. India was active in making the idea work and contributing the second largest contingent to the UN Emergency Force (UNEF) until the force was withdrawn in 1967. In this project, Indian diplomats earned the esteem from the UN Secretary-General (UNSG), the United States and the Arab countries. It was indeed true that the Indian opinion was equated with the Afro-Asian opinion—an acknowledgement of India's influence amongst the small, newly independent and non-aligned members during those testing times. This set the stage soon for the biggest UN operation to preserve the sovereignty and integrity of the newly emerged Congo from a deadly combination of foreign aggression, secession and internal factional strife. Here again India occupied the centre stage both at the headquarters and in the field. Nehru took personal interest in standing by the Secretary-General during the times of polarization within Africa and between the East–West rivals. As Secretary-General Dag Hammarskjold acknowledged, the UN could not conceive of a single conflict situation which could be defused without the constructive cooperation from countries such as India. In this light, it may well be stated that the 1950s and the early 1960s signified the zenith of India's active role in the UN in the Cold War era.

On the flip side, it must be added that India's hope to play the UN card in the Jammu and Kashmir question did not work as much. Apparently, India nursed high expectations from the UN that it would be able to offer a quick and favourable disposal of its complaint against Pakistan, which illegally and forcibly occupied one-third of Kashmir (Gupta 1966). Nehru took great interest in putting the focus of India's complaint to the UNSC to ensure that Pakistan is called upon to desist from assisting the tribesmen, although Lord Mountbatten would have liked the complaint to be more general (Gopal 1979: 21–22). As an expression of faith in the fairness of the UN, the lieutenants of Nehru representing the matter in the Security Council were exuberant about their claim of 'high statesmanship'. Going beyond the mere 'wish', expressed originally in the letter appended to the accession instrument, to a reference to the people of Kashmir for approval after restoration of normalcy by clearing the land of invaders, the Security Council was told of the country's willingness to hold a plebiscite under the supervision of UN. Further,

> the question of future status of Kashmir vis-à-vis her neighbours and the world at large, or a further question, namely, whether she should withdraw her accession to India, and either accede to Pakistan or remain independent with a right to claim admission as a Member of the United Nations—all this we have recognized to be a matter for unfettered decision by the people of Kashmir, after normal life is restored. (Deora and Grover 1991: 103)

Instead of blaming one or the other party for causing the military action, the Council members explored a common ground between the claims and counter claims of both sides so as to provide hopefully a basis for further efforts at resolving the problem amicably. A commission was sent to the area, which worked out a ceasefire arrangement followed by the deployment of a military observer group along the ceasefire line in 1949. Further, conditions were sought to be created to hold a plebiscite or bring a mediated solution without a plebiscite during the years 1948–1953 (Murthy 1989).

The matter procrastinated reaching a dead end, thereby causing a great deal of annoyance among Indians about the sidelining of the original complaint for eviction of illegal occupation by Pakistani tribesmen from occupied Kashmir. In spite of the clear priority given in the UN resolution in August 1948 as the first step required for conduct of the proposed plebiscite, Pakistan refused to vacate fearing that it might mean forsaking whatever claims it has over Jammu and Kashmir by virtue of possession of a part of the territory. Nehruvian India turned its ire on the role of power politics in the Security Council for the delay to get Pakistan forces out. Nevertheless, critics blamed India too for mishandling the matter at the UNSC (Bandyopadhyaya 1980: 295; Saksena 1978: 812–814).

Since the blame game has gained greater currency in the present times, it may be pertinent to ask if Nehru had before him options better than going to the UNSC. Based on various constructions of events of those days, it may be possible to surmise about three alternative courses of action in 1947–1948, viz. to continue with the military operations against Pakistan to take back the occupied areas, or secondly to elicit the popular opinion on accession through elections without involving any foreign supervision, and third do-nothing, that is, avoid going to the UN—all of which have strong nationalistic connotations compared to the UN option. The military option was easier said than could be accomplished, as was clear already due to the military stalemate in the field. Besides, it is doubtful if the international community (i.e. the UN) would have just remained unconcerned with the continued India–Pakistan military escalation. Then, the second option of organizing the promised reference to the Kashmiris on the question of accession without involvement of any external quarters, including the UN, was stillborn as no constitutional mechanism existed to organize such an exercise credibly. Finally, it is doubtful if the third option to do nothing, thereby expecting time to take care of the problem of Kashmir, was viable at all. If India did not go to the UN, Pakistan would have, as it was hinted during the stalemated bilateral talks in November–December 1947 (Murthy 2002: 190–191).

On the other hand, raising the matter at the Security Council and an offer to conduct a plebiscite soon after intruders leave did not seem to be naïve or misplaced idealism. Nehru rued that the question would have been settled long ago, but for the pro-Pakistan intrigues by the United Kingdom. Indeed his resentment against, and distrust of, the UN had become so strong by the mid-1950s that he advised President Nasser of Egypt (before the outbreak of the war in October 1956 against Israel) not to commit the mistake he did years earlier by referring the Suez Canal nationalization dispute to the UNSC for a settlement (Gopal 1979: 279). It was quite possible that he made the bold offer of a plebiscite under the UN supervision on the basis of two assumptions: one that a plebiscite would be held without delay, and secondly, given the political complexion in the State of Jammu and Kashmir at that time, the outcome would certainly be in India's favour. These core calculations were packaged in the language of high statesmanship to allow also a Pakistani option and even the option of independence to Kashmiris. Perhaps, the independence option was a ploy to frighten the spoilers (like Britain and also Pakistan) about the strategic logjam they might land in if Jammu and Kashmir became independent (Murthy 1989: 141–163).

In the midst of continuing deadlock at the UN, a safe option for Nehru to protect India's national interest was to set in motion the strategy of resetting the road map to rescind the very idea of the UN-supervised plebiscite. The job was executed with characteristic finesse and filibustering by Nehru's long-time aide and friend, Krishna Menon, in the Security Council in January 1957. Menon hammered home the point—a point notably acknowledged by the UN mediator, Gunnar Jarring—that the conditions in which the offer of plebiscite was made had long changed. Therefore, the plebiscite offer could not be deemed as open to be availed in an indefinite time frame without reference to the changing circumstances at all. Arguing that Kashmir's accession to India in 1947 was 'full and final', Menon reminded the Council that the original intention was a wish on the part of the Indian government to make a reference to the people, which need not necessarily mean only a plebiscite. In Menon's own inimitable words, a reference 'might be a referendum, it might be a plebiscite, it might be a general election, it might be a Gallup Poll; it might be anything' (Deora and Grover 1991: 52–53).

Menon's elaborate attempt at retraction from the earlier commitment was no aberration. Another major action to signal the shift towards asserting national interest even if it contradicted its traditional advocacy of non-use of force erupted in December 1961 when forces were sent to liberate the Portuguese 'colony', Goa. When the Western members (as a mark of support to Portugal) sought to denounce India's coercive action in an emergency meeting of the Council, Ambassador C. S. Jha asserted that India would do what is in its vital interest, 'Charter or no Charter, Council or no Council.' This symbolized in a way, India's disgust with, and distrust of, the reliability of UN mechanism in safeguarding its vital interests (Jha 1983: 150–164). India's stubbornness was hailed by the African hard-line anti-colonial countries, besides of course the Soviet Union.

Indira Gandhi's Preference to Use the UN Only When It Suited India's Interests

The successors of Nehru faced the pressing need to address domestic issues, rather than playing a larger than life role in defusing world conflicts. Diplomats became cognizant of the limitations of disproportionate dependence on moral and political principles alone to carve out a place in world politics without regard to 'the food we cannot produce, the population we cannot control and the borders we cannot protect without relying heavily on others' (Rana 1970: 71). The new thinking influenced the country's cautious response on numerous occasions. India chose to keep off the new peacekeeping operations dispatched to Cyprus (1964), Golan Heights and Sinai (1973) and Lebanon (1978). While India began the efforts for beefing up its security capabilities in the aftermath of the humiliating defeat in the 1962 war, the shock upset encouraged Pakistan to strike for completing an unfinished task of seizing Kashmir by subterfuge in 1965. When the conflict escalated into a full-scale war, again the Security Council and the Secretary-General entered the scene in October 1965. It is necessary to recall that the Indian foreign minister dramatically staged a walk out in protest against the derogatory remarks made by his Pakistani counterpart. According to an official who was intimately involved in the planning and execution of that dramatic move, the object was to 'drive it home to all concerned that the United Nations does not matter as it did earlier' (cited in Kochanek 1980: 53). Notably, that action ensured that there was actually no reference to Kashmir in any of the Council's resolutions passed in 1965.

During the premiership of Indira Gandhi during the years 1966–1984 (with a break of two and half years due to electoral defeat in 1977), there were mixed trends which partly tended to reject any attempt by the international community to restrict its policy options and continue to keep the UN at a distance in national security matters with a consequential—but robustly pronounced—tilt towards bilateralism. Authors saw a global-Indian 'hiatus' in the early years of Mrs Gandhi's rule (Mukherjee and Malone 2011: 314). India refused to be a party to the 1968 Nuclear Non-Proliferation Treaty (NPT) because it meant foregoing the nuclear option forever. The principled argument to justify its pragmatic position was that the unequal treaty froze the privileged status of nuclear weapon powers and discriminated against non-nuclear weapon states. In the same vein, India did not hesitate to cast a negative vote year after year against Pakistan's popular resolution calling for establishment of a nuclear-weapon-free zone in South Asia in the aftermath of India's underground nuclear explosion in 1974. Essentially intended to keep its nuclear option open (Murthy 1993: 106–136), India pointed out that South Asia could not be isolated from presence of nuclear weapons in its neighbourhood (meaning China), and that a proposal of that kind should have first achieved consensus among all relevant countries.

At the same time, perhaps in a clever variation from the past, Indira Gandhi-led diplomacy worked to selectively use the UN to its advantage. Indira Gandhi personally attended the Stockholm Conference on Environment in 1972 to assert that poverty was the greatest polluter and therefore the route to environment protection lay through the removal of poverty and economic development. Similarly, major powers were forced to concede that nuclear disarmament was the urgent need as the final document agreed at the first special session of the General Assembly on disarmament in 1978 acknowledged. India, as a non-permanent member, succeeded in building consensus on a Security Council resolution imposing mandatory arms embargo against the racist regime of South Africa (Jaipal 1978f). In another major initiative, India worked through the non-aligned group to press for turning the Indian Ocean into a peace zone, thereby seeking to ensure the danger from the growing military activity by the outside major naval powers, such as the United States in the region. But then the Indian tactic became futile when Kampuchea and Afghanistan emerged as regional flashpoints in the 1980s due to intervention by regional countries rather than due to the activities of extra-regional naval powers (Murthy 1993: 79–105).

But the big episode during Indira Gandhi's tenure is the liberation of East Pakistan and the emergence of Bangladesh as a separate nation after India–Pakistan war in December 1971. Here is a brilliant example of India using the UN in tune with its plans to keep focus on the role of the international community to pressurize Pakistan to end peacefully the unprecedented scale of refugee crisis in East Pakistan, and simultaneously guard against adoption of an unwelcome call for ceasefire prior to successful conclusion of military operations. To this end, Indira Gandhi visited various foreign capitals, but knowing that India's appeals were not gaining sufficient traction, she swiftly stitched up a treaty of friendship with the Soviet Union in August 1971. This ensured the Soviet backing to India in the event the conflict over East Pakistan was raised in the UNSC. Indeed, the Soviet vetoes thwarted all attempts by the US–China combine to adopt a resolution blaming India for the December 1971 war, till actually a unilateral ceasefire was declared by India after surrender of Pakistani troops in Dhaka (Murthy 1993: 53–73). The Council was left with no option but to take note of the changed ground reality presented through the emergence of independent Bangladesh, and equally importantly acquiesce in the changes brought about to the UN-monitored ceasefire line in Jammu and Kashmir as a result of the war. In short, it was largely an impressive demonstration of military and diplomatic strategy working in tandem. As an aside, it should be acknowledged that the role of Sardar Swaran Singh as foreign affairs minister in the Council during both the 1965 and 1971 wars was an asset. On the other hand, however, there was an unpleasant, if not unexpected development (therefore somewhat sub-optimally managed) when the United States invoked the Uniting for Peace resolution to implore the General Assembly for immediate attention. Brushing aside India's pleas, the General Assembly voted a resolution with a huge majority to call for an immediate end to the ongoing war while at the same time cautioning against any change in the territorial status quo of Pakistan through use of force. There the absence of Soviet veto was a clear disadvantage to India.

The memory of the Soviet support to India in 1971 lasted long to motivate a thankful Indian leadership to support the Soviet Union's military intervention in Afghanistan in December 1979, even though it was a clear violation of the Charter. The diplomatic representatives in New York were instructed to brazenly defend the Soviet military intervention in Afghanistan in the emergency session of the General Assembly. This ill-advised action clearly amounted to breaking of ranks with most of the non-aligned and Islamic countries, thereby allowing Pakistan to take full advantage of the cleavage and benefit hugely from massive military and economic aid from the Western countries. This was one of the costliest mistakes committed by Indira Gandhi's government (Saksena 1981: 98).

Rajiv Gandhi's Susceptibilities and Statesmanship

Rajiv Gandhi took over the reins of the Indian government after his mother's unfortunate assassination in October 1984. He consolidated his grip on the party and governance after winning an unprecedented mandate owing to sympathy factor. He sought to bring fresh air to domestic governance and foreign affairs. To cite an example, Rajiv Gandhi in his address to the US Congress in June 1985 extended full support to UNSG's peace efforts in Afghanistan and declined to fish in troubled waters of the Afghan situation – an indication that he was willing to deviate from his predecessor's predilections. (This could partly be attributed to the changing mood in the new leadership of the Soviet Communist Party.) As a corollary to this, India's permanent representative pleaded in 1989 full support for a bigger role by the UN in the implementation of Geneva Accords. Around the same time, India ended its two decades long spell of absence from the UN peacekeeping by agreeing to contribute troops to help end the Iraq–Iran war and Namibia's transition to independence from South Africa.

There was also a parallel streak in Rajiv Gandhi's approach. He seemed to aim to reintroduce Nehruvian touch to the foreign policy and craft an image of world's young and modernist statesman. He utilized the earliest opportunity to go to the UN General Assembly (UNGA) in 1985, which coincided with the 40th anniversary of the organization. Among others, three issues were highlighted in his address in the Assembly: firstly, environment protection, understandable in the light of Bhopal gas disaster and Chernobyl nuclear leak accident and secondly, cooperation to end the menace of terrorism (justifiable on the ground that India's serving prime minister was felled by bullets fired by her personal security guards in retaliation to her decision to send armed forces to evict the pro-Khalistan extremists from the precincts of the Golden Temple in Amritsar, Punjab.)

And thirdly, he pledged support to nuclear disarmament by reinforcing the Delhi Declaration issued by six nations from five continents calling for an immediate halt to the testing, development and production of nuclear weapons and their delivery systems, which would eventually lead to elimination of weapons of mass destruction (WMDs). He called his mission a 'crusade for peace, freedom and equality' (Gandhi 1985: 32–40). He went to the General Assembly two years later to highlight the twin issues of environment and development (Gandhi 1987: 42–50). Encouraged by positive developments, such as the agreement to eliminate intermediate-range and short-range nuclear missiles (INF Treaty) between the superpowers in 1987, Prime Minister Rajiv Gandhi attended the 1988 special session of the General Assembly on disarmament to debunk the rationale offered by the advocates of nuclear deterrence that nuclear weapons once invented cannot be eliminated. He went on to offer a very bold 'Action Plan' for 'elimination of all nuclear weapons in three stages, over the next 22 years beginning now' (Gandhi 1988: 14). The plan advocated a moratorium on nuclear arms race, negotiation on an international convention on making use or threat of nuclear weapons illegal, and revision of the NPT to 'give legal effect to the binding commitment of nuclear weapon states to eliminate all nuclear weapons by the year 2010, and of all the non-nuclear weapon states not to cross the nuclear weapons threshold' (Gandhi 1988: 7–16). While the initiative was hailed as world statesman-like, it was predictably cold-shouldered by the nuclear weapon powers. Perhaps the lack of progress on the plan might have made it inevitable for India to decide to cross the threshold a decade later.

Turning attention to another dimension, it is important to point out that Rajiv Gandhi's actions at times showed susceptibility to come under the American pressure. In April 1986, the US Air Force bombed the presidential building in the capital city of Libya as punishment for protecting those of its nationals charged with terror attacks in Western cities. Participating in the Security Council meeting on the issue both on the country's behalf and on behalf of the non-aligned foreign ministers, the then foreign minister, Bali Ram Bhagat:

> Strongly condemned this dastardly, blatant and unprovoked sort of aggression against a fellow non-aligned country, which constituted a violation of international law and of the principles of the United Nations Charter, and endangered international peace and security. This act of aggression by the United States was all the more condemnable since, by virtue of its position as a permanent member of the Security Council, it has primary responsibility for the maintenance of international peace and security and to abide by the principles of the Charter of the United Nations. (Bhagat 1986: 9–10)

The United States reacted with indignation over the entirely one-sided and unforgivable language used in the name of non-alignment. The immediate fall out of the face off was the unceremonious removal of Bhagat from the Union Cabinet. It was done to mollify the United States, if the secret papers of the American intelligence agency were to be believed (Haidar and Bhattacharjee 2017).

Recapitulation

Based on the above discussion, it may be argued that India was responsible enough not to question the organizational framework of the UN which was created before it gained independence. Free India under Jawaharlal Nehru's premiership desired to actively work in the UN to pursue its foreign policy goals for world peace and removal of economic inequalities and racial injustice. This was to be done not in a revolutionary manner but by working towards piecemeal, peaceful changes through the instrumentality of the UN. Given the constraints and opportunities presented by the bipolar political climate, Nehru's India adroitly explored the middle ground in containing the major eruptions of Cold War-related armed conflict in Korea, West Asia and Africa. Often big and small powers, besides the UNSG, turned to India for assistance and support. At the same time, it is to be clarified that India's claim to be consistent supporter of the UN and its principles is not true. In furtherance of vital interests in Kashmir and Goa, India did not hesitate to retract from the initial commitment to conduct the UN-supervised plebiscite in Jammu and Kashmir or to swiftly liberate colonized Goa, apparently undermining the UN Charter principles. These actions underlined the limits to India's unreserved support to the UN, and this understanding is linked to the conviction that the UN was under the influence of manipulative power politics. The down-to-earth realization has remained and got further strengthened during the times of the prime ministers who succeeded Nehru.

Indira Gandhi, in a calibrated manner, executed the strategy to cut Pakistan to size by militarily helping liberation of Bangladesh. She did so by tying up with the Soviet Union for political and diplomatic support so that in the UNSC the likely anti-India moves by China and the United States do not succeed. With that, Indira Gandhi's policy heralded a clear shift in favour of reserving Kashmir dispute for only bilateral negotiations. This has put a firm end to the original initiative by Nehru to take the complaint against Pakistan to the UN. As an extension of this approach, Indira's India resisted the pressure to sign the NPT, which meant surrendering its nuclear option forever in an uncertain regional strategic environment. Again India refused to endorse the non-binding UN resolutions aimed to keep South Asian region free from nuclear weapons. There is more to it. This wariness towards the UN role in matters of its security and regional interests did not in any way prevent India from using the UN platform to corner powerful and rich countries on issues of common interest, such as making Indian Ocean free from the growing presence of extra-regional powers, and the urgency of ameliorative action to help the developing countries. However, those days India could not escape from the criticism that its positions were biased against the United States and therefore compromised on the basic tenets of non-alignment. Indira Gandhi's successor, Rajiv Gandhi sensed the need to bring about pragmatic course correction, especially to repair relations with the United States. He did not hesitate to dismiss his foreign minister to mollify an angry United States over the latter's strongly worded condemnation of the American aggression against Libya in 1986. Another manifestation of fresh air is Rajiv Gandhi's attempt to revive Nehru's legacy in the area of nuclear disarmament. That would help him claim the stature of a young statesman dedicated to the cause of saving the world from the danger of nuclear annihilation. The plan he proposed in the 1988 special session on disarmament for total elimination of nuclear weapons in three stages was, admittedly, too ambitious to be acceptable to the nuclear majors. But the plan has not ceased to be a reference point in the Indian discourse on disarmament. In sum, the chapter establishes that the Indian experience in the UN during the four and a half decades of East–West contestation has evolved to appreciate the benefits and costs of using the UN for a variety of general and specific purposes. Tactical mistakes apart, the continuities are as striking as departures during the tenures of Nehru and the two Gandhis.

CHAPTER 3

Pragmatic Conservatism during the Unipolar 1990s

The end of the Cold War is a watershed in the post-1945 world affairs leaving no aspect of international conflict and cooperation uninfluenced. To India and to the UN, it appeared to be a historic opportunity, as well as an overpowering challenge. During the years since 1990, dubbed as the post-Cold War era, India's role in the UN is characterized by collaborating in the efforts to ease some protracted regional problems, cautioning about the new set of threats, and creating a more vibrant and vital place for the UN in the emerging new world order. During the first decade of the post-Cold War period, pragmatism in India's role in the UN is more defining feature than in the Cold War times. This chapter seeks to substantiate this thesis. Before attempting this, however, it would be worthwhile to appreciate how different is the early post-Cold War context as compared to the preceding years.

New Domestic and International Context

No doubt, India is regarded as one of the few original members of the UN with multilateral diplomatic experience and formidable reputation of representing the moral voice in the polarized Cold War world. This was made possible by many enabling factors, including the charismatic leadership in a stable democratic polity, the bulwarks of the Non-Aligned Movement (NAM) and the Third World solidarity, the manoeuvring space offered by the chasm between the Cold War contenders, and so forth.

The dawn of the post-Cold War era coincided with the rise in India of the post-Nehru/Gandhi political leadership to administer the country's foreign policy. In 1990, the absence of a credible political leadership, for example, showed very much on the country's diplomacy in the wake of the Gulf War. There was a lame-duck government, not having any time for foreign affairs. In fact, the unstable domestic political scenario in the 1990s saw six changes in the government. Anyway, in those years of political uncertainty, the task of redefining or reaffirming various features of the country's foreign policy principles fell on the shoulders of three personalities, Prime Ministers P. V. Narasimha Rao for five years and briefly on Inder Kumar Gujral and Atal Bihari Vajpayee. All of them had long experience in the conduct of foreign policy in and outside the UN, and Vajpayee's charismatic qualities were well known. Furthermore, in a dramatic development which gave a new, economic turn to India's foreign policy, the government of Prime Minister Rao and the then Finance Minister Manmohan Singh launched bold and largely fruitful policies of economic liberalization—which the successors of Rao government carried forward. This laid foundations for recovery of India's standing in Asia and outside too. Further, they copiously exhibited the capability of pragmatism, courage and innovation vis-à-vis India's conduct at the UN: pragmatism in terms of developing working relationship with the United States in political and economic matters of mutual interest, courage in facing alone (without the Soviet aid) the moments of embarrassment of isolation engineered by regional adversaries, and innovation in terms of orchestrating expression of a truly united national will in the UN forums. For instance, Atal Bihari Vajpayee first as the leader of opposition and then as the prime minister was among those actively associated with India's participation in the post-Cold War UN political processes.

To begin with, India rejoiced over the end of the Cold War. India felt vindicated, for it was integral to its long-standing aspiration about one world. The renaissance of the UN was promised when the former Soviet Union and the United States jointly sponsored (an unprecedented initiative in the history of the world body) a resolution calling for adherence by all member states to the principles and the provisions of the Charter in letter and spirit. No wonder, the text was adopted unanimously on 15 November 1989 (GAOR 1989). A variety of regional conflicts began to be resolved, while more and more countries embraced democratic form of government with the hope of consequential development dividend. In other words, a prospect of a new world order of peace, progress and justice was widely welcomed.

The UN quickly seized the opportunity to organize a succession of special events on salient global problems. Prime Minister Narasimha Rao himself attended four of them—the Security Council Summit and the Earth Summit at Rio de Janeiro (both held in 1992), as also the Social Summit and the UN-50 commemorative session (both held in 1995). But soon India sensed that it could be 'neither complacent nor euphoric' (Faleiro 1992: 33) about the dawn of a 'new and genuinely cooperative web of kinship and collaboration.' In addition to the rise of new conflicts and tensions, India was disappointed that 'the voice of the rich and powerful nations rings louder than ever, while the developing world feels itself more marginalized and ignored than ever' (Gujral 1996: 13).

The heart of the chapter deals with a set of cardinal issue areas for the purpose of analysing the content and quality of India's role in the post-Cold War UN. These issue areas are major conflict situations and the UN role therein, human rights, economic development and the institutional reforms.

Peace and Stability

In responding to various challenges to international peace and security under the UN auspices, India continued to advocate avoidance of threat or use of force, negotiation of a comprehensive settlement accommodating contending views of parties and at the same time preserving the independent, non-aligned, and united identity of the country in question by, of course, strictly adhering to the provisions of the Charter and to the terms of resolutions of the UN bodies, such as the General Assembly and the Security Council. On the Arab-Israeli problem, for example, India held:

> There can be no durable peace without a just and comprehensive settlement based on the inalienable rights of the Palestinian people to self-determination, as well as the right of all States in the region, including Palestine and Israel to live in peace and security within internationally recognized boundaries. (Gujral 1990b: 113)

To this end, India called for holding UN-sponsored conference. Opposing the Israeli plans to settle the Jews of the Soviet origin in the territories of Palestine, India regretted that the Middle Eastern region remained uninfluenced by the larger climate of reconciliation after the end of Cold War. Major countries, with strong influence in the region, were 'not showing the determination to resolve this issue that they have displayed on some other issues' (Menon 1990: 22). As a measure of reconciliation, India joined other countries in December 1991 to rescind the 1975 General Assembly resolution that dubbed Zionism as racism (GAOR 1991a). And, naturally, India was pleased with the Arab–Israeli negotiations under the joint sponsorship of the US and Russia, which culminated in a peace accord, signed in 1993.

Likewise, responding to peace dividend in Southern Africa, India welcomed the emergence of independent Namibia under the UN supervision (the process in which India played a key role, forming part of the UN Transition Assistance Group) in 1990, the various measures taken by the regime of President de Klerk in piecemeal reversal of the apartheid policy beginning with the release of Nelson Mandela from imprisonment, and finally the installation of President Mandela's government consequent to the successful exercise of universal adult franchise in May 1994. As a country that took the original initiative against racism in 1946, India supported the General Assembly decision in October 1993 to lift all sanctions against South Africa. India welcomed also a new, non-racial democratic South Africa (which was kept out of the Assembly since 1972) to the privileges of full participation in the General Assembly. The Indian delegate observed on that joyous occasion:

> We see the end of apartheid in that country as vindication of the human values—we have always held high and pursued steadfastly and unwaveringly. India was in the vanguard of the anti-apartheid struggle, and was the first to raise the subject in the United Nations, in 1946, even before achieving our own independence; we did this because we felt that it was our cause and not just that of a distant neighbour. (Khurshid 1994: 21)

In neighbouring Angola, another country of long-standing strife in Southern Africa, India fervently hoped for display of necessary political will to bring about political reconciliation in the interest of a lasting peace and an end to all bloodshed there. Accordingly, as a measure of goodwill India contributed military observers to all three missions the UN dispatched to Angola since 1989 (Sreenivasan 1995b: 7).

India heartily welcomed the fact that Afghanistan was the first among regional conflicts to benefit from the end of Cold War. However, India was dismayed that Afghanistan failed to return to peace after the Soviet withdrawal of troops. The reason was the unabated foreign interference in the civil war there, thus providing a fertile ground for terrorism, arms supplies and drug trafficking. Therefore, India stressed the need for a united, stable, independent and non-aligned Afghanistan. As a step towards this goal, India demanded first cessation of hostilities and the termination of foreign interference; second, timely provision of humanitarian assistance to the long suffering people of Kabul; and third a UN plan for the reconstruction of Afghanistan (Shah 1996: 29–30).

Another example of India's plea for negotiation and accommodation getting ultimately vindicated is the Cambodia conflict. According to India, a settlement of the problem should confirm 'Cambodia's sovereignty and independence and ensure that its people can exercise their democratic right to determine their own destiny free from foreign interference and intervention' (Gujral 1990b: 116). India welcomed and in fact had participated in the UN convened international conference at Paris, which hosted signing of the peace agreement in

October 1991. Subsequently, India became a key contributor to the international endeavour that facilitated the smooth electoral process under the supervision of one of the most ambitious and expensive (at that time) peacekeeping operations (UN Transitional Authority in Cambodia) during 1992–1993 which helped orderly establishment of a democratic, constitutional government under the stewardship of former prince, now King, Norodom Sihanouk in 1993.

Concerns over New Conflicts and Threats

Notably, while some of the Cold War-era regional conflicts began to ease, what has caused concern to India was the emergence of new and disturbing threats to world peace and stability. The euphoria generated by the end of the Cold War was short-lived to sustain hopes of a harmonious and peaceful world. Indeed, the new generation of conflicts tended to erode the very fundamental attributes of the state, namely sovereignty and territorial integrity and at the same time thoroughly shake the foundations of the interstate system. Obviously, it was a matter of great concern and challenge to India, as well as to the UN. Among the major challenges to the post-Cold War peace, Iraq–Kuwait conflict in the Gulf region was epoch making, as it heralded unipolar order with no trace of resistance to the United States.

It was in response to the Gulf conflict (1990–1991) that the UN came closer than before to a most vigorous invocation of Chapter VII of the Charter for collective restoration of peace when Iraq forcibly occupied and annexed Kuwait. Heralding a new incarnation of the UN, the Security Council swiftly condemned the Iraqi aggression against Kuwait and demanded under the mandatory terms of Chapter VII of the Charter the Iraqi troop withdrawals from Kuwait. In a determined and decisive move to force Iraq to withdraw, the Council imposed the widest set of non-military sanctions ever attempted in the past. While there were many enabling factors (including the most important one being the fortuitous coincidence of the UN interest with that of the United States), the actions of the world organization had wider impact on a large number of countries, not parties to the conflict.

India was one of those countries. It was not represented on the Security Council in 1990 when the above momentous decisions were taken. From the initial, 'low-key and reasonable' posture as could be deduced from avoiding open condemnation of Iraq (in view of the various understandable considerations, such as safety of Indians in Iraq and occupied Kuwait), India's policy moved gradually 'in step with the world community' (Murthy 1993: 140–142). India's Minister of External Affairs noted in the 45th regular session of the General Assembly:

> We firmly oppose aggression. The crisis has arisen from the Iraqi invasion of Kuwait. It follows that Iraq must withdraw its forces from Kuwait as demanded by the Security Council. India does not recognize Kuwait's annexation. Kuwait's independence and sovereignty must be restored. Any differences between the two neighbouring States must be resolved exclusively through peaceful means. (Gujral 1990b: 112)

The prescription of peaceful means was certainly addressed to Iraq; but it was also an open-ended policy addressed to all other actors outside the region, with a view to discouraging plans for a collective use of force against Iraq to ensure compliance with the Security Council resolutions. Accordingly, India was not elated by the Council's authorization in November 1990, by implication, for use of force if Iraq failed to withdraw voluntarily before the set deadline, that is, 15 January 1991 (SCOR 1990). In the aftermath of the feverish, but fruitless, efforts to persuade Iraq to back down before the deadline expired, India remained helpless witness to the commencement of massive action by the US-led coalition in January 1991 to militarily evict Iraq from Kuwait. It is worth recalling that the commencement of the Gulf War coincided, roughly, with the beginning of India's two-year term in the Security Council as a non-permanent member. In the Council, India joined other non-aligned member countries, first to convene the Council to discuss the tragic effects of the military attacks on the civilians and to explore the ways and means of bringing the conflict to an early end. India along with Malaysia and Zimbabwe, viewed the news about the Iraqi conditional offer to withdraw as a 'window of opportunity'. Hence, it proposed 'immediate cessation or at the least a suspension of hostilities' in order to provide a congenial environment and an authorization to the Secretary-General to work on the possibilities of a peaceful settlement (Gharekhan 1991c: 115–121).[1]

Meeting with no positive response from the pro-Kuwait US-led coalition, India supported Soviet leader, Mikhail Gorbachev's peace initiative to facilitate rescinding of the Council's punitive measures in return for a time-bound Iraqi withdrawal from Kuwait. India's permanent representative even offered to bring together the 10 non-permanent members of the Council to narrow down the differences between Soviet and American proposals (Gharekhan 1991d: 311). However, those were the moments when, horizons of ensuing victory in the war overpowered diplomatic proposals. Once the chief objective of the military action was achieved with the defeat of Iraqi forces in Kuwait, the diplomatic formalities of approving the modalities of ceasefire followed. While expressing 'rejoice' over the liberation of Kuwait, India expressed reservations on resolution 686 (1991) for having no provision for a 'permanent or formal ceasefire' and as such the possibility of the resumption of hostilities very much remained (Gharekhan 1991c: 76).

However, this principled stand as manifested in its abstention on the above-mentioned resolution was overshadowed by India's affirmative vote on more controversial, if not unprecedented one that stipulated a series of stringent conditions against Iraq.[2] India was unhappy that the non-military sanctions were not being lifted against

---

[1] The record of the closed meeting of the Council was made available, thanks to the exception agreed to the rule 51 of the Council's provisional rules of procedure.

[2] These included the unconditional acceptance of the Iraq–Kuwait boundary, which would be demarcated by a UN commission, the acceptance of a UN observer mission along the Iraq–Kuwait border, the release of all foreign nationals and the return of the Kuwait property seized during the occupation, the agreement to pay compensation against the claims of loss or injury by any government, individuals and others, and the commitment to eliminate, under strict international supervision, its stocks of the biological and chemical weapons as also to destroy its nuclear weapon capabilities. Notably, even after the formal ceasefire came into force, the economic sanctions continued only with a periodical review mechanism in place. See SCOR 1991.

Iraq, and it cautioned against any attempt to arbitrarily impose the boundary line between Iraq and Kuwait. Nevertheless, it was happy that the formal ceasefire was coming into force and that the resolution was a product of meaningful negotiations between the members of the Council. As such, India's affirmative vote on the resolution had the following explanation:

> The authors of the draft have assured us, bilaterally as well as in course of informal consultations, that they have put together the various elements of the resolution in full understanding that the international community is dealing with a unique situation of which there has been no parallel since the establishment of the United Nations; hopefully there will be none in the future. We have been urged to look at the resolution in the light of the uniqueness of the situation. (Gharekhan 1991a: 72)

Later in August 1991, India supported the Secretary General's plan that permitted limited sale of oil by Iraq, the proceeds of which would be used partly to fund food and humanitarian needs of the country's population. Similarly, India welcomed the work of the Iraq–Kuwait Boundary Commission which merely demarcated an already agreed boundary, without attempting to impose a new boundary line.

On the entire question of the Gulf conflict, India's role could be seen as an effort to adjust its foreign policy to the newly emerging reality of pre-eminence of the United States. But at the same time India was aggrieved: its constructive attitude was not adequately reciprocated by the UN in the context of the serious adverse socio-economic effect of its compliance with the sanctions against Iraq/Kuwait. India informed the Council that the total loss it suffered under various heads during 1990–1991 was approximately US$3.45 billion and sought relief under the terms of Article 50 of the Charter. The UN response was 'both frustrating and disappointing'. In the words of India's external affairs minister, the consideration of these concerns took place after long delay and it resulted only in a call to member states and the UN specialized agencies to give attention to its problems (Solanki 1991b: 24).

Prime Minister Narasimha Rao also raised the matter subsequently in the historic summit meeting of the Council and suggested that 'while implementing its resolutions in good faith, it is incumbent on the Security Council to anticipate all the consequences of its decisions. Some consequences may be unintended, but they can affect those whom are least intended to affect' (Rao 1992: 97). These sentiments guided India when it abstained on a move to impose diplomatic and aviation sanctions against Libya in April 1992. India regretted the omission of a clearer acknowledgement of the Council's responsibility to take 'concrete, practical and effective measures' under Article 50 of the Charter. On the next occasion nonetheless, India's views prevailed in the sense that a paragraph appeared in the text, which imposed in 1992 economic sanctions against Serbia so as to force an end to latter's involvement in the conflict in Bosnia–Herzegovina.[3]

The fratricidal violence in the states of former Yugoslavia, particularly Bosnia–Herzegovina was a matter of grief and deep concern to India. This was natural as India's ties with former Yugoslavia were 'burnished by history and strengthened by cooperation and friendship' (Solanki 1991a: 44–45). India appealed to all parties to eschew violence and resolve the problem peacefully within the framework of the UN Charter principles. When the situation worsened, India endorsed the proposal to enforce punitive economic sanctions against Serb Republic of Yugoslavia. It was hoped that only such a stern action would send an unmistakable message that the Council would not countenance violence in the pursuit of sectarian ends. However, India was anxious about the adverse effects of sanctions on cooperation of the parties concerned with the UN peacekeeping operation in the field. In its perception, action 'should be rapid, but not hasty; decisive, but not unbalanced; effective, and not over-reaching itself. The cure, in other words, should not be worse than the disease' (Gharekhan 1992e: 23). As India became increasingly uncomfortable with the direction of the UN actions, its delegate protested:

> For too long the international community concentrated on the military peace-keeping aspect, ignoring the political, peace-making

[3] The reference here is to the decisive action (SCOR 1992b).

aspects of the crisis. Cease-fires were repeatedly negotiated only to collapse before the ink had even dried. Humanitarian conditions worsened while the parties resorted to such abominable practices as 'ethnic cleansing' in their attempts to jockey for the political and military high ground. (Gharekhan 1992i: 4)

Equally unsettling situation arose in Somalia during 1991–1992 with casualties were nearly five times higher than in former Yugoslavia. Keeping in view the sui generis character of Somalia as manifested in no single political authority in control and consequently complete breakdown of law and order, India supported the suggestion for a UN-authorized humanitarian intervention to ensure adherence to ceasefire among warring factions and organize unimpeded delivery of food and medicine. Admittedly consent from the government was not required, as no government existed to exercise sovereign rights. Of course, the challenge to the basic norms from the North Atlantic Treaty Organization (NATO) intervention Kosovo in 1999 was viewed quite differently.

India was greatly concerned at the aerial bombing of Federal Republic of Yugoslavia by the NATO, in March 1999, in the name of humanitarian intervention to save the lives of Kosovars from the Serbian government of Belgrade without prior authorization from the Security Council. In New Delhi, the government issued a strongly worded statement that any country taking on the garb of a world policeman was unacceptable. Although India was not elected to the Council at that time, it joined Russia to sponsor a draft resolution, which called for an immediate end to this senseless violence and sought to re-establish the authority of the Security Council. It was discouraging that the draft received supporting votes only from Belarus, China and Russia, and therefore was defeated for lack of the required majority. Questioning NATO's apparent claim to be above the law, India doubted if NATO could use such illegal force while accusing the Serb government of those very methods against innocent civilians. Rejecting the NATO powers' claim that the military action with humanitarian motives enjoyed the support of the international community, the Indian representative (Sharma 1999: 15–16) reasoned:

It is natural to be revolted by violence and to want to put an end to human suffering. However, between nations as within them, populations can be protected, the law upheld and those who break it punished only through legal means. The cure otherwise is as bad as the disease. It is also very rarely effective and often makes things worse. Those who take the law into their hands have never improved civic peace within nations; neither will they help in international relations.

In the years since 1990, India highlighted terrorism as one of the most dangerous and pernicious threats to global peace and security. India referred to the problem first in the summit meeting of the Security Council and followed up with a proposed draft comprehensive convention on international terrorism in the General Assembly.[4] Prime Minister Narasimha Rao minced no words (Rao 1995: 45)

> The world's greatest danger today is the spread of terrorism. When sponsored and supported by States, terrorism becomes another means of waging war. The international community must therefore resolve to combat this menace, since it threatens the very basis of peaceful societies.

India, also, stood on guard to protect the sovereign rights of states from the challenges coming from diverse sources. It staunchly opposed attempts to stretch the scope of the right to self-determination with the aim of destabilizing the existing, multi-ethnic states. Referring to the 1993 Vienna Declaration on Human Rights and clearly implying Pakistan's motivated attempt to apply that right to Jammu and Kashmir, India stressed:

> Taken out of context, self-termination could be used to encourage secession, terrorism and violence .... The unstable aftermath of the cold war had been seen by some States as an opportunity for territorial aggrandizement. Self-determination must not be distorted and interpreted as including the right of any ethnic group to proclaim its independence or join another State. (Devi 1998: 5)

---

[4] For detailed discussion, see Chapter 9 in the book

Expediency in Applying Principles of Peacekeeping When Necessary

Faced with the complex challenges in peace and security during the post-Cold War years, the UN turned to the time-tested technique of peacekeeping and enlarged its scope and capabilities. After a long gap of more than two decades, India re-started its association with the UN peacekeeping operations during the period and played a worthy role in major peacekeeping operations in the Gulf, Namibia, Central America, Cambodia, Haiti, Rwanda, Somalia, Bosnia–Herzegovina and Angola. As highlighted separately in Chapter 7, India took part in 24 out of the 35 peacekeeping operations launched in the 1990s. Indian army officers commanded UN Iraq–Iran Military Observer Group (Iraq side of the border), UN Transition Assistance Group in Namibia, and UN Protection Force (UNPROFOR) in former Yugoslavia. During these years, India was guided in its decisions based on the question whether India's contribution was sought, the solidarity and empathy with the affected country and commitment to the UN and the cause of international peace and security (Gujral 1996: 15). India expected the peacekeeping operations to be deployed on the request of the countries concerned, and they should strictly adhere to the traditional principles of respecting sovereignty, territorial integrity and non-interference in internal affairs of host countries. Setbacks to the missions in places, such as Bosnia–Herzegovina or Somalia, were due to the deviation in the core and time-tested principles (Mukherjee 1995: 16). India did make exception if the situation so demanded. For instance, India agreed to take part in the second UN operation in Somalia even though it was mandated bereft of prior consent, because there was no government in existence there.

Of course, India endorsed a few enabling proposals made by the Secretary-General in 'An Agenda for Peace' (Boutros-Ghali 1992) to strengthen the capacity of the UN in peacemaking and peacekeeping. It supported the recommendation for inception of peacekeeping reserve fund for meeting the start-up costs, as well as institutionalization of consultations between the Security Council and the troop contributing countries. On the whole, however, the Indian reaction was guarded on the suggestions to deploy peacekeepers without the consent and with the mandate to use force, as it was not sure if the major proposals regarding peacekeeping fully conformed with the spirit of the UN Charter and if they could further the credibility and impartiality of the UN. It was of the view that military force was to be considered as a last resort and when used it should be invariably under the UN command and control (Heptullah 1992a: 51). Responding to the 1995 Supplement to the Agenda for Peace with revised recommendations (Boutros-Ghali 1995), India underlined the importance of learning lessons from the post-Cold War phase of peacekeeping thus:

> We are gratified to note that the clear lesson drawn in the Supplement from recent experience of peace-keeping operations that respect for certain basic principles of peace-keeping is essential to success. These are consent, impartiality and the non-use of force except in the case of self-defence. We are equally gratified that the Secretary-General has highlighted the point that the logic of peace-keeping flows from political and military premises quite distinct from those of enforcement, and that the dynamics of the latter are incompatible with the political process that peace-keeping is intended to facilitate. (Sreenivasan 1995a: 19)

Among other concerns specific to India were the safety of the peacekeepers, the timely reimbursement of costs to the contributing countries (nearly US$60 million were owed to India during the 1990s) and adoption of a fair and non-discriminatory scheme of compensation in case of death or disability.

Stubborn Objection to Unfavourable Developments in Nuclear Disarmament

Clearly linked to India's views on peace and security problems is India's advocacy of nuclear disarmament. India was encouraged by the adoption in 1993 of the international convention which prohibited development, production or stockpiling and use of chemical weapons, and which required their destruction under a multilateral system of verification and on-site inspection. India deemed this convention as a model treaty to be followed in regard to barring nuclear weapons also.

In the Cold War era, as alluded in the preceding chapter, India made several proposals for nuclear disarmament—a call for ending nuclear testing in 1954, a broad framework of principles in 1965 for negotiating the NPT, a call in 1982 for adopting a convention on banning the use of nuclear weapons, and in 1988 advocated a comprehensive action plan for a world free of nuclear weapons. The hopes for a genuine progress in nuclear disarmament in the post-Cold War era proved to be unfounded. India refused to sign the NPT right from the time it was opened for accession in 1968, as it found to be discriminatory in character. As India argued, the NPT prohibited the non-nuclear weapon countries from producing or acquiring the nuclear weapons without reciprocal obligation on the nuclear weapon states to eliminate their nuclear weapons. With the result, the continuing expansion and modernization of stockpiles of major nuclear weapon powers made the world ever more dangerous. Although India did not take part in the Review Conferences till then, India hoped that the post-Cold War fresh thinking would cause the 1995 Review to rectify the anomalies. On the contrary, the conference renewed the treaty indefinitely without altering any of the original provisions. This was not the only setback to India, more were in the offing.

Soon India turned its attention to the need to comprehensively ban nuclear tests. The text India co-sponsored and adopted without a negative vote in the General Assembly in December 1995 (GAOR 1995) requested Assembly's Conference on Disarmament (CD) to negotiate a 'universal and multilaterally and effectively verifiable' comprehensive nuclear test ban treaty which would further the twin goals of nuclear non-proliferation and nuclear disarmament. However, the text negotiated in the CD banned underground tests while allowing computer-simulated laboratory tests. Nor did it contain any action plan for nuclear disarmament. Therefore, India stood out and refused to join the consensus in the CD, which meant that, as per the procedure, the text could not be recommended to the Assembly for adoption. Yet, in a subterfuge, the failed text in CD was brought to the Assembly by Australia. India took strong exception on grounds of breach of propriety. As India asserted, the CTBT text banned only explosive tests leaving the scope wide open for the nuclear weapon countries to opt for the non-explosive testing technologies. Secondly, the critical part of the negotiations involved only a handful of countries and the resultant formulations were presented to the rest in the CD on a 'virtually take-it-or-leave-it basis'. Thirdly, without a genuine commitment by the nuclear weapon countries to eliminate all their weapons in a time frame, the text became 'an unequal one' sanctioning in effect, the possession of nuclear weapons by some countries for their security and that of their allies while ignoring the security concerns of other states (Ghose 1996: 3). Finally, it was pointed out, the text required India's ratification for the treaty to come into effect, ignoring the fact of India's objections and negative vote in the Assembly. It is anybody's guess if these disappointments pushed India to prepare for underground tests later on. Once in 1995, the preparations for such test were reportedly aborted at the last minute after detection by the Clinton Administration (Sitapati 2015: 195–196), but India successfully conducted series of tests in May 1998 soon after Atal Bihari Vajpayee (who incidentally took part in the UN disarmament debates during previous years) became the Prime Minister. To the Vajpayee government, it did not matter much how the UN or the United States would react. While India withstood sanctions imposed by the United States as a punishment, the Indian delegation did not attend the meeting of the Security Council at which the nuclear tests of both India and Pakistan were condemned in a resolution (SCOR 1998).

India faced setback on another security and disarmament-related issue in which it was deeply interested for two decades and long: the question of making the Indian Ocean a zone of peace free from any manifestation of military presence of outside great powers. After the Cold War ended, the United States and its allies (including the new allies from Eastern Europe) became bolder to put obstacles. They were determined to ensure that the original 'orthodox' concept of the peace zone was 'modernized' for the simple purpose of pinpointing that the threats to the idea of peace zone in the Indian Ocean emanated more from within than outside. India strongly resisted those revisionist attempts, but its position had been reduced to that of small minority—a bitter fact reminded by, of all, the post-Cold War Russian Federation which was previously supportive of India on the issue but reversed its position to endorse the Western argumentation (Murthy 1993: 102–103). This development considerably eroded the manoeuvring ability of the non-aligned countries such as India on the question. Paradoxically, the end of the Cold War, instead of brightening the prospects of an early convening of a much delayed conference on implementation of the 1971 Declaration, abandoned it altogether. However, one has to note that the issue is as much a collective setback to the Indian Ocean countries as to India.

Resistance against Motivated Use of Human Rights Agenda

Human rights issues gained salience in the post-Cold War world more than in the past. India and many other countries at the UN held definitive views on such questions as the desirability of prescribing human rights practices, the question of primacy of certain rights over others, and the extent to which the world community could go to intervene for protection of human rights. India urged caution in projecting human rights in an intrusive manner that would militate against national sovereignty. 'Contexts and situations differ from country to country, and international concern for human rights preservation should not detract from the efforts in the same direction made by the country concerned' (Solanki 1991b: 32). These views had a bearing on the UN Conference on human rights held in Vienna in 1993. According to India,

> The United Nations must balance the promotion of all human rights—civil, cultural, economic and social—preserve and propagate the values of every society and promote tolerance for diversity and cross-cultural interaction. Politicizing the human rights agenda and using it to target countries is undesirable. (Mukherjee 1995: 16)

India had proudly and repeatedly cited the guarantees for protection of fundamental rights in the country's constitution. However, with a view to improving the existing monitoring mechanism and as a response to the growing power of human rights movement across the world as evidenced in the Vienna Conference, India set up in 1993 the National Human Rights Commission under a parliamentary legislation. In addition, India invited the UN High Commissioner for Human Rights to India. Surely the sharp and critical focus fell on the country's track record particularly in the state of Jammu and Kashmir. India did not accept that 'all human rights are a privilege of terrorists' alone (Mukherjee 1994: 16), it insisted that the rights of innocent and unarmed citizens must be protected.

Indeed, the resurfacing of developments in Jammu and Kashmir in international human rights forums was mainly due to the insurgency caused by the Islamist fundamentalist and terrorist elements, enjoying the ideological, financial and logistical support from Pakistan's army. These claims were corroborated by the findings of the Western foreign affairs think tanks which came handy to the Indian delegates in the sessions of the UN Commission on Human Rights (UNCHR) and the General Assembly. Pakistan made important gains by engaging India in regular and at times vitriolic exchanges all of which put India on back foot. Pakistan compared the human rights situation in Kashmir with that of Palestine, and demanded not only greater vigil by the international community to ensure protection of human rights but also a settlement of the long pending problem as per the past resolutions of the Security Council. India's diplomatic energies were excessively consumed by the repetitive exercise of right of replies accompanied by unsuccessful attempts by Pakistan to push through draft resolutions the adoption of which would have meant a major loss of face to India. Nonetheless, India was placed in an unenviable position to take note of UNSG's reference to Jammu and Kashmir in his annual reports during the years 1993–1996. Yet, India left no one in doubt about its will to retain Kashmir, no matter what Pakistan attempted to do to internationalize the problem:

> Nothing Pakistan can say or do, no violence, no outrage, no falsehood repeated a thousand times over, will change the fact that Jammu and Kashmir is, and will continue to be, an inalienable part

of India. The Government of India will do everything necessary to defend the right of the people of Kashmir to live in peace and security which other Indian citizens enjoy. (Surie 1995: 50)

Focus on terrorism was the chief concern when India expressed dissatisfaction about the deficiencies in the powers assigned to the International Criminal Court (ICC) in its Statute finalized at the Rome Conference in 1998. The purpose of the Court is to apprehend, prosecute and punish individuals accused of ordering or acquiescing in the perpetration of crimes of genocide, war crimes, ethnic cleansing and crimes against humanity. India actively participated in the deliberations at the Rome Conference hoping that the Court would be 'universally acceptable, independent and efficient institution that could deal not only with traditional crimes, such as war crimes and genocide, but also with international terrorism and drug trafficking' (Chandumajra 1998: 4). Besides not including the crime of terrorism, what particularly seemed to have annoyed India was the subordination of the Court to the discretion of the five permanent members of the Security Council.

Disappointment over Absence of Development Dividend

A remarkable feature of India's role in the UN from the early years has been its emphasis on the urgent need for correcting gross imbalances in the socio-economic conditions particularly in the developing countries, without which foundations of durable peace cannot be built. In that perspective, the post-Cold War years witnessed continuation of diplomatic efforts by India to highlight the deteriorating conditions in many parts of the developing world. The hopes of 'peace dividend' and 'the disarmament dividend' remained farfetched. On the other hand, economic factors have assumed new prominence by virtue of several factors, including the unopposed acceptance of Capitalist and market-oriented economic policies over the socialist model after the collapse of the Soviet Union, and equally notably the pace of economic globalization as manifested in the growing attraction for private investments, cheaper modes of production and easier movement of goods and services. However, serious concerns remained in spite of initial hopes. India also addressed itself to the relevance of various models of economic development. While joining consensus at the General Assembly to call upon the UN system in 1991 to promote free entrepreneurship and market-oriented approach (GAOR 1991b), India introduced a word of caution that 'entrepreneurship was not a universal panacea. Institutional support for entrepreneurship, in particular from the UN system, should supplement, not supplant other efforts to promote growth and development' (Ahmed 1991: 11). In sum, India preferred a market-plus model of development (Gujral 1994: 8–9).

As India pointed out in the 18th special session of the General Assembly on development and international economic cooperation, 'détente devoid of economic cooperation' could not be durable (Gujral 1990a: 79–80). At the UN-50 commemorative session, India's Prime Minister described 'all-round development' as the 'priority one' (Rao 1995: 45), specially because the ODA figures were the lowest in five decades. Moreover, the ODA was getting linked to non-economic considerations, such as good governance, human rights, environment, defence spending, and so on. While funding for multilateral aid agencies declined by an average of 15 per cent in the early 1990s, the indebtedness of the developing countries crossed US$2000 billion (Solanki 1991b: 31).

The Third World's bargaining power considerably diminished in the trade negotiation forums, as evident in the Cartagena meet of the UN Conference on Trade and Development (UNCTAD) held in 1992. India regretted the tendency in some major industrialized countries 'to force their will on trading partners to adopt unilateral coercive means to penetrate their markets in the name of liberalization', completely contrary to the spirit of multilateral negotiating framework. India impressed on the fact that the success of ongoing economic liberalization programme in several developing countries required a much more open and cooperative world economy. The Marrakesh agreements, the outcome of the Uruguay Round trade negotiations, paved the way for the establishment in 1995 of the World Trade Organization (WTO) as a successor to the General Agreement on Tariffs and Trade (GATT). India thought the outcome was the best possible under the circumstances and joined the WTO with the hope that the new organization would uphold non-discrimination, consensus and transparency in the world trade regime eschewing new conditionalities (Mukherjee 1994: 14).

Alongside, India's prioritization of development was amply reflected during its participation in the Rio Summit on environment and development, held in 1992. India contended that the basic development needs of developing countries must be met before environment by itself could take precedence over other concerns. Further, the participation of developing countries needed to be facilitated through transfer of environment-friendly technologies and financing. In its view, global partnership for sustainable development ought to rest on equality and equity (Nath 1992: 43). This development-first orientation guided India's participation in other UN-sponsored thematic summit conferences on population, women and social development during the 1990s.

With the universal realization that development, in all its dimensions, is the foremost need of the times, the 1990s witnessed an attempt to restore to the UN a central role in the task. Secretary-General's 'An Agenda for Development' (Boutros-Ghali 1994) prepared at the instance of the General Assembly in 1994 generated a great deal of debate on strengthening the UN's role in promoting socio-economic development of the underdeveloped countries. Reacting to the document, India agreed that the role of the UN was vital in promoting awareness, consensus-building and in catalysing action. Moreover, India wanted the UN to conceive development in its 'comprehensive, pristine and integral sense' without allowing fragmentation of the concept. However, the UN must scrupulously respect the principles of consent, and avoid intrusiveness and conditionalities. Having said so, India regretted that the 'Agenda' did not make any concrete proposals in the area of financing, technology, trade, ODA and debt.

Support to UN Restructuring If It Strengthened the UN

The Indian perspectives represent a combination of principles and pragmatism on a range of UN reform issues. Acknowledging the need for reform, India perceived reform not simply as an exercise to trim the budget, but it should strengthen the capacity of the UN to respond effectively to the priorities identified by the overwhelming majority of its membership (Gujral 1997: 6–7). India believed that the 'capacity to pay' principle should continue to be the basis of financing the UN. The financing system should be firm towards the habitual defaulters, fair to the poor countries and flexible in respect of genuine difficulties experienced by any member state.

The marginalization of the UN was nowhere as striking as in the management of world economy. It was India's conviction that assigning the UN only a complementary, instead of the central role in the economic and social fields was contrary to the letter and spirit of the Charter. India wanted revitalization of the UN by way of reforming the Economic and Social Council and by reinstating to the UN coordinating role vis-à-vis the major monetary, financial and trade institutions. While it had welcomed thematic debates in the high-level ministerial segments of Economic and Social Council (ECOSOC) annual sessions, India did not favour introduction of inter-sessional bureaus to work for ECOSOC, as they might marginalize the interests of the developing countries (Gujral 1994: 10). Similarly, India expressed itself against the disbanding of UNCTAD (Mukherjee 1995: 14), as also the proposals for merger of the UN Centre for Human Settlements (UN Habitat) with the UN Environment Programme (UNEP), both of which are based in Nairobi (Sreenivasan 1998: 21).

The highlight of India's plans for UN reform is the enlargement of the Security Council. Taking advantage of the US attempts to include Japan and Germany as permanent members of the UNSC, India put forward its claim in 1994. It made an elaborate case based on 'objective criteria', and opposed any piecemeal expansion or any discrimination in the privileges of the existing and new permanent members (Mukherjee 1994: 16). However, expectedly, the 1990s saw no progress in the matter.[5]

Assessment

Some of the salient principles and aspects of India's foreign policy faced serious challenge for readjustment or reaffirmation in the UN during the 1990s. The potential for exercising its mediatory role had virtually vanished, as demonstrated in the Gulf War. The disintegration of Yugoslavia and the Soviet Union and sectarian strife in other regions had become a matter of concern to India in regard to the principles of respect for state sovereignty and territorial integrity. While it appeared to be conservative on issues of sovereignty while responding to unilateral use of force in Kosovo or espousing the continued usefulness of the traditional principles of peacekeeping, or on human rights overreach, it showed signs of pragmatism in respect of withdrawal of earlier General Assembly resolution designating Zionism as racism or the ideological shift towards economic liberalization. On the other hand, on certain issues which had adverse implications to its security needs and interests, India did not hesitate to be tough and obstinate, as in the case of opposing the CTBT, the Land Mines Ban Treaty and the Rome Statute, or more importantly the indefinite extension of the NPT.

It also emerges that, given the serious limitations imposed by the post-Cold War world, India tried hard to draw the best from a difficult situation. For instance, India earned appreciation for its critical contribution to major peacekeeping operations, reworked new partnerships on human rights, and made an elaborate case for the permanent membership in the Security Council. Finally, India's desire to nurture an image of a mature, world-oriented and forward-looking country to work in, with and for the UN is worth mentioning. This attempt is evident in Prime Minister Rao's (1995: 45) observations in October 1995 on the occasion of the 50th anniversary of the organization:

---

[5] The issue is discussed separately in Chapter 5.

...We have thus the task of making the United Nations truly and effectively the global repository of humankind's aspirations. Right thinking nations and peoples working together have in the past achieved miracles. I am confident that they can do so again. India will be proud and happy to be part of such an endeavour.

CHAPTER 4

Opportunities and Obstacles for India at the UN in the New Century

The present chapter is special for understanding India and the UN. While the preceding two chapters provide historical perspective on India's role at the UN, the present chapter seeks to offer immediate and contemporary context to India's participation in the world body. The 20 years since the dawn of the new century do seem to project India in a new light. Parallel to the UN attempts to reposition itself in tackling the trinity of principal functional domains, viz. peace, development and human rights, India could be understood as a key partner not only willing, but also able to help in the furtherance of the goal towards a stronger UN.

The discussion in the chapter will dwell on the following questions. In what way, do the recent couple of decades stand out in terms of the trends and patterns of India's historical association with the UN? What does one make out of the broad spread of issues India has shown interest and concern at the apex bodies, such as the General Assembly and the Security Council? Is India part of a problem or solution with reference to setting standards or implementation of norms in the areas of nuclear disarmament, development cooperation, human security and sustainable development, or strengthening of the UN? How relevant are the strides India made in the economic and technological fields to its profile and participation in the UN? Do the recent two decades take the country's association with the UN forward or not?

Key Guiding Factors

Four factors exhibit and underpin the past two decades of India's wide-ranging interest in, and engagement with the UN. These pointers are the greater interest invested by the country's political leaders in the UN deliberations, the ability to forge or join diverse and flexible issue-focused coalitions, the attempt to not let principles constrain pragmatic options on important issues and, finally, the electoral popularity it had tested and demonstrated successfully.

First, the political investment India's top leaders had brought in the recent years to the UN activities is as striking, if not more, as it was in the early decades. To cite a specific piece of evidence, the Indian Prime Ministers showed up at the General Assembly sessions 10 times in the past 20 years, in stark contrast to the levels of political investment evident in the preceding 55 years. Notably, Prime Minister Manmohan Singh addressed the General Assembly on five occasions during his 10 years rule, while his charismatic predecessor, Atal Bihari Vajpayee appeared thrice since the beginning of the new century. Indeed, in the eye of Vajpayee, the Millennium Summit of 2000 was taking place at a unique point in history, to allow a 'pledge to bring nations together in a global family, united by peace and prosperity' (Vajpayee 2000: 28). Manmohan Singh also spoke in similar vein on the 60th anniversary that India would be a 'willing participant' in the process of reorienting the world organization in meeting the challenges of the new era (Singh M. 2005: 29). Prime Minister Narendra Modi, too, travelled thrice so far since 2014 to deliver sober and popular addresses, including at the special event dedicated to the commencement of the post-2015 Development Agenda. In his latest address in September 2019, he (Modi 2019: 10) asserted: 'All our endeavours are centred on 1.3 billion Indians. But the dreams that these efforts are trying to fulfil, are the same dreams that the entire world has, that every country has, and that every society has.' While the country's leadership is focused on the economic and social progress in India, it is conscious of the influence it would have on the world at large. Besides, the democratic and pluralistic nature of political life in India has been put to concerted use by involving multiple shades of parliamentary opinion in the deliberations on varied subjects. For example, delegations to the issue-focused six special sessions of the General Assembly held since 2000 were led by prominent political personalities belonging to opposition at that time. They included L. K. Advani, Arun Jaitley and Sonia Gandhi.

The second guiding factor is the reinforcement and vigorous pursuit of the belief that the UN is best suited to pursue collective solutions to common problems of mankind, but not to exhaust itself on parochial complaints. This non-parochial perspective tended to prioritize global problems, such as climate change, international terrorism, and nuclear disarmament in political and economic domains. This would require strengthening of multilateral institutions, such as the UN. However, the actions of the UN as also the member countries should be strictly in compliance with the basic principles of respect for state sovereignty, territorial integrity, non-use of force and non-interference in internal affairs. It is not that India is inflexible on adherence to these principles, if specific situations demanded India supported pragmatic responses whether it is robust peacekeeping operations with a mandate to use force as in Democratic Congo, or strict compliance with sanctions against financing and sheltering of terror groups. On climate change negotiations also, India sought to reiterate the principle of historical responsibility of industrially advanced countries for greenhouse gas emissions while coming forward with voluntary commitments for emission cuts.

The next feature of India's role is its ability to forge and join groups and coalitions on different sets of issue areas which made an impact on the deliberations and negotiated outcomes. For example, in the Security Council reform process, India was a key participant in the 'Group of 4' aspirant countries as also the group of small and developing countries supporting expansion of the Council's membership in both the permanent and non-permanent categories. In trade and environment matters, India is part of the India, Brazil, South Africa (IBSA), Brazil, Russia, India, China and South Africa (BRICS) and Brazil, South Africa, India and China (BASIC) countries (Murthy 2010: 220). This was in addition to continuing close contact with established groups, such as the NAM and the Group of 77.

The fourth feature of India's role in this century is its significant striking rate in winning electoral contests for coveted seats and posts. While it was elected to ECOSOC continuously without a break, India garnered the highest number of votes when it contested for a non-permanent seat in the Security Council in 2010, as also other bodies, such as the Human Rights Council and the International Law Commission. In all, India is presently serving elected posts in 20 other bodies in 2019. Remarkably, India vigorously campaigned and prevailed in the contest for judgeship in the World Court against a nominee of United Kingdom in 2017, notwithstanding the support expressed by all other permanent members to the latter.[1] Again, having its candidature endorsed by the Asian group, India is set to get elected for its eighth term in the Security Council in October 2020. As a reflection of India's growing esteem, it would suffice to cite the failure of Pakistan to gain traction among member countries on the alleged excesses by India in Jammu and Kashmir in several sessions of the General Assembly or in the peacekeeping thematic debates in the Security Council, except occasioning routine, but robust, exercise of right of reply by Indian delegates. Further, it may be recalled that as many as 170 member countries co-sponsored a 'simple yet substantive' text India piloted for observance of 21 June every year as international yoga day (GAOR 2014; Mukerji 2014c: 1).

---

[1] In an unsuccessful electoral attempt for the post of the UN Secretary-General, India nominated at a late stage former international bureaucrat, Shashi Tharoor, who lost to South Korea's Ban Ki-moon in the Security Council's straw polls in 2006.

As regards the substantive issues that engaged India's attention and intervention either in the General Assembly or the Security Council structures over the two decade long period, the following are being focused—major armed conflicts as also newly emerging issue areas in international security, globalization and sustainable development, including issues of trade and climate change, and the ongoing process of organizational revitalization stretching from General Assembly to the Secretariat. (Keeping in view the contents of the succeeding chapters, the chapter avoids discussing in detail the issue areas of counterterrorism, human rights or peacekeeping.)

Major Armed Conflicts with a Bearing on International Security

India's concerns regarding the implications of violent conflicts both interstate and intrastate categories for regional and international security are eloquent and well-meaning, stressing the principle of peacefully negotiated outcomes of all outstanding differences in accordance with the provisions of the Charter. But some theatres touch the core of India's policy traditions and interests. The outstanding conflicts in Afghanistan and in the Middle East are undoubtedly of special interest.

Clearly, the continuing conflict in Afghanistan has figured regularly as a matter of natural concern to India in its interventions in both the Security Council and the General Assembly in the new century. The outline of its approach is the following: first, the Taliban which has brought colossal suffering to the Afghans through its oppressive rule must be quickly and completely taken out of Afghanistan; secondly, the best way to move towards establishing a broad-based and multi-ethnic government in Afghanistan would be through an intra-Afghan process, without outside interference or dictation. And thirdly, a new international framework to help Afghanistan recover economically and politically with participation of all countries (such as India) that have a 'legitimate and benign interest in, and influence on' developments in that country (Sharma 2001a: 16–17). India viewed the presence of the United States-led International Security Assistance

Force (ISAF) as a bulwark against destabilizing forces in Kabul (Nambiar 2002a: 10). Notwithstanding the ISAF presence, in India's assessment, the terrorist actions in Afghanistan witnessed a spurt due to the support and sanctuaries available beyond borders. Hence, India asserted that Afghanistan's security and stabilization would remain elusive unless the syndicate of Al-Qaida, Taliban, Lashkar-e-Toiba and other terrorist and extremist groups operating from within and outside Afghanistan's borders are isolated (Puri H.S. 2010c.: 35–36). At the same time, India saw the need for greater cohesion and coordination in operational terms between ISAF and the UN Assistance Mission in Afghanistan (UNAMA). In view of the increased instability caused by the attacks from Taliban forces, the mandate of UNAMA should be strengthened to ensure upkeep of the political institutions, in addition to better delivery of humanitarian and development work (Puri M. 2013a: 23). At the bilateral level, India has extended assistance worth more than US$2 billion catering to capacity-building projects, infrastructure creation and reconstruction. Lately in the midst of reports about US interest to substantially reduce its troops from Afghanistan, India insisted that the implications of such drawdown of troops must be thoroughly examined in order to ensure safety of the Afghan people (Mukerji 2013: 22).

On Middle East, India's support to the cause of Palestine has continued, but India clearly disapproves terrorism and violence in the name of liberation struggle. While appealing to all sides for restraint and patience, India told Israel that the 'construction of a wall that cuts across a wide swath of Palestinian land, annexes agricultural areas, destroys dwellings and separates families is both unjust and illegal. Such actions can only increase the sense of despair and frustration among Palestinians and aggravate a situation already vitiated by the imposition of hardships and the suffering imposed by a regime of blockades and roadblocks' (Nambiar 2003a: 12). India suggested to Israel to honour the World Court's 2004 opinion that construction of the wall in the Occupied Palestine territory was contrary to international law and therefore needed to be demolished (Gopinathan 2005: 13). Accordingly, India did not support prolonged blockade of Gaza lasting for years, affecting essential services and economic activities. India contributed US$4 million to the National Early Recovery and Reconstruction Plan for Gaza in 2016, apart from substantially increasing its contribution to the UN humanitarian fund for Palestinian refugees.

Another major blow to the political stability in the Middle East came from the war on Iraq launched by a coalition of countries led by the United States in 2003. India reasoned that the unfortunate war against Iraq in 2003 was a fall out of 'the extraordinary inability of the five permanent members of the Security Council to agree on action'. The war had shown that the founders' vision about enlightened multilateralism has not materialized (Vajpayee 2003: 14). Moreover, the brutal terrorist attack on the UN Office in Baghdad in 2003 struck a body blow at the UN humanitarian efforts in Iraq. While endorsing the Secretary-General's call for the early lifting of sanctions to ease large-scale human suffering, restoration of full sovereignty to the Iraqi people, India wished the UN to work for political and economic reconstruction of post-war Iraq.

In more recent times, the civil wars in both Syria and Yemen present the scenario where internal and external forces join hands to prolong the violence and pave the way for entry of international terror networks. The civil war in Syria has become a major preoccupation in the Security Council deliberations since 2011. India has been gravely concerned at the continuing violence and the worsening humanitarian situation. India strongly condemned all violence and violations of human rights, no matter which side has done it. It is its conviction that there is no military solution to the conflict; only 'an inclusive political dialogue to resolve the crisis should remain the focus of the United Nations, including the Council' (Kaur 2013: 33). India contributed US$4 million towards humanitarian relief tor Syrian refugees.

The spread of intrastate conflicts across the continent of Africa has preoccupied time and energies of the Security Council in an unmatched way. In Sierra Leone, where the UN sent a major peace operation with Chapter VII mandate to implement the peace accord between the government and rebel forces, it faced serious challenge when the Revolutionary United Front resumed major offensive. India advised the Security Council strongly against withdrawal of the UN peacekeepers. It had also warned against authorizing use of force by multinational coalition while the peacekeeping mission was present. Instead, it suggested that the existing peacekeeping contingents be afforded unified command with professional and well-equipped reinforcements so that they would be able to ensure that the government institutions and power would not fall into the hands of the rebel forces. In any case, India made it clear that its contingents would not be withdrawn from the difficult mission (Sharma 2000a: 24–25). The growing incidents of piracy off the coast of Somalia were also a matter of great concern to India. More than 11 per cent seafarers employed by international shipping companies happened to be Indians, and some of them were taken hostage by Somali pirates, besides the fact that a good part of India's trade goes through the waters. So India favoured coordinated naval operations to accompany commercial ships to guard against piracy attacks, and also prosecution of the apprehended pirates as per the respective national or international laws (Ray 2010: 34–35). Other theatres, such as Sudan, South Sudan and the Democratic Republic of Congo also elicited constructive and clear positions from India, while it participated as a non-member in the Council meetings. In most of these situations, India has singled out the threat from terrorism, allied to the narcotic and human traffickers apart from helping transnational organized crime.

New Dangers to International Security

In the era of increased non-traditional threats to international security, India underlined the role of non-state actors that not only use, but also target women, children and civilian populations at large in waging protracted conflicts for sectarian and power grab objectives. Increase in the intrastate conflicts, terrorist attacks, ethnic cleansing and egregious violations of human rights has affected women and children the most. Extending full support to the principles and objectives of the Security Council Resolution 1325 (2000) in regard to the impact of armed conflicts on women and the corrective steps needed to reverse that impact, India noted that greater participation of women in the areas of conflict prevention, peace negotiations and post-conflict reconstruction is germane to the issue.[2] While some measures would need to emerge from the conflict-ridden societies themselves, others are more long-term and structural, involving promotion of democratic ideals and practices, freedom of speech and expression, effecting improvements in economic and social conditions and the expansion of opportunities for education and productive employment (Sen 2004b: 34). India supports greater presence of women in the peacekeeping missions and women advisers in major missions. India was among the sponsors of relevant Security Council Resolutions 1888 (2009) and 1889 (2009). India has always held that the growing attacks against civilians are condemnable and protection of civilians should be approached through the framework of international law in the sense that protection of civilians is primarily a national responsibility. The role of the international community may be through assistance in national capacity-building, rather than intervention mechanisms (Akbaruddin 2016a: 36).

In the aftermath of the armed intervention in Kosovo by the NATO countries in 1999 and against the backdrop of genocide in Rwanda and Srebrenisca in the mid-1990s, the debate on humanitarian intervention to protect populations from mass crimes got revived in the early 2000s. This was so notwithstanding the fact that the General Assembly in the Millennium Declaration in September 2000 avoided endorsing the concept of humanitarian intervention (Sharma 2000b: 20). When the new concept of 'Responsibility to Protect' (RtoP) surfaced in place of humanitarian intervention in the next few years, India raised serious objections with the support of many non-aligned countries, such as Egypt and Pakistan in the course of consultations on the wording of 2005 World Summit Outcome document that

---

[2] The Indian representatives referred to various United Nations reports which state that women globally constitute less than 4 per cent of signatories to peace agreements and less than 10 per cent of negotiators at peace tables. Moreover, women constitute only 3 per cent of the military and 10 per cent of the police personnel who are deployed by the United Nations in peace missions. These numbers reflect the enormity of the challenges that the UN is confronted with (Akbaruddin 2016b: 33).

protection of its population is one of the foremost responsibilities of every state, and international community's role should be to assist the capabilities of willing states (Sen 2005b). India, like many non-aligned countries, has little disagreement with the rationale of the cardinal features of the first and second pillars of the RtoP. But in so far as the third pillar regarding military action on behalf of the international community as a legitimate means of enforcing rights in the face of a state's failure goes, India opined, it is contrary to the internationalist impulse of our age. Further, India pointed out, the thresholds for pillar three intervention—such as just causes, right intentions, last resort, proportional means, reasonable prospects and the right authority to take a decision—remain elusive and contested. Though there is no common understanding on such concepts related to the four crimes referred to in the 2005 World Summit Outcome document, some have even sought to expand the scope of the RtoP to include situations that may arise from pandemics, climate change and natural disasters (Akbaruddin 2018a: 13–14). Experience shows that implementing the notion of the RtoP in order to prevent or stop major internal abuses within a State has in several instances been used to frame or justify interventions by external powers (Murthy and Kurtz 2016: 47; Pai 2013: 303–318). They include instances when the Security Council failed to agree to intervene under Chapter VII of the Charter and other instances when mandates have been interpreted in a manner not originally authorized, as it happened in Libya in 2011 (Puri H.S. 2016).

Among other issues, India highlighted the growing menace of the illicit trade in small arms and light weapons whose value in the early decades of this century was estimated at US$1.5 billion. The proliferation of small arms has aggravated use of more than 300,000 children in armed conflicts in more than 87 countries, because they are easy to handle and less expensive. It is not the states which are bound by the international treaty obligations but the non-state actors such as terrorists who are emerging at the centre of the new security threats in using mainly small and light weapons illicitly (Bose 2000: 19–20). India chaired the group of governmental expert to draft international instrument to enable states to identify and trace illicit small arms and light weapons in a 'timely and reliable manner' (Nambiar 2002b: 20–21).

Again, India struck a strong note of caution that when the Security Council continuously expands the scope of its work, it would not only overlap its functioning with that of other mandated UN bodies, but would also be committing its valuable time and resource allocations to functions best handled elsewhere (Nambiar 2004a: 12).[3] The changing nature of international conflict has not escaped India's attention. In the present times, the issues of peace and security cannot be seen in isolation from the wider development-related issues that are dealt with outside the Council. A more holistic approach towards gender equality and empowerment, access to health care, education, employment, and the strengthening of democratic institutions and processes are all important aspects of a holistic approach to prevent conflict (Lal 2016: 52).

Non-discriminatory Nuclear Disarmament

The new century saw the emergence of India as a nuclear weapon state and yet it is evincing interest in nuclear disarmament goal at the UN. Its nuclear policy was stated to be 'restrained and responsible' fully committed to universal, verifiable nuclear disarmament (Vajpayee 2000: 28). India stated its intention to join a multilateral treaty to reinforce its announcement about no-first use and non-use of nuclear weapons against non-nuclear weapon countries. Three draft resolutions India has been associated with as a co-sponsor all through the years, among others, are: the draft resolution on a convention on the prohibition of the use of nuclear weapons, the draft resolution on reducing nuclear danger arising from accidental or unauthorized use of nuclear weapons, and the draft resolution on measures to prevent terrorists from acquiring WMDs. This is a marker of continuity in India's approach to nuclear disarmament in step with Rajiv Gandhi

---

[3] On an occasion India objected to references to the recruitment and use of children by Maoist extremist groups in eastern and northern India in the Secretary-General's Report, on the ground that the matter did not fall within the Special Representative's mandate (Puri M. 2010: 23).

Action Plan of 1988. As such, India expressed its commitment to work for the goal of nuclear disarmament 'by a step-by-step process underwritten by a universal commitment and an agreed multilateral framework that is global and non-discriminatory' (Advani 2012: 11). Similarly, India would support the negotiation of a non-discriminatory and internationally verifiable treaty banning the production of fissile material for nuclear weapons and other nuclear explosive devices (FMCT) without compromising India's security interests. Equally notably, in line with its security interests and preference for non-discriminatory and multilateral verification regime, India voted consistently against those texts that demanded India to join NPT as a non-nuclear weapon state urgently and unconditionally (Gill 2012: 22).

Having actively participated in the negotiations on arms trade treaty, India expressed dissatisfaction that the treaty fell short on two important expectations, viz. making 'real impact on illicit trafficking in conventional arms and their illicit use, especially their use by terrorists and other unauthorized and unlawful non-State actors' and ensuring 'a balance of obligations between exporting and importing States' (Parkar 2013: 9). India abstained on the text on the ground that it was reviewing the treaty from defence, security and foreign policy interests. Again, India supported no-first placement of weapons in outer space. As a major space-faring nation, India has vital development and security interests there. India supports that objective, as well as that of strengthening the international legal regime, with the aim of protecting and preserving access to space for all and preventing the weaponization of outer space, with no exceptions (Gambhir 2016: 2).

Expectations from Globalization and Pursuit of Sustainable Development Agenda

India saw connection between globalization and development. As India saw it, the choice was not between globalization and isolation. Notwithstanding creation of wealth and opportunities by globalization, it has also brought in instability and insecurity. Moreover, the benefits of globalization have not been equitably shared and its costs are unevenly borne, as the global financial and economic crises had shown. While global living standards have been rising, extreme poverty has still affected 23 per cent of the world's population in 1998, compared with 28 per cent in 1987, and the total number of poor people in the world remained constant, with 1.2 billion living on less than one dollar a day, and 2.8 billion on less than two dollars—500 million in South Asia alone.[4] The skewed globalization has naturally engendered protests in different financial capitals.

India particularly drew attention to the phenomenon of what it called 'feminization of poverty and the marginalization' wherein a new category of poor, who do not inherit poverty, falls into it because of inadequate income, a lack of access to social services and ecological deterioration. While governments in developing countries do their best to improve health services for women and to provide medicine at affordable costs, they need greater support from their development partners in the international community (Joshi 2000: 18).

The UN embodied a vision of global solidarity in adopting Millennium Development Goals (MDGs) in the Millennium Summit 2000. The goals touching upon incidence of absolute poverty, promoting human settlements, environment and development partnership represent a global compact that should bring together all member states, developed as well as developing. A sustained and broad-based annual per capita income increase of 3 per cent is required to meet the goal of reducing by half, by the year 2015, the proportion of people living on less than a dollar a day. It has been estimated that an additional US$50 billion a year in ODA alone would be needed. It would be no exaggeration to state that the success or failure of the MDGs hinges on whether developed countries meet their commitments in the areas of trade, debt relief and aid (Nambiar 2003b: 25–26). The MDGs embodied a quantifiable vision of certain important economic

---

[4] India had shared its success in reducing poverty from 38.9 per cent in 1987 to 23 per cent in 2000, with a hope to further reduce poverty to a level of 10 per cent by 2012 (Reddy 2002: 5).

and social rights and, in this sense, they carry forward the right to development. Nonetheless, India was disappointed with the follow-up characterized by slow, if little, help from the developed countries. India found it unacceptable that not one of 97 reports prepared on MDGs covers any developed country.

India asserted that rising food prices and associated volatility, accentuated by the global economic crisis, were seriously undermining efforts to mitigate hunger, poverty and malnutrition throughout the world, particularly in poor countries of Africa. Ironically, in India's contention, food waste was equal to one-third of total annual global food production, and would suffice to feed the world's one billion hungry people. That situation could be corrected only by improved regulation of commodity markets (Chowdhury 2012: 7). Paradoxically, while food security was a priority in the post-2015 development agenda and was prominent among the sustainable development goals (SDGs), there was reluctance to address the issue as part of global trade rules. Developing countries such as India must have the freedom to use food reserves to feed their poor without the threat of sanctions (Narang 2014: 11).

India expressed satisfaction that South–South trade had rebounded in 2010 at a faster rate than anticipated and now accounted for 55 per cent of exports from developing countries and one-fourth of world exports. The trend towards regional integration to promote economies of scale was another promising new development. It supported the UNCTAD prescription for stricter regulation of the financial sector and for a greater focus on income growth as the basis for sustainable and balanced development worldwide (O'Brien 2013: 7–8). Also India called for reinvigoration of the Doha Development Round to deliver a fair, balanced and equitable outcome so that barriers preventing developing countries from participating fully in global trade are be removed, as should trade-distorting subsidies in the agricultural sector in developed countries (Choudhry 2013b: 10).

As the process to develop a set of SDGs had begun, Indian delegates stressed that the MDGs must be integrated in the new framework so that the unmet development priorities continue to be the main focus. In the global discourse on the post-2015 development agenda, the focus ought to be on the word 'development' (Krishna 2012: 11). The effective management of globalization was an essential element for the post-2015 development agenda (Choudhry 2013a: 8).

Addressing the high-level plenary meeting marking adoption of the post-2015 SDGs, India's Prime Minister welcomed the vision behind the 2030 Agenda (GAOR 2015) for its lofty and comprehensive outlook. India expressed satisfaction about the fact that the vision gives priority to problems that have persisted over the past decades and reflects our evolving understanding of social, economic and environmental issues. The Indian Prime Minister welcomed the prominence the agenda gave to poverty eradication as well as environmental goals, with special focus on climate change and sustainable consumption (Modi 2015: 17–18). He also utilized the opportunity to share India's efforts in housing, power, water, healthcare, education and sanitation sectors.

According to India, the 2030 Agenda and the SDGs sought to integrate and balance the three pillars of economic growth, social inclusion and environmental protection. However, the eradication of poverty and hunger are necessarily the first priorities, without which no development could be sustainable. India has integrated the framework of the SDGs into its national development strategies and dedicated one day of each parliamentary session to discuss progress on the goals. The success of India in sustaining robust economic growth to eradicate poverty would contribute in no small measure to the global achievement of the goals (Sinha 2016: 17–18). The national development goals of India are mirrored in the SDGs, which would be achieved through a whole-of-government approach with unity of purpose and efforts at all levels.

Climate Change: Part of Solution, Not Problem

India's insistence has been that respect for the Rio Principles, in particular the principle of common but differentiated responsibilities, must underpin global cooperation on sustainable development. In the context of the UN Convention to Combat Desertification, Indian delegation welcomed the inclusion of land degradation, desertification and deforestation as a focal area for financing by the Global Environment Facility. The effectiveness of those arrangements, however, would depend largely on the allocation of additional resources to that focal area for financing the needs of affected countries.

India would be interested in balanced and comprehensive outcome to climate change negotiations in accordance with the principles and provisions of the UN Framework Convention on Climate Change (Haque 2013: 3). On the threat of climate change to international security, India is equally sharp. India is clear that reduction of greenhouse gas emissions and energy consumption by developed countries will considerably reduce threats to international security. On the other hand, although 'nothing in the greenhouse gas profile of developing countries even remotely reflects a threat to international peace and security, they are the ones whose development would be adversely impacted by greenhouse gas mitigation targets they agree to implement. Further, even if climate change is a threat, the correct forum in which to discuss what can be done about the physical effects of climate change would be the Framework Convention, not the Security Council' (Sen 2007a: 22–23). In accordance with its commitment to the 2015 Paris Agreement on Climate Change, India announced its intended nationally determined contribution by reducing its emissions by 20–25 per cent by 2020 over 2005 levels (Javadekar 2014), to build 40 per cent of power capacity from non-fossil fuels and for creating an additional carbon sink of 2.5 billion tonnes through afforestation (Sinha 2016: 18). The climate action plans of India reflected its strong commitment to substantially reduce greenhouse gas emissions, make greater use of non-fossil fuels and create additional carbon sinks. Among other initiatives, India is working with partner countries to establish the International Solar Alliance in order to facilitate the transition towards renewable energy globally (Sinha 2017: 13).

As for implementation of the Habitat Agenda, India questioned:

> Today, as we meet 29 years after Stockholm, 25 years after Vancouver, nearly a decade after Rio and five years after Istanbul, should we not ask ourselves to what extent the ground-level reality has changed for most of the people living in developing countries?

Is it not true that many more are without shelter now, inhabiting stinking slums, drinking polluted water, inhaling poisonous air, unemployed or underemployed and exposed to new scourges such as AIDS? Should we not look into the deeper implications of the fact that during all these years, while we have been adopting resolutions and observing 'days' and 'decades'? (Jagmohan 2001: 19)

Strengthening Organizational Capacity

On the question of reforming and strengthening the UN, India's approach is critical and constructive. Its position broadly is guided by three considerations: (a) the reform of the UN cannot be merely cost-cutting exercise; it should go beyond that to increase the effectiveness and efficiency of the organization; (b) no reform of the UN would be complete without the expansion of the Security Council membership; and (c) need to identify and do away with the mandates and activities that are no longer relevant. However, India has contended that the proposal to consolidate UN information centres to form a single unit at the regional level may not be appropriate to meet the needs of the developing countries. Further, the idea to utilize grants from the UN development system for advice and advocacy, which may result in blurring the borderline between advice and decision-making, would go against the time-tested characteristics of neutrality, responsiveness, impartiality and universality (Nambiar 2002c: 24–27). In this broad framework, India's views touch upon initiatives and issues concerning the work of the General Assembly, the ECOSOC, the Secretariat and creation of the new bodies, such as the Peacebuilding Commission and the Human Rights Council.

India has shown a good deal of interest in revitalization of the General Assembly and made or supported several suggestions in that respect. India is of the view that the Assembly needs to undertake a thorough review, 'not only of the agenda and programme of work for plenary meetings and of the Main Committees, but also of their methods of work, with a view to improving them and enhancing their effectiveness' (Nambiar 2003c: 4). Despite the declaratory language in the resolutions of the Assembly due to the body's policymaking function, it should be possible to rationalize and simplify the language of resolutions so that the focus is on their operational content. Further, the Assembly's proceedings could be made more purposeful by organizing high-profile parallel events, interactive dialogues, panel discussions and seminars with participation from civil society, including non-governmental organizations (NGOs), academia and the private sector. There is also a case for reaching a common agreement on reduction of number of meetings, reports and resolutions (Nambiar 2003c: 4–5). On the one hand, revitalization of the General Assembly could trigger improvements in the other organs of the system, but on the other hand, India warned that the General Assembly could not be made weak to make the Security Council strong, because weakness of one organ would lead to weakness of the other. In other words, a weak Security Council would have to rely on the General Assembly for legitimacy (Sen 2005a: 22). On a related aspect, India had strong reservations on the Eminent Persons Panel Report on Civil Society–UN Relations (GAOR 2004a), since the definition of civil society offered by Cardoso Panel was problematic to India. Opposing the recommendation which sought to open up the General Assembly deliberations to accredited non-governmental organizations, India contended that it would 'militate against both the intergovernmental principle and the principle of democratic representation, since civil society NGOs, in strict meaning of the term, have not been elected' (Sharma 2004: 18).

In addition to the expansion of the permanent and non-permanent categories of membership, India has supported the proposal of five small countries (led by Switzerland) for improvement of the Council's working methods. On its part, India has made a few suggestions which touch upon opening up the Council's deliberations to those countries not members of the Council. They include, as a general rule, the meetings of the Council must be open to all UN member states; there should be regular consultations as per Articles 31 and 32 of the Charter, with those non-members which have a special interest in the substantive matter under consideration in the Council; participation of non-members in the Council's subsidiary organs should be promoted; regular and substantive consultations should be held with troop- and police-contributing countries when the mandates of peace operations are to be framed or changed. Besides, there should be regular consultations with the Presidents of the General Assembly and the ECOSOC (Puri H.S. 2010b: 10).

India has been a strong supporter of the ECOSOC's mandate for system-wide coordination in development cooperation. Accordingly, in order to restore its role in that regard, India welcomed the move in 2006 to incept Development Cooperation Forum within the Council with an important function to regularly review and assess international economic policies and their impact on development (Sen 2006b: 7).

As far as managerial issues go, India advocated the need to strengthen oversight in the UN system by making the oversight bodies independent. The UN should have a fair, transparent and rules-based selection process that is based on equitable geographical representation and has due regard for gender balance (Sen 2006c: 14). Citing the Secretary-General's report on the composition of the Secretariat (GAOR 2006c), it was contended that only about 40 per cent of posts at the senior and policymaking levels were occupied by the staff from developing countries, even though developing countries constituted the overwhelming majority of the organization's membership. It was perhaps time to rationalize the selection process, especially as the mathematical formula for calculating desirable ranges of representation gave undue weight to the budget (Vijayaraghavan 2007: 6). India supported creation of UN-Women which resulted from consolidation of four UN fringe agencies in 2010.

India has firm views on financing problem too. It strongly believes that the current methodology based on the principles of 'capacity to pay' and the 'low per capita income adjustment' must continue. Alongside, other core elements of the current methodology of fixing the scale of assessments, such as base period, gross national income, conversion rates, gradient, floor, ceiling for least-developed countries, and debt stock adjustment must be kept intact. India is critical of the efforts by some delegations to introduce the element of maximum ceiling in the peacekeeping scale (Kumar 2018a). Further, delays in clearing outstanding dues by major contributors to the regular budget have been perennial problems that hindered the operations of the UN. While India has been diligent in paying its assessed contributions in full and in time, many powerful and wealthy nations deliberately delay to demonstrate their displeasure against certain activities of the UN. It has been brought out that 34 per cent of the arrears were concentrated with only two member states and a further 41 per cent were concentrated with a group of seven member states, several of which were permanent members of the Security Council (Beg 2010: 3–4).

India welcomed 'historic' reform measure in the form of establishment of the Peacebuilding Commission (PBC) on the occasion of the 60th anniversary of the UN (Sen 2005c: 9–10). India has welcomed the inception of the PBC in 2005 which is expected to fill an important institutional gap and hoped that the Commission would coordinate the security, economic reconstruction and development needs of countries emerging from conflict, wherever it agrees to act upon a request for advice (Puri H.S. 2009b: 28). India's positive view on the PBC was also to express solidarity with the African countries which wanted such a body. Its representative, however, drew attention to some of the concerns about the design of the new body. India was displeased that the PBC as a subsidiary body to both the General Assembly and the Security Council might cause confusion in its working. Further, constraints on the right of those countries already on the agenda of the Security Council to seek advice from the PBC for post-conflict recovery could be a breach of the sovereign equality principle (Murthy 2007a). India was also unhappy that the Security Council in its resolution ensured automatic representation to the five permanent members in the PBC organizing committee without going through election process, which was again a departure from the previously agreed consensus in the informal consultations on the structure of the PBC. Thus, in India's assessment, the PBC was being reduced to a form not envisaged in the 2005 outcome document (Sen 2005c: 9–10). As India gained experience as member of its organizing committee in its capacity as a top troop contributor to the peacekeeping operations, India has offered advice on various aspects of future functional strategy. For instance, according to India, external assistance channelled through the PBC should go hand in hand with the imperative of national ownership of post-conflict peacebuilding. For national ownership minimizes wastage and duplication of effort. And to make progress, the UN needs to forge an integrated approach, for the world sees only one UN, not its constituent organs or member states (Sen 2008a: 28).

In contrast to its initial reservations on the design of the PBC, India expressed satisfaction about the General Assembly resolution in 2006 that established Human Rights Council replacing the UNCHR. India was particularly pleased that the text on Human Rights Council did not depart from what was agreed in the informal negotiations. India expressed happiness that the Human Rights Council has not been subjected to the 'Security Council-led conditionalities'. All in all, India was gratified that the UN could prove its critics wrong by achieving broad agreement to create 'something with a high threshold, something that is new' (Sen 2006a: 31).

Summary

As the above analysis demonstrates, India in the 21st century has new tasks cut out for it in the UN in a range of issue areas, ranging from unconventional aspects threatening international security in a big way. Protection of civilians, including women and children, drug trafficking and use of small arms and light weapons are among them. India clearly sees predominant role of non-state actors as a major menace to the stability of global security order and calls for united effort to contain the threat from non-state actors. As for theatres of conflict, the intrastate conflict is a pronounced phenomenon, and India's response represents advocacy of nationally owned peace process with the benign involvement of the international community under the umbrella of the UN, coupled with pragmatism to authorize and participate in robust peacekeeping operations in delicate conflict theatres like South Sudan and Democratic Congo. In the area of nuclear disarmament also, India clearly follows its traditional commitment for total prohibition of use and threat of nuclear weapons, without setting aside its security and foreign policy interests by insisting that such a regime should be universal, non-discriminatory and verifiable. There is naturally a firm insistence on rejecting the demand to become party to NPT that does not recognize its newly earned status as nuclear weapon power. Development continues to remain the core of its engagement on trade, debt relief, climate change and post-2015 agenda. In these matters, India on the one hand forged useful coalitions such as BRICS, but also is keen to present itself as a responsible and conscientious partner in global problem-solving. The emphasis on reserving the UN for searching solutions to common problems and resisting any use for narrow, short-sighted gains is a phenomenon that seems to be fetching rewards in more ways than one. The electoral gains are apparently one powerful incentive of this strategy. On the question of UN reforms, India's perspectives are both critical and constructive—applying the criterion whether changes are adding to the capacity or eroding the functional autonomy and capacity of the UN.

CHAPTER 5

India's Aspiration for Permanent Seat in the Security Council

The purpose of this chapter is to analyse in some detail India's political and diplomatic attempts to secure a permanent seat as a part of the larger campaign for enlargement of the prestigious UN principal organ, the Security Council. It is 26 years since the Indian campaign began, and seven prime ministers have led the effort carried forward by several foreign ministers and ambassador rank diplomats. Yet the humongous effort does not seem to be approaching the desirable conclusion. The reasons for making the Security Council more representative than it is presently so as to enhance its credibility and legitimacy, the tactical trajectory of the aspiration India pursued so far, and the reasons that account for the lack of progress are worthy enough for a systematic and sober assessment. But before this, a brief summation of the remarkably exceptional features of the Council, with reference to its composition, powers and decision-making procedure would be instructive.

Multi-speciality Security Council

The founding fathers of the UN seem to have paid special attention to the design of the Security Council. Although the UN highlights its multi-purpose character in the very opening chapter of the Charter, the pre-eminence of one purpose, viz. the maintenance of international peace and security, was left in no doubt. To pursue this all important purpose with a single-minded orientation, a 'security-specialist' council was conceived. What is remarkable is that, to match with the security-specific mandate and in the interest of its efficient functioning, the Council's membership is deliberately made very rigid, while being endowed with unusual set of binding powers along with exceptional procedure for decision-making (Goodrich et al. 1969: 199–227).

As for its composition, the Council was designed as a strictly limited membership body. Membership is not a matter of right, but a privilege. That privilege is stratified in the form of two categories, viz. permanent and non-permanent. Article 23 of the Charter names five countries as permanent members of the Council. The basis on which only those five, not others, were conferred the status of permanent membership was not shared. Simply it was a self-conferred status that formalized formidable stature some of these five countries attained by virtue of their victory in the Second World War. At least two of them (China and France) did not earn this status; they were simply the beneficiaries of the gesture rooted in the geopolitical necessities of the other three—the United States, the United Kingdom and the former Soviet Union. Some participant states at San Francisco Conference, particularly Australia and New Zealand, offered heroic resistance to the arbitrary arrangement, but in vain. There was hardly any assurance about making the permanent membership open for alterations or additions in future. In sum, the five permanent members froze their superior status and built near-insurmountable hurdles to any future change in the permanent category of the Council membership.

On the other hand, the situation regarding the non-permanent membership (increased from six to ten through an amendment to the Charter in 1963, which came into effect from 1966) is somewhat different. Apart from the reasons of historical precedent under the League of Nations, the founding fathers of the UN desired inclusion of the non-permanent members for reasons of legitimizing the Security Council's decisions. In other words, inclusion of a small number of non-permanent members could make it a 'microcosm of world opinion' (Nicholas 1975: 76–101). But the access to the non-permanent membership was made far from easy. Unlike the permanent membership which is not regulated by any criteria, the Charter lays down two-part criteria for the election of non-permanent members. The criteria insists on firstly, the contribution to the maintenance of international peace and security and other purposes of the organization, and secondly, equitable geographical representation. Notably, however, the Charter does not provide guidance for determining as to what amounts to the 'contribution' to the maintenance of international peace and security and how to measure that contribution. (Presumably at that time contribution implied active participation in the Second World War.) Furthermore, it must be noted in parenthesis that middle ranking powers, such as Canada and India, pushed through this contribution criterion at the San Francisco Conference to ensure better chances of their election as the non-permanent members (Rajan 1973: 439). The sponsoring powers were receptive to the idea as it served their objective of ensuring restricted access to the membership of the Council. They doubly ensured it by requiring the election of non-permanent members with the support of two-thirds of members voting in the General Assembly. And the term so earned through the democratic process cannot last for more than two years. To further ensure that the non-permanent members would not attain even pretence of permanence, the Charter explicitly disallows immediate re-election of a retiring member. In other words, the Council's composition is exclusive, not inclusive. Further, any change (minor or major) in the composition would require amendment of the Charter, which is far from easy.[1] The fact that the Charter was amended only thrice so far is a testimony to this.

Equally exceptional about the Security Council are its extraordinary powers of far-reaching importance in the area of peace and security. The Charter in Article 24 makes it abundantly clear that when the

---

[1] According to Article 108, amendments to the Charter would have to be adopted in the General Assembly by a vote of two-thirds of the members, and the amendments so adopted would come into effect only when ratified by two-thirds of the member states, including all the permanent members.

Council discharges its 'primary' responsibility in the peace and security matters, it does so on behalf of all members of the UN. As if this authority were not sufficient, member states agree in advance to accept and implement all future decisions the Council takes (Article 25), without reservations no matter what the consequences could be. It is on this foundation that the Council exercises the authority to determine any threat to peace or name an aggressor country, and to launch undefined range of punitive measures (military and non-military alike) to be carried out by all members against the culprits.

The uniqueness of the Security Council composition and powers is further embellished by the decision-making procedure, too. Unlike all other principal deliberative organs where either a simple or two-thirds majority is required for decisions, the Security Council's resolutions are to be adopted by a special, if not distinct, procedure. As per Article 27 of the Charter, the minimum number of affirmative votes required for a decision on procedural matters is nine out of 15 (originally seven out of 11 prior to the 1963 amendment): which is to say that nine is neither simple nor two-thirds majority in that body; but something special falling between the two types. Further, while a decision on procedural matters would not distinguish a vote cast by a non-permanent member from that of a permanent member as long as the requirement of nine affirmative votes is met,[2] on substantive matters, such as peace and security questions, nine affirmative votes should include concurring votes of the permanent members. In other words, a negative vote by any one permanent member can negate the prospects of a decision on a substantive proposal even if the requirement of nine votes is otherwise met. This capacity of a permanent member to incapacitate the Security Council is commonly referred to as 'veto' power. It was a subject of sharp criticism both at and since the San Francisco Conference on the ground that it was a serious breach of the principle of sovereign equality. Nonetheless, acceptance of the veto provision was the non-negotiable price the small and

---

[2] One will be well advised not to take seriously the overtones of sovereign equality here because firstly the range of procedural matters is rather limited, and secondly, any difference as to whether a matter is procedural cannot be settled by any nine votes.

middle powers had to pay to see the UN come into being. Many of them accepted it (as India's Vijaya Lakshmi Pandit put it) as a 'necessary evil' (Berkes and Bedi 1958: 3). It would be suicidal for the UN to take strong action for peace when the permanent members are disunited. The lack of unity among the permanent members (P5) is evident 207 times during 1946–2019.

There is yet another aspect of the Security Council's uniqueness. Perhaps in the case of no other principal organ of the UN, the gap between promise and performance has been so glaring as regards the Council's track record. The standard explanation for the Council's inability to deliver relates to the East–West Cold War. The end of the Cold War by 1990 and the resultant growth of collegiality among the P5 members had fuelled the hopes of an efficient and effective Security Council devoted to the actualization of the dreams of the founders. But the euphoria tapered off soon afterwards, owing to serious shortcomings in its performance in addressing major regional and local conflict situations, such as Bosnia–Herzegovina, Somalia, Rwanda, Iraq, Libya, Syria, Sudan and Yemen. In many of them, questions have been raised about the Council's credibility and legitimacy. It has become clear that legitimacy is larger than legalistic formalism, and is far beyond the control of manipulative tactics of winning coalitions.

It is in this context that expanding the membership of the Council, particularly the permanent category, as part of enhancing its credibility and legitimacy has gained salience among the official and non-official quarters, particularly since the early 1990s. India seized the opportunity to add its voice and weight to press for improvements in the Security Council, thereby stake its claim for a permanent position at the high table.

Outline of India's Candidature for the Permanent Seat

By virtue of their status as the second and third biggest contributors to the UN budget, Japan and Germany staked their claim in 1992 for permanent seats in the UNSC with open support from the United States followed by the General Assembly's decision to set up an open-ended working group in 1992 to discuss all issues related to enlargement of the Council's membership. In the meantime, a major developing country from Latin America (a totally unrepresented region in the permanent member category) joined the budding league of aspirants. After first making a critique about the democratic deficit of the Council membership in its communications to the working group chair,[3] India came forward to officially stake a claim for permanent seat in the 1994 session of the General Assembly.

It would be instructive to refer here to the historical dimension of India's discreet approach to the suggestions about UNSC permanent seat, which is a contrast to India's active advocacy of such status since 1994. The records, declassified in due course, of deliberations in 1945 reveal that the British India's delegation to San Francisco Conference headed by Sir Ramaswamy Mudaliar was unhappy at the London preparatory consultations about the choice of China as a permanent member, keeping in view the fact that India's contribution to the war effort was greater. His colleague on the delegation, Sir Feroz Khan Noon (later to become Pakistan's foreign minister) was more explicit about India's claim for permanent seat (Rajan 1973: 439). However, the very fact that it was not yet independent probably guided India's reluctance to press the suggestion made by Australia and Yugoslavia at the San Francisco Conference that India should be considered for permanent membership. A few years later, in the thick of the Korean crisis, Nehru reportedly politely rejected the US enquiries, sent through India's representative, Sir B. N. Rau, if India would accept permanent seat ousting China. Nehru wrote to Rau that India was 'certainly entitled to a permanent seat, but ruled out assuming that

---

[3] India marshalled a whole range of arguments in support of the enlargement of both the permanent and non-permanent category of seats. The themes stressed often concern the principle of equitable geographical representation, population, contribution to the Charter purposes of maintaining international peace and security, especially in relation to the peacekeeping operations, financial contribution, economy size and potential. India's perspective on some of these themes bears relevance here. For example, India argued, the total population of the present permanent members is less than 1.75 billion—leaving therefore two-thirds of the world's population without representation in the permanent category (India 1993: 47).

position at the cost of China because it would not only 'do us little good [but also] would bring a great deal of trouble in its train' (Rana 1970: 61).

In the late 1950s and early 1960s, India actively worked for increase of non-permanent seats of the Council by exerting diplomatic pressure on the reluctant major powers on behalf of the Afro-Asian group. Again, it was among the countries that demanded further expansion of the non-permanent seats in 1979, but the question remained in limbo until Japan and Germany with the American support revived the issue in 1992 by bringing to the fore the hitherto untouched issue of enlargement of permanent seats in the Council.

On the strength of its advocacy of criteria-based enlargement of the Council giving due attention to population, contribution to international peace and security and economic potential which in a way implies India's own aspiration, India took the next logical step by offering its candidature officially and openly for the first time in the 49th session of the General Assembly. India's foreign minister asserted (Mukherjee 1994: 16):

> On the basis of any criteria—population, size of economy, contribution to the maintenance of international peace and security and to peace-keeping or future potential—India deserves to be a permanent member of the Security Council. In India's perception, India becomes an obvious choice when any objective criteria are applied to expand the Council.

The pitch was raised to the higher political level, and continuously. Speaking at the 50th anniversary commemorative meeting, the Indian Prime Minister added his voice to assert that the UN 'cannot afford to be seen either exclusivist or incomplete, either in appearance or in outlook' (Rao 1995: 45). While declaring India's readiness to assume all responsibilities of the permanent membership, another Prime Minister elaborated India's case in the 1997 session of the General Assembly.

> We are the largest democracy in the world, with a civilization replete with ancient values and achievements, as well as a world view based on a universalist inspiration, participative governance,

respect for diversity and pluralism, as well as the readiness for constructive engagement in the world affairs. These strengths, we believe, would be an asset to an expanded Security Council. India's standing as one of the leading economies of the world will be progressively strengthened, and we are prepared to bear fully the responsibilities of permanent membership. India's long-standing participation in United Nations peacekeeping operations testifies not only to the dedication and professionalism of Indian soldiers, but also to the political will of the government to actively contribute to these operations. (Gujral 1997: 9)

Every successive Prime Minster, whether it was Atal Bihari Vajpayee, Manmohan Singh or Narendra Modi unfailingly called for timely changes in the Security Council's membership and that India 'is ready to play its role' in an expanded Council (Singh M. 2005: 29; Vajpayee 2000: 28). They have also reminded about the need for timely expansion, because the matter is pending for a long time without much progress. India gave 'main priority' at the time of the 60th anniversary in 2005 by wanting the reform to be completed by the end of the year (Singh N. 2005: 28). Unless the 20th century institutions such as the Security Council are made more democratic and participatory, they will 'face the risk of irrelevance in the twenty-first century' (Modi 2014: 17).

Multi-pronged Pursuit of the Aspiration

The burden of vigorously pursuing the aspiration for the coveted seat fell on the shoulders of the senior diplomats under the guidance of the foreign ministers both in the bilateral and multilateral formats. What has been done in the course of the two-and-a-half decades long pursuit of India's aspiration on the issue can be summed up in terms of four interrelated lines of the campaign.

First and foremost, it is notable that India has achieved and impressively showcased its enhanced stature in world political arena. The 1998 underground nuclear weapon tests and the series of successful intermediate- and long-range missile tests boosted its hard power capabilities. India's strides in the use of advanced space technology are already well received. The United States has warmed up to India by entering into a major civil nuclear cooperation agreement in 2007, and the nuclear majors (except for China) want India to be part of the nuclear suppliers group. Besides, there has been a highly impressive economic rise of India, thanks to the opportunities provided by the economic globalization and its own policies of liberalization. In the early years of the new century, the huge Indian market attracted foreign investments at unprecedented levels, it built up comfortable levels of foreign exchange, and it uplifted the incomes of lower- and middle-class people; and above all, the country has lately emerged as the third largest economy and is among the fastest growing economies in the world, growing at the annual rate of 7–8 per cent on an average for the past decade or so. India has become part of the regular gatherings of world economic powers, such as the Group of 20 major economies, besides becoming a special attraction to global corporates at the Davos meets of World Economic Forum. On the side of soft power demonstration, India's readiness to contribute fully formed troop and police contingents for most of the major UN peace operations has reaffirmed India as a responsible and reliable partner in international peace and security efforts. On India's initiative, the UN has in 2014 recognized the benefits of Indian ancient yoga tradition and cleared the decks for annual observance of international yoga day. Aside from the fact that India is no longer an aid-receiving country, in fact, it has emerged as an important development partner to developing countries in the neighbourhood and beyond.[4]

The second aspect of India's campaign is the concerted lobbying to seek endorsement of its candidature through bilateral contacts. The focus of India's statespersons visiting foreign capitals, and more importantly talks with nearly every visiting foreign dignitary from major, medium and small powers was to seek support to India's aspiration. Worth mentioning here is the comment made by President Barack Obama of the United States during a visit to India in November 2010 that he looked forward to India becoming a permanent member of the reformed UNSC. This was partly due to much improved bilateral

---

[4] For these aspects, see separate Chapter 10 on India's Development Diplomacy at the UN.

relationship between India and the United States, although the United States had not done anything beyond this oral support. Most of the neighbouring countries, countries from Africa, small island developing countries, besides the permanent members, such as France, Russia and the United Kingdom, have indicated their sympathy to the aspiration. Officials claimed in 2012 that India had support of nearly 130 countries, thanks to the lobbying launched over the long years.

Third interesting point pertains to India's deliberate construction of its case in conservative, if not constructive, mode without deviating from the existing structural outline of the Security Council. Right from the beginning, India's articulation highlighted its preference that the Council's expansion should be only in both the permanent and non-permanent member categories, that there should not be any discrimination between the new and the existing permanent members, and that the selection or election should be according to the principle of equitable geographical representation as applied in the allocation of non-permanent seats. Further, the new permanent seats should belong to a single designated country as at present, not collectively attached to a group of countries. As an extension of this position, India saw no reason to discriminate between the existing permanent members and the new permanent members in terms of their voting power. In other words, India is very much averse to a 'radical reorganization of the Council, with new categories of members, or new geographical arrangements, [which] will lead to more complications' (Chaturvedi 1994: 22). Equally notable is its contention that there should be a level-playing field among all claimants for permanent seats, thereby rejecting any attempt to prioritize the claims of some countries at the expense of others. In the words of one of the former Indian ambassadors, 'We should not yield to the temptation of... cosmetic reforms which bring no resolution to the core problem. We have stated time and again that partial solutions are no solutions at all and would be a disservice to the membership of the Organization' (Sharma 2000c: 27).

India was patient and pragmatic enough in pursuing its aspiration knowing fully well that reconciling divergent opinions would be a time-consuming process involving give and take among different negotiating parties. It took active interest in the proceedings of the open-ended working group ever since it was established in 1992. It suggested that the expansion of the permanent category should be as per objective criteria (India 1993: 47–49). Subsequently, small steps forward in the long winding process were warmly welcomed. This was evident when Ismail Razali, the General Assembly President and concurrently the chair of the working group, proposed a plan in 1997 for enlargement of the Council from 15 to 24 by adding five permanent members without veto powers, which could inevitably pass through three stages beginning from adoption of framework resolution by two-thirds majority in the Assembly, followed by selection of permanent members by two-thirds of Members present and voting, and finally the Charter to be amended as per Article 108 procedure. India warmed up to the proposal but a large section of members rejected the plan (Muller 2010: 15). Nonetheless, Indian delegations actively participated in the deliberations in the working group on five specific issues, such as categories for expansion, the veto, the relationship between the Council and the Assembly and working methods (Swart 2013) admittedly with mixed results at best.

In the midst of brainstorming organized in preparation for observance of 60th anniversary of the UN, India became active when two alternative models were recommended by the Secretary-General for enlargement of the Council's membership in his much applauded report, 'In Larger Freedom' (Annan 2005: 42; Luck 2005). From then on, India expended its energies to mobilize sufficient support for clinching the issue by citing the need to clear the decks for Council enlargement as a breakthrough befitting the 60th and later 70th anniversaries of the UN in 2005 and 2015, respectively. In the words of a senior Indian diplomat,

> We need to have a results-based timeline, and the year 2015 — which will be the seventieth anniversary of the United Nations and mark tenth year since the 2005 World Summit, when all our Heads of State and Government mandated us to achieve early reforms of the Security Council — will be an important occasion for delivering concrete outcomes on that most pressing subject. We hope that we can collectively work together in a constructive and forward-looking

manner, not just on the process but on the substance as well, in the interim, to deliver on that long-due mandate. (Puri M. 2013b: 15–17)

Subsequently in 2015, India drew satisfaction by welcoming the General Assembly's 'outstanding' decision to set in motion a substantive and irreversible process of intergovernmental negotiations beginning from the 70th session (Mukerji 2015: 6).

The third discernible aspect of India's strategy has been the discreet adjustments of its positions in the light of the prevailing opinion among different sections and the need to appear flexible on stated positions. Conscious of the hesitation among large number of countries about adding more permanent members without the assurance that the Council would remain a club of powerful resisting any more changes in future, the Indian representatives acknowledged that any agreed expansion arrangement would have to be open for a review at pre-determined point of time (Sharma 1997: 18). Further, India has seemingly diluted its original stance on veto power by stating its readiness not to exercise veto power till a review of the veto occurred in the year 2020. India's Prime Minister once acknowledged that the continued possession of single veto was 'anachronistic in today's world' and urged democratic countries to provide feasible models for decision-making which should suggest neither a total unanimity nor a simple majority (Vajpayee 2003: 14–15). The text India introduced along with other aspiring countries in 2005 circuitously offered a self-restraint on exercise of veto until a review takes place.[5] This is in line with what a few Indian scholars have also suggested (Murthy 1998b: 123–124). As a seasoned ambassador (Puri H.S. 2012b) wisely acknowledged, it is not the 'case where a large number of member states are dying to use the veto. I hope all of us understand how difficult it is to use the veto. What the cost involved is? I suggest you ask those who had some recent experience.' Moreover, as the opinion

---

[5] The operative paragraph 5 states that while the new permanent members should have the same responsibilities and obligations as the current permanent members, 'they shall not exercise the right of veto until the question of the extension of the right of veto to new permanent members has been decided upon in the framework of the review,' that is, the review after 15 years (Puri H.S. 2012a).

gathered steam among influential small countries against the veto, India endorsed the demand that no veto by the existing permanent members would be allowed in situations of genocide, or the permanent members could keep away from voting on questions where they are directly involved (Puri H.S. 2010a). The Indian side repeatedly appealed to those who were obstructing discussions from going forward and negating the overwhelming opinion among member states favouring expansion in both the existing categories. It is in this context the remark made by the Indian ambassador recently may be viewed: 'we cannot allow the veto to veto the Security Council reform process' (Akbaruddin 2019b).

India sought to counter the naysayers' objections or 'aspersions' against the process of holding text-centred intergovernmental negotiations (Puri M. 2013b: 15–17). The intergovernmental negotiations are aimed to frame the broad parameters of what the expanded Security Council would be like and provide workable options on each of the five key issues as per the Assembly's directive in 2008 (Decision 62/557), and therefore it would be totally unfounded understanding that the intergovernmental negotiations would decide which countries will assume permanent members and not others. Further, the text-based negotiations are not necessarily 'inimical to the position of any group… nor as the final word'. Every member will be completely at liberty to suggest additions, deletions or amendments and to build upon such text when presented. Hence, 'to insist that no forward movement can take place until we have complete consensus is only tantamount to delaying any kind of progress'. India points out that in any case the question whether consensus exists can be tested through a vote on the floor of the General Assembly at an appropriate stage which of course has not been reached.

The fourth and perhaps the most important line of action indispensable for multilateral negotiations is its strategy to promote groups of like-minded countries to influence the course of deliberations. Two initiatives deserve to be highlighted here. First, prior to the 2005 World Summit, India joined other known aspiring countries, viz. Brazil, Germany and Japan, with scope for future representation to one or two African countries to jointly work and support each other

(Mahbubani 2015). The Group of Four (G4) has turned out to be the most vocal coalition pushing hard the case for six new permanent members.[6] Similarly, in a more important initiative, India played a key role in forming a larger group of 42 small and developing countries, including the Caribbean and Pacific Island countries (known as L69 group), to support the proposal for adding six new permanent members (besides additional non-permanent seats) with a proviso for review of the implementation of the changes made to the Council's membership (Kutesa 2015: 23–26 annex).[7] India invariably aligned its views and those of G4 with the L69. With this, it was possible to ensure the greatest numerical support to the plea for addition of new permanent members, which the opposing sides could not manage to achieve.

Hurdles to India's Aspiration

Despite the four strands in India's patient pursuit, India's aspiration for permanent membership remains stuck in the deliberations. The lack of success in the long-winded deliberations involving diverse groups of member countries is due to 'substantive and strategic differences among those professing to share specific goals' (Swart 2013: 25). The prolonged stalemate may be attributed to four interconnected bottlenecks. It is worthwhile to pay attention here to each of these hurdles, one by one.

---

[6] For one of the latest communication on the latest G4 position on issues of size of the enlarged Council, the categories of enlargement, the question of veto see Kutesa (2015: 2–5). For example, on the question of veto, the G4 states that the new permanent members 'would as a principle have the same responsibilities and obligations as current permanent members. However, the new permanent members shall not exercise the veto-right until a decision on the matter has been taken during a review, to be held 15 years after the coming into force of the reform'.

[7] The position of the L-69 on the extension of veto to new permanent members is stronger than that of G4. The L69 categorically states that the veto power should be abolished, or else 'it should be extended to all new members of the permanent category of the Security Council, who must enjoy all the prerogatives and privileges of permanent membership in the permanent category, including, the right of the veto'. This is a position identical to that of the African Union.

Firstly, one cannot shy away from the hard reality about the serious differences—both horizontal and vertical—within the Global South on the nature and scope of reforms to the Security Council. Contrary to the belief that the permanent members are responsible for the lack of consensus on the expanded Security Council, it remains a bitter truth that the developing countries across the regions of Asia, Africa and South America are deeply divided on the enlargement issue. These differences mainly are due to serious sub-regional geopolitical consequences on the already uneasy interstate relationships in the event of addition of permanent seats. For example, Latin American countries are not agreed on Brazil's candidature; particularly, Argentina and Mexico are open in their opposition. Similarly, Pakistan is naturally worried about the unalterable geopolitical ramifications if India were to be accorded the coveted position. Furthermore, both Koreas are strongly opposed to Japan's hopes of becoming a permanent member. Similarly, Italy and Spain have reservations about Germany's candidature at their expense. The African countries have their own internal differences and are unable to endorse the claims of South Africa, Nigeria or any other country, but came up in 2005 with Ezulwini consensus demanding no less than two permanent seats with full veto powers (von Freieslebein 2013: 4). To add to the complexity, the Arab countries are unhappy that they do not fit in an existing geographical group, and demand a permanent seat for themselves. Moreover, several small countries feel that it is they who deserve a permanent seat, rather than the present claimants who can take care of their security on their own strength (San Marino 1994: 9). As a matter of principle, there is strong conviction among cross section of members that the veto power per se was a mistake committed at the time of the founding of the UN; therefore nothing should be done to reinforce it by adding new permanent members with veto power. And a few of the influential small countries have pleaded for focus on improving the working methods instead of enlargement. Indeed, the fact that the developing countries are vertically divided on the subject is testified by the fact that neither the non-aligned group nor the G-77 countries have a commonly agreed position. Quite unlike now, the success for the expansion of non-permanent category members in the mid-1960s was mainly because of the united effort by the non-aligned developing countries at that time. India has, however, sought to soft-pedal these differences by mending its approach to them, rather than ending its pursuit. To some extent, it has managed it with reference to the African Union (AU) as well as the small developing countries. But the main challenge to India's aspiration comes from a relatively small number of cross-regional countries belonging to developed as well as developing categories. They are the spoilers to India's prospects.

The credit for being the greatest spoiler in the attempts to expand the Council's permanent membership goes to the high-profile coalition of some 30 countries, which identify themselves as the 'Uniting for Consensus' (UfC) group. Argentina, Canada, Colombia, Italy, Mexico, Spain and Pakistan are active in the group. They are united to keep the permanent category intact and unchanged, and resolutely reject the G4 move for enlargement of the permanent category as anti-democratic. At the cost of getting castigated as staunch friends of the unjust status quo, the UfC advocates the addition of only non-permanent seats with a provision for immediate re-election of some of them (Italy 1993). Fearing that India and the G4 countries could find a shortcut to the voting procedures,[8] the UfC countries have opposed railroading by any type of majority vote and prefer the broadest possible agreement, that is, consensus. Indeed, as a counter to G4 proposal in 2005, the group moved a proposal for creating 10 additional non-permanent seats, which will be open for middle ranking powers from various regions and those retiring members would be eligible for immediate re-election (Canada 2005: 1–2). Subsequently, the proposal was rephrased to allow 'a new category of membership, based on longer-term non-permanent seats, with the possibility of an

---

[8] In a procedural masterstroke aimed to make matters difficult for the claimants of permanent membership, the countries belonging to UfC and other countries, including some non-aligned countries, successfully got a resolution adopted in the General Assembly in December 1998. The resolution (GAOR 1998) prescribed that enlargement of the Council would have to enjoy support of not less than two-thirds of the total members, in contrast to the practice of two-thirds of those present and voting. This was widely read as a pre-emptive tactic to subvert any hasty initiative on the part of the permanent membership aspirants (von Freiesleben 2013: 5).

immediate re-election, to allow for fair and equitable representation' (Italy's letter annexed to Kutesa 2015: 122–123). India has naturally questioned the group in the following manner:

> Uniting for Consensus sounds impressive. It is relevant, therefore, to ask as to who or which countries are uniting and for what kind of consensus? These are very important countries in their own right and we need to understand why they chose to unite for a consensus that essentially calls for maintenance of the status quo, i.e., an expansion only in the non-permanent categories with different categories with slightly shorter or longer-term non-permanent seats. (Puri H.S. 2012b)

The countries most critical to the realization of India's aspiration are the permanent five (P5) and reportedly some of them are quite active in manipulating the responses of some of the groups mentioned above. True, the P5 countries do not have a publicly stated common position on the issue on the Security Council reforms. Notwithstanding the fact that three of the five permanent members have endorsed the candidature of some of the G4 countries, the reading of their statements from time to time shows that they would allow—if necessary—only a limited expansion of the Security Council, in the permanent and non-permanent categories. In any case, they do not endorse the extension of the veto privilege to the new permanent members. But all of them continue to advocate a decision by consensus (Kutesa 2015: 101–110, 114 in annex), knowing well that it is not easy to reach. Otherwise, they would not mind continuation of status quo (with regard to the permanent category) with some improvements in the working methods to be decided not by the General Assembly. France and the United Kingdom have been more forthcoming than others. Russia would prefer only limited expansion and is not opposed to India's candidature. The United States has openly supported the claims of Germany and Japan (United States 1994) and opposed the G4 initiative (von Freiesleben 2013: 7). In particular, the United States stood against India's candidature after the 1998 nuclear tests (Muller 2010: 16). China too has studiously worked to slow the process by actively encouraging the UfC group as well as the AU into taking inflexible positions (von Freiesleben 2013: 8), notwithstanding its stated position that it would like to see greater role for developing countries in the Council. More particularly, China is cleverly avoiding to expressly endorse India's claim for permanent seat. All in all, India acknowledged that if UNSC reforms were to depend only on the P5 they would not happen, because 'some of them are [seemingly] in favour of reform but in practice are actually against reform' (Puri H.S. 2012c).

The fourth impinging factor is the dynamics within the G4 leading to the impression that the group often suffers from lack of cohesion and consistency. Some of them have fallen prey to the strategy of a few P5 countries to weaken the unity of the group. If the observers are correct, Japan became less active in G4 consultations, aware of the American opposition to the G4 aggressive campaign for UNSC reforms. On the other side, President Obama's enthusiastic support, announced in New Delhi in 2010, to India's candidature was not music to other G4 members. In fact, some of the permanent members have played on these suspicions. China, for instance, reportedly told Indian officials that it would have no objection to support India's case if India desists from supporting Japan's claim for permanent seat. Fearing that the company of developing countries was not exactly helpful, Germany and Japan indicated in 2012 their willingness to consider the intermediary approach as a 'stepping stone' towards permanency. On the other hand, India has categorically rejected such option, by dubbing it as potentially a problem, not a solution.

Options and Outlook

There is no doubt that the question of enlargement of the Security Council's composition is one of the most complex tasks India has ever taken up so far, that too as a high priority matter. On the positive side, India's efforts have borne fruit in garnering much greater support than in the early days for expansion in both the permanent and non-permanent categories. Alongside, it was widely accepted by differing sections that the size of the Council after expansion should be in mid-twenties. The convergence achieved with small island and developing countries to form the largest lobbying group is also something to India's credit. However, on the flipside, numerous rounds of intergovernmental negotiations for the past 10 years have gone on without producing a text to serve as a basis for text-based negotiations. With no end in sight, some countries such as Australia have stopped attending the informal consultations, and India is dismayed with the process that has gone 'awry' (Akbaruddin 2019c).[9] As correctly noted by a former foreign minister of the country, the Security Council reform is 'not about any country's prestige or power, but about transforming the balance of power in the world' (Singh N. 2005: 28).

In that case, what is the outlook for India in realizing its aspiration? A couple of scenarios may be construed by way of concluding observations. The first is to continue to be patient without losing heart over the persistent obstacles. Compared to the situation in the early 1990s when India staked its claim for the coveted seat, India has buttressed its acceptability on the basis of its demonstrated power potential and reputational value. In the fast changing global and Asian dynamics, India may have to wait for a moment in future when either or both the United States and China come to realize that India would be vital to the management of 21st century Westphalian order and therefore concede, in a grand bargain, India's claim for a permanent seat. This is the most optimistic scenario in support of India's aspiration. In that sense, it may sound better than aborting the political project abruptly and altogether.

The alternative option is to reach out to the naysaying UfC group and concede that, as an interim reform measure, the expanded Council could have additional elected seats to be filled by election with renewable terms up to 5–10 years, if (that is of course a big if) the AU also agrees to such a prospect. Some writers from the Western think tanks expressed themselves in favour of this idea (Langmore and Thakur 2016: 110–112). Already, all three partners in G4 have signalled their willingness to consider the interim solution. Even France and the United Kingdom, having supported India's case earlier, have indicated

---

[9] The Indian permanent representative drew attention to the observation made by Sierra Leone Ambassador that the 75th anniversary of the UN may mark 'the start of the organization's rebirth and not its demise' (Akbaruddin 2019a).

their openness to considering the intermediate option as a compromise. In that sense, some reforms may be better than no reforms. Certainly, given the impressive track record of India winning election for the non-permanent seat, membership in the Human Rights Council and the judgeship in the World Court in recent years, no one doubts India's ability to make the cut in the contest for new set of seats. However, it could mean 'loss of face' for India, which has for long opposed creating new categories or hierarchies.

CHAPTER 6

India's Experiences as Elected Member of the Security Council

No matter whether and when India manages to occupy a permanent seat in the UNSC, India's experience in that body as a non-permanent member, elected by the General Assembly for a term of non-renewable two years in itself is worthy of assessment. India has been elected so far seven times, that is to say, it served as a member of the Council with full voting powers for a total duration of 14 years. The last occasion of its non-permanent membership was in 2011–2012. Indications are available about the likelihood of India getting elected to serve its eighth term from 2021 onwards. The purpose of the chapter is to take stock of the nature of its association and participation in the Security Council as a non-permanent member. Such an attempt will be useful to map the kind of interests and priorities India may like to pursue in 2021–2022.

How useful is India's experience in the Security Council as a non-permanent member to understand the broad texture of India's contribution to the UN system over the years? How principled or pragmatic have our positions been on various problems that were brought before the Council during the time it served on the Council?

What bearing does that experience have on India's aspiration for a permanent seat in the enlarged Council? This chapter explores these questions. (A word of caveat, however, is in order here: The discussion here is confined to India's association with the Security Council as a non-permanent member, and will not include the numerous times India took part in the deliberations as a non-member of the Council.)

There has been no doubt in the minds of Indian leaders about the need for an organ such as the Security Council endowed with power matching with its responsibility. As discussed in previous chapters, in India's outlook, the Security Council has a special value to reinforce the relevance of the UN for building a better world for the succeeding generations from the 'scourge of war'. As an organ entrusted with the primary responsibility for the principal purpose of securing world peace, the Council is exceptional, in terms of its composition, mandate, powers and decision-making procedure and the relationship with other organs of the UN. India understands the logic behind the argument for provision of a permanent, privileged place for a few chosen powerful countries in the Council. Equally welcome is the associated feature of the Council's elected membership in the non-permanent category—a device by which the vision for equalization or democratization of decision-making is given a concrete shape.

India's Membership Profile

At the 1945 San Francisco Conference, India showed a good deal of interest in matters relating to the Security Council's composition. Of utmost interest to India at that time was the basis of election of non-permanent members. The Indian delegation advocated weightage for factors, such as population, industrial potential, willingness and ability to contribute to international peace and security, past performance, apart from the need for representation to various regions while selecting states to sit in the Security Council. India did not press its amendment for a vote since the sponsoring powers accepted the suggestion and modified their original proposals (Rajan 1973: 446–447).

Indeed Article 23 of the Charter embodies elements of the criteria for election as non-permanent members.[1]

India's approach to the UN is characterized by 'wholehearted cooperation' through full participation 'in its councils to which her geographical position, and contribution towards peaceful progress entitle her' (ICWA 1957: 27–28). Interestingly, these remarks by Prime Minister Jawaharlal Nehru coincided with India's first successful election to the Security Council as a non-permanent member. In the past 75 years, India was elected seven times to serve two years each time as non-permanent member of the Council.[2] It is likely to be elected in 2020 again for a term beginning from January 2021, due to the support from the Asian regional grouping. India held the seat on behalf of the Asian group, except for the first time when it occupied the seat earmarked for the Commonwealth group. One of those terms (i.e. 1984–1985) coincided with India's chairpersonship of the NAM. Remarkably, India and Pakistan sat in the Council in four years which never occasioned any fireworks between the two traditional rivals. The years it served coincided with 'testing times' for the Security Council and the UN at large. Major conflict situations occurred during the time India was a member, the Korean War during 1950–1951, the two Arab-Israeli wars in 1967 and then in 1973, Israel's first invasion of Lebanon in 1977, the first Gulf War against Iraq in 1991 and the massive upheavals in Libya and Syria in 2011–2012. The significance of the seat was such that invariably senior seasoned diplomats at the level of ambassador/permanent representative represented the country. Besides, ministers of foreign affairs took part occasionally in the meetings. For example, Khurshid Alam Khan attended the meeting commemorating the 40th anniversary of the UN, while P. V. Narasimha Rao attended the January 1992 meeting

---

[1] Article 23, paragraph 1 envisages that non-permanent members will be elected with 'due regard being specially paid, in the first instance to the contribution of Members of the UN to the maintenance of international peace and security and other purposes of the Organization, and also to equitable geographical distribution'.

[2] India was unsuccessful in its electoral attempts thrice in the past. Twice it withdrew from the contest against Ukraine and Pakistan in 1947 and 1975, respectively, after realizing that it lacked sufficient support. In 1996, India contested and badly lost to Japan.

at the level of government heads. Some of the highlights of India's non-permanent membership in the Council are presented in Table 6.1.

From the information in Table 6.1, a mixed picture emerges. First, it may be noted that India held the monthly presidency of the Council nine times. The high point of India's presidency occurred when it presided over UN deliberations on Korean War (June 1950) and the Syrian conflict (August 1991), while the low point occurred in February 1985 when only a solitary meeting took place. Quite surprisingly, India participated in a third (34.5 per cent) of the meetings of the Council. This observation is pertinent not just to the post–Cold War Council, but also to the Cold War era. The lowest level of participation of 17–19 per cent was evident in 1950, 1991 and 1992, whereas the highest participation (47–49 per cent) was noticed in 1951, 1967, 1972 and 2011. Also, it is very clear that India strove to be a part of the democratic majority helping in the adoption of broadly acceptable decisions and resolutions. It was part of 68 per cent of resolutions adopted either unanimously or without a vote.

Even in regard to the aggregate of 124 resolutions (31 per cent) which attracted division, India cast an affirmative vote on 110 (89 per cent). Only on no more than 14 occasions, it stood aside without joining the concurring majority. To be sure, India had not voted against any resolution, but it has resorted to abstentions only to signal its reservations. Interestingly, moreover, India was never a loner as an abstaining country; it had the company of China, the Union of Soviet Socialist Republics (USSR)/Russia, Yugoslavia, Zimbabwe on many occasions. Out of the 14 abstentions, as shown in Table 6.2, three were to adhere to the principle that a member of the Council should refrain from voting on a resolution dwelling on an item to which it is a party. The reference is to the resolutions on the Jammu and Kashmir question during 1950–1951. Six abstentions (50 per cent) pertained to its sixth term (1991–1992). In general, all abstentions exemplify India's sensitivity to negative implications of the adopted resolutions for such important principles as respect for state sovereignty, non-discrimination among member states of the UN, precedence to a call for unconditional and immediate ceasefire, recourse to coercive action only after exhausting all other peaceful options, respect for the jurisdiction of other organs and so forth.

Table 6.1 Overview of India as Non-Permanent Member

Year	Month of Presidency	Chief Delegate	Ministerial Participants	Meetings			Resolutions Adopted Unanimously or by Consensus	India's Voting Response	
				Total Held	India Intervened	Total		Affirmative	Abstained
1950	June	Benegal N. Rau		72	13	11	–	09	02
1951				39	19	07	02	02	03
1967	September	G. Parthasarathy	M. C. Chagla	46	22	12	12	–	–
1968				76	18	18	14	03	01
1972	December	Samar Sen		60	29	17	03	14	–
1973				77	34	20	07	13	–
1977	October	Rikhi Jaipal		73	25	20	04	16	–
1978			A. B. Vajpayee	52	22	21	01	20	–
1984		N. Krishnan		57	14	14	06	08	–
1985	February		Khurshid Khan, K. R. Narayanan	74	20	21	15	06	–
1991	October	Chinmaya Gharekhan	M. S. Solanki	53	09	42	36	04	02
1992	December		P. V. Narasimha Rao	86	17	74	64	06	04
2011	August	Hardeep Puri	E. Ahamed, Preneet Kaur, S. M. Krishna, Anand Sharma	135	67	65	60	03	02
2012	November		E. Ahamed, Preneet Kaur	199	71	53	47	06	–

Source: Compiled on the basis of Index to Proceedings of the Security Council for the relevant years and also Bailey and Daws (1998).

Table 6.2 India's Abstentions in the Security Council Votes

S. No.	Resolution	Date	Subject	Voting Pattern	Others Abstaining
1.	80 (1950)	14 March	Jammu and Kashmir	8-0-2	Yugoslavia
2.	84 (1950)	7 July	Korea	7-0-3	Egypt, Yugoslavia
3.	91 (1951)	30 March	Jammu and Kashmir	8-0-3	USSR, Yugoslavia
4.	95 (1951)	1 September	Palestine	8-0-3	China, USSR
5.	96 (1951)	10 November	Jammu and Kashmir	9-0-2	USSR
6.	255 (1968)	19 June	Security of non-nuclear weapon states parties to NPT	10-0-5	Algeria, Brazil, France, Pakistan
7.	686 (1991)	2 March	Military Operation against Iraq	11-1 (Cuba)-3	China, Yemen
8.	688 (1991)	5 April	Humanitarian crisis in Iraq	10-3 (Cuba, Yemen, Zimbabwe)-2	China
9.	748 (1992)	31 March	Sanctions against Libya	10-0-5	Cape Verde, China, Morocco, Zimbabwe
10.	770 (1992)	13 August	Bosnia-Herzegovina	12-0-3	China, Zimbabwe
11.	776 (1992)	14 September	Bosnia-Herzegovina	12-0-3	China, Zimbabwe
12.	777 (1992)	19 September	Membership of Yugoslavia	12-0-3	China, Zimbabwe
13.	1972 (2011)	17 March	Enforcement of no fly zones in Libya	10-0-5	Brazil, China, Germany, Russia
14.	S/2011/612 (draft)	4 October	Condemnation of Syria	9-2 (China, Russia)-4	Brazil, Lebanon, South Africa

Source: Compiled on the basis of Index to Proceedings of the Security Council for the relevant years and also Bailey and Daws (1998).

One of the most prominent features of India's participation in the Council is its steadfast pursuit of the project of universalizing the membership of the UN. India not only advocated China's representation setting aside its bilateral problems with that country, but also actively endorsed every application for admission to the UN that first came up in the Security Council. The latest one to get ready support from India was South Sudan's application for admission, soon after that country gained independence from Sudan in 2011. Only in one case, India did seem to have regrets, that is, the apartheid South Africa. Indeed on an occasion, it was commented that South Africa should not have been made a member of the UN in the first place (Jaipal 1977c: 4). As a logical corollary, India found it necessary to defend the UN against the unjustified denunciation from South Africa. Referring to latter's characterization of the UN as a 'joke' that deserved the 'damnedest' from the world, the Indian representative retorted: 'I wonder who these jokers are in the United Nations: those who condemn apartheid and are powerless to act, or those who condemn when they have the power to act' (Jaipal 1978a: 9).

Equally stout was the defence of the UNSC against Israel's criticism of the trends of 'craven submission' and 'cynical hypocrisy' as a result of which the Council 'forfeited its right to pass judgement'. According to the Indian delegate, no purpose would be served by such 'unrestrained insult' to the UN (Jaipal 1978b: 4). Equally puzzling was the approach of some permanent members, especially during the brief period of East–West détente in the early 1970s. During the 1973 Arab-Israeli crisis, for instance, India was unhappy that the Security Council was being degraded just to underwrite quickly what the big two had agreed outside (Sen 1973c: 10). This does not mean that India was totally uncritical of the Council, when it comes to the exercise of fairness. The Indian representative pointedly countered a few members' suggestion to condemn the United Kingdom's failure to force an end to the illegal white regime in Rhodesia/Zimbabwe thus: 'What has the Council done? The Council, in a sense, has failed to agree on measures that could bring about the fall of the illegal regime in Zimbabwe and is, perhaps equally responsible for that failure. Why, therefore, select the United Kingdom for special condemnation?' (Sen 1972b: 3).

Strands of Principled Positions

India pursued its foreign policy principles and goals in the Security Council, just as it has done in the General Assembly and other bodies. During the time of its non-permanent membership of the Security Council, the Indian delegation has espoused certain fundamental principles and beliefs that should govern relations among member states. These are the principles of non-use of force, respect for sovereignty, independence and territorial integrity of states, and peaceful settlement of disputes. The principle of inadmissibility of territorial acquisition by force is absolutely fundamental to India's approach.

Upholding of Sovereignty and Territorial Integrity

India was sensitive to threats to sovereignty of member countries coming from outside or inside. For example, in 1977, India took a strong view of the attempt to overthrow the government in Benin by armed men supported from outside the country. India headed a fact-finding mission to investigate the matter. In the 1967 Arab–Israel war, India criticized the attempts made in the Council to pass a resolution in support of Israel's claim for free passage of its ships through the Gulf of Aqaba as a move designed to undermine the sovereignty of the United Arab Republic over its territorial waters (Parthasarathi 1967b: 8). Upon Soviet military intervention in Czechoslovakia in 1968 too, India referred to non-interference in another country's internal affairs as guiding principle defining international relations and expressed 'anguish' at the Soviet intervention in Czechoslovakia (Mishra 1968: 12). However, India abstained on the Western procedural draft for deferment of the discussion for a few hours, and it was explained as a move aimed to be useful to Czechoslovakia if UN decided to take any steps towards peaceful resolution of the situation (Rana 1970: 66).

In the aftermath of the 1991 Gulf War, India asserted that it would never support any decision whereby the Council would impose arbitrarily a boundary line between Iraq and Kuwait. This would nonetheless not rule out a role for the Council to recognize a boundary, agreed by the two countries in exercise of their sovereignty (Gharekhan 1991b: 78).

Having made its points, ironically enough, India allowed itself to be persuaded by the sponsors of a major resolution—a move widely seen as an unprecedented assault on Iraq's sovereignty—to vote in favour on the ground that an 'extraordinary' response was needed to deal with the exceptional situation Iraq had put itself in at that time (Gharekhan 1991d: 72). Again a few days later in April 1991, in the wake of reports of exodus of civilians from Iraq, the Council voted on a resolution that authorized humanitarian organizations to undertake assistance activities without Iraq's consent (Gharekhan 1991e: 62–63). India raised objections to ignoring Iraq's sovereignty and unsatisfied with some of its provisions, India abstained on that resolution. India regretted foreign interference in Afghanistan for long which brought immense suffering to the people. The resolution of the continuing foreign interference would lie in 'a strong, independent, sovereign, stable, united, democratic and prosperous Afghanistan, at peace with itself and its neighbours', and India would extend all moral, political and economic help to that end (Puri M. 2011c: 15). In the case of Yemen also, India condemned all violence and terrorist acts in Yemen and supported the cause of that country's political independence, sovereignty and territorial integrity. (Puri H.S. 2012g: 11).

The complementary principle of territorial integrity was equally important to India. This was the main issue for India in guiding its position on, for instance, Cyprus. India maintained that Cyprus must continue as an independent, sovereign, united country with the necessary guarantees to all communities, while firmly opposing 'any hint or suggestion of any kind of partition... both on moral and practical grounds' (Sen 1973d: 16). Accordingly India expressed 'profound shock and concern' at the unilateral declaration of independence by Northern Cyprus (Krishnan 1984a: 7).

Opposition to Use of Force

India has, on more occasions than not, rejected use of force as unwarranted and unhelpful. The first major test to this position occurred in June 1950, a few months after assuming its non-permanent seat for the first time. The Indian delegation voted in favour of two texts in June. On 25 June, it voted in favour of the US-introduced draft

(SCOR 1950a) describing the movement of North Korean forces into South Korea as a breach of peace, and it also supported the other text (SCOR 1950b) that authorized necessary military action against North Korea, although initially it stated that it was unable to participate in the vote due to lack of instructions from New Delhi (Rau 1950a: 16). Analysts point out that India's behaviour in the Security Council in June 1950 constituted 'a rare, if not the only, exception to India's dedication to the tradition of hearing both sides as an essential prelude to UN action' (Berkes and Bedi 1958: 94). (The distinction of insisting on both sides being heard before action in this case belonged to Yugoslavia, which abstained on both the above draft resolutions.) India's role, as Krishna Menon once reflected, can be traced to B. N. Rau's (Indian delegate to the Council then) 'textbook view of things'. Menon who claimed to have 'more influence on policy at that time than anybody else' preferred an approach of 'playing safe' in order to avoid 'landing ourselves in a major war' (Brecher 1968: 34–36). However, it must be acknowledged that Rau made one particular contribution during the June 25 meeting. On his suggestion, the wording of the American agenda item was altered by prefixing the phrase 'Complaint of' to 'Aggression upon the Republic of Korea' (Berkes and Bedi 1958: 97).

By the same standard, India denounced South Africa's 'military adventurism' against its neighbours, viz. Angola, Botswana, Lesotho, Seychelles, Zambia and Zimbabwe during the 1970s and 1980s. India strongly disapproved of the use of tactics, such as 'hot pursuit' and 'pre-emptive strikes', by South Africa against the South West Africa People's Organisation (SWAPO) freedom fighters in Angola. Also a matter of great concern in the 1980s was the threat of widening of the Iraq–Iran war. In India's perception, it was a 'war that should never have begun, has gone on far too long and should not continue any further. The longer it lasts, the greater the temptation to resort to unacceptable methods of warfare and impermissible action, bringing about not only the danger of further escalation of the fighting and the widening of the conflict but also the grave potential of external involvement, which could only be to the detriment of the countries of the region, including the parties to the conflict' (Krishnan 1984b: 9).

When both the warring countries agreed to end the war, India readily consented to be part of the UN military observer group to monitor ceasefire and withdrawal of troops.

Whenever reports of use of force reached the Council, India's first priority was to ensure cessation of fighting. It wanted immediate ceasefire invariably in all cases, and the ceasefire was to be without any conditions from any side. In the 1967 war, India welcomed the unanimous decision to order an immediate ceasefire; but it was unhappy that there was no accompanying call for withdrawal of troops (Parthasarathi 1967a: 9). Similarly in the first Gulf War in 1991, India was unsatisfied about the conditional ceasefire that was brought about in March 1991, because it apprehended the possibility of resumption of hostilities (Gharekhan 1991d: 76). While welcoming the establishment of formal permanent ceasefire a month later, India suggested that sustainability of ceasefire must not be made contingent upon the implementation of open-ended conditions (Gharekhan 1991d: 79–80). In the case of Libya too in 2011, India opposed the haste with which the NATO allies wanted to take 'far-reaching measures' with Council's authorization under Chapter VII of the Charter without waiting for the efforts by the mediators of the AU and the UNSG (Puri M. 2011a: 6). In the case of Syria, India supported deployment of ceasefire supervision mission (which only lasted for a short while) so that further bloodshed could be avoided (Puri H.S. 2012d: 8–9).

Advocacy of Peaceful Resolution

India's reputation as a seasoned advocate of negotiated settlement of all problems was partly built upon its contribution in the Security Council going back to its role during 1950–1951. Its attempts to bring a peaceful end to the Korean War through the Neutral Nations Repatriation Commission are well documented, but this role had beginnings in the Security Council. When the Council was stalemated on the Korean War after the sudden return of the Soviet Union to the Security Council in August 1950, India called for creation of a special committee of non-permanent members to study all draft resolutions and proposals for a peaceful settlement of the problem

(Rau 1950b: 9). The Indian delegate was willing to propose a formal resolution if it found sufficient support, which was unfortunately not forthcoming.

During its second stint at the Council, after the 1967 war was brought to an end, India sought to find a just and broad framework for peaceful resolution of the Arab–Israel conflict. A set of five principles was outlined. First, withdrawal of Israeli forces to the positions they held before the outbreak of hostilities accompanied by an end to the state of belligerency. Second, all states in the area have a right to live in peace and complete security free from threats or acts of war. Third, all states in the area must respect the political independence and territorial integrity of one another in accordance with the Charter. Fourth, there must be a just settlement of the long-deferred problem of the Palestinian refugees. Fifth, there should be not only freedom of navigation through international waterways in the area, but there should be a guarantee of such freedom (Parthasarathi 1967c: 8). Accordingly, India proposed a draft resolution along with Mali and Nigeria highlighting the principles of withdrawal, security and non-belligerency, and the right of every State to be secure within its borders (Parthasarathi 1967d: 6).

On the question of Palestine, India's position emphasized that no solution to the problems in the Middle East could be envisaged without taking into account the inalienable rights of the Palestinian people; secondly, that the exercise of those inalienable rights of the Palestinian people to return to their homes and property and to exercise their right to self-determination, including the establishment of a State of their own, would contribute to a final solution of the entire crisis; thirdly, that participation on an equal footing of the Palestine Liberation Organization, the sole and authentic representative of the Palestinian people, was indispensable to all efforts to find a solution; and fourthly, that no just and lasting peace in the Middle East could be established without the withdrawal of Israel from all the Palestinian and other Arab territories that it occupied since 1967, including Jerusalem, and that all states of the region should be guaranteed secure and recognized boundaries (Krishnan 1985: 6).

In the post-Cold War period too, India's support to efforts to find negotiated end to various conflicts in the Balkans, West and South Asia or the African continent continued as before. In the 1991 Gulf War, India desired that diplomacy be given a chance in view of Iraq's offer to unconditionally accept all UN resolutions, and supported Soviet leader, Mikhail Gorbachev's efforts to bring to an end Iraq's occupation of Kuwait, without further bloodshed (Gharekhan 1991c: 116–121). Similarly, India welcomed the efforts for finding a peaceful solution to the problem of former Yugoslavia through the mechanism of the International Conference at London in August 1992. India has vital interest in the security and prosperity of Afghanistan and therefore expressed repeatedly its hope for a peaceful resolution through 'inclusive, Afghan-led and transparent' process accompanied by renunciation of violence (Puri H.S. 2011f: 22). On Syria too, from the beginning India advocated international community's help for an inclusive political process for national reconciliation and an end to violence as well as gross violation of human rights by all sides (Puri M. 2012a: 8). India supported the six-point plan proposed by the UN–Arab League joint special envoy, Kofi Annan in 2012 (Puri H.S. 2012f: 7).

Diverse Perspectives on Security Council's Action

Authorizations for Military Action Should Be an Exception

The Indian views on not perceiving the UN as an instrument for military action are well known. Even on the Korea question, where as a matter of principle at least initially India supported military action against North Korea, India refrained from getting involved in that multinational action except in non-combat engagement. After the end of the Cold War, especially because of the threats posed by terrorism and gross violations of human rights, India had to take a flexible approach on the need for the Council authorizing military intervention in Somalia and Bosnia–Herzegovina in 1992 while continuing with its traditional conservatism. As regards the situation in Bosnia–Herzegovina, the Indian representative agreed that it is inconceivable that in this day and age, the phenomenon of 'ethnic cleansing' should have raised its ugly head. Such activities, whether practiced by a State or by groups with the support of outside States, deserve the strongest possible condemnation, wherever and everywhere they might take place.

To stop this trend, India endorsed use of force on an exceptional basis (Gharekhan 1992f: 11). As for the ethnic conflict in Mogadishu and other parts of Somalia coupled with the total collapse of state structures there, India went along with the rest of the Council membership to suggest that the situation was 'sui generis' that defied conventional solutions, and therefore, deserved to be treated as an exceptional case to set aside the tradition of eschewing enforcement action and authorize presence of multinational troops led by the United States (called UN Task Force) under Chapter VII of the Charter to restore order and provide security to humanitarian supplies to the starving people in the country (Gharekhan 1992c: 31–32).[3]

Case for Transparency in Sanctions to Avoid Unintended Suffering

Unlike military measures, India seemed to be more open to economic sanctions as an option for the Council in appropriate situations. Indeed, in the early years, India took lead to press for imposition of comprehensive mandatory economic sanctions against the racist minority regime of southern Rhodesia. It blamed certain (Western) powers for the failure of the selective sanctions approved by the Council earlier in 1966 (Parthasarathi 1968: 10). In yet another significant initiative, India mooted the idea of mandatory ban on sale of arms against South Africa in 1972 (Sen 1972a: 6–9). The efforts fructified five years later when India returned to the Council, which unanimously—thanks to the understanding shown by the Carter administration and its ambassador, Andrew Young—decided by resolution 418 (1977) of 4 November to impose mandatory arms embargo against that country (Jaipal 1978f: 19–20). Subsequently India, on behalf of the NAM,

---

[3] Fuller account can be found in Gharekhan (2006).

argued that only comprehensive mandatory sanctions against South Africa would make it pay heed to the demand for ending occupation of Namibia and the apartheid policies (Narayanan 1985: 13).

Instances of sanctions became more frequent since 1991 with mixed outcomes. In order to control civil wars, such as the one that erupted in Somalia, India was ready to support proposals for arms embargo. India supported mandatory arms embargo on Liberian warring parties, with the hope that the action would help in reducing bloodshed besides sending a clear political signal to the parties that the international community was serious in demanding peace (Gharekhan 1992j: 88). The international community experienced the first taste of the most comprehensive sanctions ever in the history to make Iraq vacate Kuwait in 1990. Most of those continued very long (till 2003) even after the objective of reversal of Iraqi invasion of Kuwait was achieved. After the surrender of Iraqi forces in March 1991, India recommended an early review of the sanctions on the ground that the measures played havoc with the economy of not only Iraq but also its innocent population. Particularly, India pleaded in favour of lifting of the embargo on supply of humanitarian goods to the people of both Iraq and Kuwait. It was largely because of the pleas from India and other non-permanent members that the Council devised a simplified procedure to facilitate exemptions from sanctions regime for meeting humanitarian needs.[4] The policy of seeking exemption for humanitarian goods, such as foodstuffs and medicine, from sanctions continued with other sanctions regimes brought into force by the Council (former Yugoslavia was an example).

There is a problem of particular concern to India. India raised the question of concrete action to provide redress to those sanctions-complying countries wherever such implementation adversely affected them. The Indian delegation got a paragraph included reaffirming the Council's responsibility in terms of Article 50 of the Charter in the case of sanctions on former Yugoslavia (Gharekhan 1992e: 23).

---

[4] Afterwards India expressed disappointment that the Council had not readily accepted the proposal to transfer those items from the 'no objection' to 'notification' category (Gharekhan 1992i: 78).

The same point was made about the Council's responsibility to alleviate special problems of the Third World countries in connection with the contemplation of sanctions against Libya. Moreover, in regard to the Libya case, India protested against resolution 731 (1992) for not precisely defining the circumstances under which sanctions either would not come into force or would be lifted (Gharekhan 1992d: 57–58). In the case of sanctions proposed against Libya and Syria in 2011, India had strong reservations. India drew the attention to the suffering sanctions would cause to those countries that had long-standing economic relationship with Libya (Puri M. 2011a: 6). In the latter case, India opposed the threat of sanctions against the Syrian government without being tough with the anti-government groups that are equally responsible for the continued violence (Puri H.S. 2011g: 6).

India expressed strong support to the financial sanctions against terror outfits and listed individuals affiliated with Al-Qaida and the Islamic State and showed active interest in the work of the 1267 Sanctions Committee. It also actively supported the work of the Counter-Terrorism Committee (CTC) established in pursuance of the Security Council resolution 1373 adopted after the September 2001 terror attacks against the United States (Puri H.S. 2011h: 9–11; Puri H.S. 2012e: 16–17). Nonetheless, India desired their implementation to be fair and transparent, adhering to the due process in working procedures and decision-making (Puri H.S. 2011c: 3). (Chapter 9 devotes detailed attention to this.)

Realistic Appraisal of the Need and Risks of Peacekeeping

At the cost of repeating what would appear in great details in Chapter 7, it is pertinent to point out that India always viewed the peacekeeping activity—to which India has been a long-standing contributor of troops, police and experts—strictly within the framework of respect for sovereignty principle. The precept of peacekeeping rested on the consent of the host country for the purpose of deployment and continuation of UN presence. In that sense, India's support to the Secretary-General's decision in 1967 to withdraw the UNEF, upon the request of the United Arab Republic, was natural. At that time, India went to the extent of warning that it

> could not be a party to any procedure which would make UNEF into an occupation force nor could the Government of India agree to UNEF's continued presence in the United Arab Republic in the absence of the latter's consent and, in any case, Indian troops could not remain part of UNEF without the United Arab Republic's approval (Parthasarathi 1967a: 19).

Notwithstanding the fact of multidimensional association of India with UN peacekeeping, India considered that the purpose of peacekeeping was 'not to enable any party to freeze the situation but, rather to enable the parties concerned to negotiate a lasting peace' on the basis of the Security Council resolutions (Jaipal 1977a: 7). While India did not oppose extension of the mandate of peacekeeping operations, such as the one in Cyprus, between Syria and Israel, Israel and Egypt, and Israel and Lebanon, India made it clear that the services of peacekeeping could not be taken for granted by the parties concerned. It went on record to oppose the tendency to regard the 'renewal of the mandate as a routine and procedural exercise' (Jaipal 1977b: 9). Such renewals could not be a substitute for permanent peace. Maintaining that routine mandate renewals of the UN missions did not add to the glory of the Council, India warned that it would be a misnomer to refer to the UN forces in West Asia as a peacekeeping operation, as there was in fact no peace to keep (Jaipal 1978c: 7). On another occasion, referring to the deadlock in negotiations between parties to the Cyprus problem, India advised the Council: 'If the stalemate should be of a permanent character, there is no valid reason, in our opinion, for indefinitely continuing the stationing of a United Nations Force in Cyprus (UNFICYP) at enormous cost' (Jaipal 1978d: 20).[5] Similarly, in the wake of reports of harassment and abduction of the

---

[5] India observed that the Council became virtually a hostage of the parties, which having agreed to the extension of the mandate of the Force 'insisted on prior approval of every single word and punctuation mark in the draft resolution' resulting in waste of some 17 hours and demonstration of extraordinary ineptitude of the Council (Jaipal 1978d: 20).

UN peacekeepers in Lebanon, India questioned the reason why the force should remain there. In its assessment, UN Interim Force in Lebanon (UNIFIL) should preferably be withdrawn (Jaipal 1978e: 12).

Moreover, there are two fundamental views held by India on traditional peacekeeping. According to India, the UN should not be seen 'drifting into the unfortunate position where in every case of aggression there has to be introduced a United Nations force in order to make the aggressor withdraw from the territory occupied'. Secondly, equally important, the UN force should not become involved in functions and duties related to the maintenance of internal law and order, for that could have serious repercussions on the impartiality of the UN force (Jaipal 1978b: 3).

Let it not be construed that India has a closed and negative opinion about peacekeeping per se. After the first Gulf War against Iraq, in fact India hoped that a token UN presence would provide renewed hope and assurance to the people in the area. Accordingly, an observer mission was deployed, known as UNIKOM with Indian troops. Similarly, India supported the establishment of UNPROFOR in former Yugoslavia whose first force commander was senior Indian army officer. At the same time, one issue over which India was concerned related to the possibility of attacks by warring parties in Bosnia–Herzegovina and other states of former Yugoslavia on the peacekeeping troops in retaliation to sanctions and other restrictions imposed by the Council (Gharekhan 1992e: 23; 1992h: 11–12). India's apprehensions indeed were borne out by the attempts by the Bosnian Serbs to undermine the presence and autonomy of UN force through tactics, such as non-cooperation and kidnapping.

India was distressed that the core principles of peacekeeping, viz. consent of the host countries, non-use of force and non-interference in internal affairs, have often been eroded unfortunately risking the very effectiveness of operations (Puri H.S. 2011e: 21). Further, issues of mandate and resources were reflected in India's interventions in the Council. When two fresh peacekeeping operations were being mandated for South Sudan and Sudan in 2011, the Indian representative pointed out the risk of managing a number of old and new operations on 'shoestring budgets and ever increasing mandates' (Puri M. 2011b: 15; Kapoor 2012: 8). Further, citing the experiences of the ongoing mission in South Sudan along with the assessment provided by the force commander, the Indian representative aptly compared the mandates of many such operations as 'Christmas tree' wherein the peacekeepers are asked to achieve what 'many of our States have struggled for decades, if not centuries, to achieve' (Kumar 2012: 18). In line with its conviction that peacekeeping is not an end in itself, India fully endorsed the idea of peacebuilding to nurse the conflict-torn societies in the post-conflict phase to help them return to normalcy. Indeed, as one of the top five troop-contributing countries, India serves on the organizing committee of the Peace-building Commission (PBC), a newly created body. India viewed peacekeepers in Cambodia, Democratic Congo, Liberia, Somalia as 'early peacebuilders' but the peacebuilding work of the UN would be effective only when it is nationally owned (Puri H.S. 2011b: 7).

Concerns on Account of New Threats

India recognized the growing importance of threats other than aggression and foreign intervention to international peace and security. In a sober intervention, India's foreign minister acknowledged that contemporary threats to international peace and security differ qualitatively from those prevalent in the 20th century. 'Conventional war has been overtaken by intrastate and even borderless violence. Low-intensity conflict, non-State actors and the terrorist-criminal drug-trafficking nexus threaten international stability and progress. It is recognized that such conflicts are extremely complicated and require complex solutions. Unfortunately, recent developments seem to indicate a worrying trend towards increased reliance on the use of force as a mechanism for resolving some of these conflicts' (Krishna 2011: 18).

Again, India fully shared the growing concern about threats posed by proliferation of nuclear and other WMDs. The threat assumed new dimension, in the sense that it was no longer the question of possible acquisition of nuclear weapons by a handful of threshold countries, but an uncontrolled spread of ready-made nuclear and other WMDs to non-state elements across the globe by a variety of illegal means and methods. The proliferation issue had thus assumed qualitatively and frighteningly new dimension (Rao 1992: 99).

Terrorism, proliferation of WMDs, ethnic cleansing and other gross violations of human rights are widely agreed as major new threats to global security. As for terrorism, reacting to the first major terrorist attack in Munich in September 1972, India condemned the attacks, while doubting how such methods served the Arab cause. However, India cautioned that while Israel like all other countries had every right to suppress terrorism or any other kind of lawlessness inside its territory, it could not exercise such a right outside its territory, particularly to the detriment of the rights of neighbouring states (Sen 1973a: 3). The problem of terrorism has assumed dangerous and global dimensions in the 1990s. India had the occasion to express vigorous condemnation of terrorism in all its forms when a complaint was brought in January 1992 against Libya's non-cooperation to hand over two terror suspects for trial on charges of exploding mid-air a Pan American aircraft in the 1980s. However, it was uneasy about rushing through with imposition of sanctions against Libya without exhausting the possibilities of negotiated resolution of differences (Murthy 1992).

In the context of growing incidence of gross violations of human rights committed in many civil war situations in Africa, former Yugoslavia, Syria and elsewhere, naturally opinion grew in strength to consider non-compliance with human rights standards as a threat to international peace and security. The problem India perceives, however, is in regard to accusations of egregious violations by countries engaged in combating terrorists who actually commit heinous crimes by targeting people. In this connection, Indian Prime Minister pointed out that Indian culture and human rights 'in their loftiest form are almost synonymous'. However, India contended that it could not 'countenance a situation where all human rights are reserved only for the practitioners of terrorism, while governments dealing with this menace are arraigned day and night on grounds of violation of human rights—real or imaginary—mostly latter.' India, in this connection, suggested the need to delineate the parameters that harmonize the defence of national integrity with respect for human rights (Rao 1992: 98).

Among other non-conventional threats, India recognized the security implications of the problem of climate change. In its cautious characterization, climate change, 'in an overarching sense, is beginning to impact the security of the global community in the same way as poverty, food security and underdevelopment continue to undermine international well-being.' However, it was wary about sweeping and unsubstantiated generalizations that climate change would cause droughts, floods, changes in weather patterns, water and food scarcity, and violent conflicts (Puri H.S. 2011d: 18).

Opposition to Council's Overreach to Impinge on the Role of Other Organs

It may be recalled here that during the 1950s, India had reservations regarding the US-led initiatives to undermine the authority of the Security Council and project the General Assembly as a better substitute for deciding on peace and security matters. The creation of the 'Little Assembly' and adoption of the 'Uniting for Peace' resolution in 1947 and 1950, respectively, are cases in point. India held that organs under the UN system should play the role assigned to them by the Charter, without overrunning the jurisdiction of each other (Rana 1970: 57–58).

This observation assumed new dimension with added pertinence during the 1990s after the Cold War ended, when the Security Council tended to step into the jurisdiction of the General Assembly and other principal organs. According to India, the General Assembly and the Security Council are meant to work in tandem for promotion of peace and security. There is no room for any conflict or competition between the two organs (Khan 1985: 15).

Not happy about the tendency to bring several global issues onto the Council's agenda under the pretext of them having a bearing on international peace and security, India stressed the need to respect the separation of functions between the Security Council and the General Assembly or even any other organ in letter and spirit. 'The Security Council should step in only where there is threat to international peace and security, and in the context of specific situations' (Puri M. 2012a: 8).

With reference to the emphasis on rule of law as an approach to sustainable peace, India stressed that the UN system should adhere to transparency and fairness by Security Council not infringing the mandate of other organs (Puri H.S. 2012a: 5).

When the Security Council resolved in September 1992 to urge the General Assembly to exclude the Federal Republic of Yugoslavia from its work, India had serious reservations about the Council's action. In the words of the Indian representative, under the Charter, the Council 'is competent to recommend either suspension or expulsion of a State. Nowhere in the Charter has the Security Council been given the authority to recommend to the General Assembly that a country's participation in the Assembly be withdrawn or suspended. That authority belongs to the General Assembly, which does not need any recommendation to that effect from the Security Council. Indeed, the General Assembly is under no legal obligation to act on any such recommendation, just as the Security Council is under no legal obligation to comply with the General Assembly's recommendation' (Gharekhan 1992g: 7). In another instance of the kind, when the Council was considering sanctions on Libya in 1992, India advised against haste as it might undermine the authority of the World Court, which was seized of the case already (Gharekhan 1992d: 58).

Tactics Kit: Accent on Consensus and Partnership

As an original member of the Organization, India brought to bear its vast diplomatic experience every time it served on the Council. Its tactics kit included introduction of draft resolutions with others as co-sponsors, promoting identity of views among sister non-aligned as well as the non-permanent members serving on the Council, building and joining consensus with the rest of the Council members, and so forth. Reference has already been made to the inputs India had made to adoption of the famous resolution 242 on the Arab–Israel conflict, in the form of a text India co-sponsored with Mali and Nigeria in 1967. Notably, India was willing to withdraw its text in favour of the British text, which was finally adopted unanimously (Lall 1968).

Several initiatives characterize India's adoption of mature and pragmatic tactics during each time it was on the Council. To cite a few, in 1973, a draft resolution (Doc. S/10974) was introduced on behalf of Guinea, Indonesia, Kenya, Panama, Peru, the Sudan and Yugoslavia on the West Asia/Middle East. India explained that the text was arrived at after

> most intensive consultations and any delegation, which wished to contribute its views for such consultations had ample opportunity to do so. This draft resolution will not... bring much satisfaction to any of the parties directly involved, but it will, we believe, inform them of the general thinking of the Council and instruct them of the ways in which they should, in the opinion of the Council, move and make progress (Sen 1973b: 2).

Likewise, India introduced in 1985 a draft resolution (Doc. S/17013) on behalf of the six non-aligned non-permanent members of the Council (Burkina Faso, Egypt, India, Madagascar, Peru and Trinidad and Tobago) on South Africa's apartheid policies. During the Gulf War in 1991, India suggested that the non-permanent members should 'sit together and see what we can do to find some way out of what appears to be an impasse' over the differences between the former Soviet and the American plans on ending the war (Gharekhan 1991c: 311).[6]

India sought to take pains to bring non-aligned member countries together and articulate its position as the considered view of the non-aligned. This was not only true during the period 1984–1985 when it represented NAM as its chair, but even otherwise. For example, on the occasion of drafting a suitable resolution on the non-cooperation of Libya in suppression of terrorism, India told the Council that the non-aligned members of the Council were engaged in a serious

---

[6] Believing in the potential of this category, India moved in mid-1980s a proposal aimed at long overdue increase in the non-permanent seats in the Council reflecting 'more adequately the enhanced membership of the Organization' (Khan 1985: 15). However, the primacy of the issue was lost when it became a part of the larger demand to expand the Council in both permanent and non-permanent categories.

attempt to find a consensus on the issue (Gharekhan 1992e: 96). Side by side, India seemed to place high hopes in the potential of the non-permanent members in the Council for playing the role of constructive peacemakers. Equally notable is the fact that as a chair of the Council in August 2011, India was successful to bring all diverging sides to agree on a presidential statement calling for restraint by all sides engaged in the Syrian civil war (Security Council. 2011).

India's efforts to forge small groups of emerging powers too have given scope for hopes that new alignments would steer the Council in a desirable direction. During its previous term (2011–2012), for one year India had the company of Brazil and South Africa, which together had already been working as IBSA coalition on economic, political and trade issues of shared interest. There was significantly one occasion in October 2011 when the three countries abstained on a text sponsored by the United States and other countries to condemn Syrian government for targeting its own people in the civil war (Puri 2016). Of course, the draft resolution was not adopted because China and Russia exercised their veto. Notwithstanding this, the IBSA group in the Security Council disappointed observers as the three countries usually voted in different ways in the single year they served as non-permanent members. For example, South Africa supported the resolution (SCOR 2011a) that authorized military action to enforce no-fly zone against the Col. Gaddafi's regime in Libya, while Brazil and India abstained.

India's voting strategy is predominantly consensual, aimed at contributing to consensus building and also voting along with democratic majority, while stating its problems with, and reservations on, the texts adopted when necessary. For example, India went along with the declaration that was issued at the summit level meeting of the Council, despite the fact that the statement did not reflect India's crucial concerns regarding the linkage between terrorism and human rights and on the issue of non-proliferation. India observed that it was 'only within the framework of such a consensus and through no other means that the Security Council could deal effectively with the threats to peace emanating from the proliferation of nuclear weapons in its current, global dimension' (Rao 1992: 101–2). On the same occasion,

India insisted that the Council could relate to the changing world by adhering to consensus as a transparent working method. Years later in 2011, India went along with the rest of the Council members (particularly the African ones) to refer the Libyan situation to the ICC, although India had serious reservations on the Court per se (Puri H.S. 2011a: 2).

India's abstentions were rare, although they seemed to be more prominent during 1991–1992. Abstentions were owing to the assessment that the adopted texts did not pay sufficient heed to the Charter principles, such as respect for domestic jurisdiction or the jurisdiction of other organs. Notably, unlike the voting response of some members, such as Cuba or even Pakistan, there was not a single occasion when India voted against a text that met with the approval of the required majority in the Council. It may be argued with some justification that the voting behaviour of India as a permanent member (if and when it materializes) may not be any different.

Sum Up

The discussion brings out a few remarkable features of India's non-permanent membership in the Security Council. As it is obvious, it was elected on behalf of the Asian regional group at irregular intervals. Between the first two terms there was a gap of 15 years; the gap became 19 years after 1992 to return to the Council in 2011. In the intervening period of 25 years (1967–1991) India returned to the Council after a gap of 3–5 years each time. If India is elected in 2020, it would mean a gap of eight years.

Again, given the relationship between the number of meetings, India might have participated in and the total number of meetings held in a year, India does not seem to come out as an overactive or overbearing discussant. In terms of quality of participation, strikingly India's contribution at the Security Council mirrors the larger picture of India's role at the UN, especially the General Assembly, encompassing a good mix of maturity, flexibility, moderation, pragmatism and propriety. The discretion in participation in meetings evidently varies from a low of 17–19 per cent in three years to a high of 47–49 per cent in four years. As a reflection of its maturity and propriety, India not merely abstained in the vote on the resolutions adopted on the question of Jammu and Kashmir dispute, but also ceded its turn to preside over the Council meeting in March 1951 because the Kashmir question came up for discussion. Moderation was manifest in the total absence of a negative vote, while abstentions remained few and far between. The characteristics of flexibility and pragmatism were evident in plenty in terms of the willingness to work with others in helping the process of drafting or refining texts that had the potential of obtaining widest possible support. In any case, India let on numerous occasions its words of caution or reservations to go on record without ambiguity or rancour. Again with a few deviations—warranted or otherwise—India espoused and applied the core principles of respect for sovereignty and territorial integrity, non-use of force, and peaceful resolution of disputes as a preferred path. On a larger plane, it must be noted also that the three Western permanent members, viz. France, the United Kingdom and the United States, have assumed more proactive role, reducing the other members' scope to take initiatives, except to react to the initiatives of the Permanente Three (Keating 2015).

It is difficult to categorically assert whether such undoubtedly enviable performance decorated by the gifts of devotion and dexterity is a rarity among the countries (developed and developing) who have served on the Council as non-permanent members. Equally open would be the question whether the measure of maturity and flexibility India demonstrated as a non-permanent member would be a progenitor of its profile as a permanent member of the future in the enlarged Council. No matter what the outcome might be in the ongoing effort for recasting the present Security Council, India should continue to build on its track record as a non-permanent member so far in its future association with the Council.

CHAPTER 7

India's Expectations and Experiences in the UN Peacekeeping Operations

The nature of India's experiences in the UN peacekeeping, the most visible and vital endeavour in the area of maintenance of international peace and security, is the focus of the present chapter. India's former Prime Minister and foreign minister observed that India's long-standing participation testifies to 'not only the dedication and professionalism of Indian soldiers but also to the political will of the government to actively contribute to the operations' (Gujral 1997: 9). Peacekeeping[1] consumes 'more resources, employs more people and occupies a greater share of the Security Council's time than any other single issue, and no other Council instrument has had a greater impact on the provenance

---

[1] According to former UN Secretary-General Javier Perez de Cuellar, peacekeeping is 'activated with the consent of the parties concerned, involves deployment of international military personnel in an integrated command with civilian elements, all acting under the authority of the Organization, in order to stop or avert fighting or help facilitate or implement a settlement without resorting to offensive use of force' (de Cuellar 1990: 5).

and application of international law and international humanitarian law than its peacekeeping mandates' (Puri H.S. 2011e: 21). Indeed one could fairly say that India's association with the UN peacekeeping is nearly as long-standing as the UN activity itself.

The analysis in this chapter will try to bring out multiple shades of India's engagement with the UN peacekeeping: the role of time-tested and traditional principles in guiding the multidimensional and complex activity, the patterns of non-participation and participation by India during the Cold War times, followed by active, but selective participation in the context of new generation operations. An interesting addition to the discussion relates to reasons for India's annoyance with the observer mission stationed on its soil for some years now. The discussion will also pay attention to India's perspectives on managerial and financial problems that often impinge on the UN ability to plan and perform. The chapter will also look at institutional and individual motivations and their mixed outcomes for India's participation in the UN operations.

India's association with the UN peacekeeping has both quantitative and qualitative features. A quick glance at the statistical summary would suffice to substantiate this. Since the time when first peacekeeping operation was launched in 1948, the UN launched 71 peacekeeping operations. As per Table 7.1, India took part in 45 of them, while it hosted two operations on its soil. During the past 25 years, India figures usually among the top four contributors to the UN peacekeeping operations with a grand total of nearly 2,50,000 troops, military observers, civilian police, formed police units, staff officers, and so on. As per December 2019 statistics, India is the fifth largest contributor (after Ethiopia, Bangladesh, Rwanda and Nepal), having presence in eight out of 12 missions.[2] A total of 13 Indian officers have served as force commanders, besides two as military advisers to the UNSG at

---

[2] These missions are in Cyprus, Democratic Congo, Golan Heights, Lebanon, Middle East, Sudan, South Sudan and Western Sahara. Nearly 85 per cent of the personnel are deployed in three theatres, viz. the Democratic Congo (MONUSCO), Lebanon (UNIFIL) and South Sudan (UNMISS). The Indian contingent remains the second largest in two of these missions.

Table 7.1 India's Participation in the UN Peacekeeping Operations, 1956–2019

S. No.	Operation	Duration	Nature of Contribution
1.	UN Emergency Force-I	1956–1967	Infantry, supply, transport and signals units
2.	UN Observer Group in Lebanon	1958	Military observers
3.	UN Operation in the Congo	1960–1964	2 infantry brigades, aircraft (air and ground) personnel, field hospital personnel, signal company, air dispatch team, postal unit, supply unit
4.	UN Yemen Observer Mission	1963–1964	Military observers
5.	UN Iran–Iraq Military Observer Group	1988–1991	Military observers
6.	UN Transition Assistance Group for Namibia	1989–1990	Military observers, civilian police, election supervisors
7.	UN Angola Verification Mission-I	1989–1991	10 Military observers
8.	UN Observer Group in Central America	1990–1992	Military observers
9.	UN Advance Mission in Cambodia	1991–1992	Military observers
10.	UN Iraq–Kuwait Observation Mission	1991–2003	Military observers
11.	UN Angola Verification Mission-II	1991–1995	25 Military observers
12.	UN Transitional Authority in Cambodia	1992–1993	1,373 personnel with civilian police, military observers, troops
13.	UN Observer Mission in El Salvador	1992–1995	Military observers
14.	UN Operation in Mozambique	1992–1994	1,078 of all ranks including military observers, 2 engineer companies, logistics and headquarters companies, etc. Military observers, troops, civilian police
15.	UN Operation in Somalia-II	1993–1994	A brigade of 5,000 troops

(continued)

(continued)

S. No.	Operation	Duration	Nature of Contribution
16.	UN Mission in Haiti	1993–1996	Troops, police
17.	UN Assistance Mission for Rwanda	1994–1996	956 total with military observers, infantry battalion group, engineer company, signal company, etc.
18.	UN Observer Mission in Liberia	1993–1997	Military observers
19.	UN Angola Verification Mission-III	1995–1997	20 military observers
20.	UN Observer Mission in Angola	1997–1999	Infantry battalion, engineer company; a total of 1,014 of all ranks
21.	UN Support Mission in Haiti	1996–1997	Police
22.	UN Mission in Bosnia-Herzegovina	1996–2002	Civilian police
23.	UN Transition Mission in Haiti	1997	Civilian police
24.	UN Civilian Police Mission in Haiti	1997–2000	Formed police unit
25.	UN Interim Force in Lebanon	1998–ongoing	650 troops of all ranks from infantry battalion and level II hospital
26.	UN Observer Mission in Sierra Leone	1998–1999	2 infantry battalion groups, 2 engineer companies, quick reaction company, along with medical, logistics and attack helicopter units
27.	UN Mission in Sierra Leone	1999–2001	Military observers, civilian police
28.	UN Organization Mission in the Congo	1999–2010	Military observers, troops, police
29.	UN Mission in Ethiopia and Eritrea	2000–2008	1 infantry battalion, one construction engineer company, one force reserve company and military observers
30.	UN Mission in Kosovo	2001–ongoing	Civilian police

31.	UN Force in Cyprus	2003–ongoing	Troops, police
32.	UN Mission in Burundi	2004–2006	Troops, military observers
33.	UN Operation in Cote d'Ivoire	2003–2017	Military observers, police
34.	UN Mission in Sudan	2005–2011	Infantry battalion group, engineer company, observers
35.	UN Mission in Georgia	2005–2009	Police
36.	UN Disengagement Observer Force in Golan Heights	2006–ongoing	Logistics battalion with 196 personnel
37.	UN Integration Mission in Timor-Leste	2006–2012	Police
38.	UN Mission in Liberia	2007–2018	Male and female formed police units
39.	UN Stabilization Mission in Haiti	2008–2017	Formed police unit
40.	UN Stabilization Mission in DR Congo	2010–ongoing	Infantry brigade with level II hospital, army aviation contingent, police, experts
41.	UN Mission in South Sudan	2011–ongoing	Infantry battalion group, police, experts, signal company, level II hospital
42.	UN Interim Security Force in Abyei	2012–ongoing	Troops, experts
43.	UN Assistance Mission in Afghanistan	2013–ongoing	Police
44.	UN Truce Supervision Organization	2015–ongoing	Experts
45.	UN Mission for Justice Support in Haiti	2017–2019	Formed police unit

Source: United Nations (1996), United Nations (1998), Nambiar (2009) and the UN Peacekeeping Website, https://peacekeeping.un.org/en/troop-and-police-contributors, accessed on 8 August 2019.

the headquarters.³ The first all-women contingent in peacekeeping operations, a formed police unit was made available to the UN mission in Liberia in 2007. Most significant of all is the fact that the largest number (169) of those who were killed on peacekeeping duty for the UN belonged to India. How has this come about is worth tracing here to provide a purpose to the chapter.

Counting on Traditional Principles with Occasional Relaxation

India's approach to the UN peacekeeping operations is a by-product of the convergence of the country's foreign policy principles, such as the non-use of force, non-alignment, peaceful coexistence and so forth, with its outlook towards the world organization's potential in managing stable international order. Just as India desired to preserve its independence in foreign policy matters by not joining any Cold War alliance, it wished to keep the UN away from undue domination by one or the other power bloc. According to India, the contribution of the UN in maintaining international peace would become meaningful when methods of moderation and mediation were used to the fullest potential, with little or no stress on combat or coercive powers (Berkes and Bedi 1958; Mehta 1976). For peaceful, systemic transformation through the UN, countries with future potential should be allowed to take part in the collective processes of conflict management. Notably, this long-term perspective was not inimical to India's immediate interests or material constraints. For, a clear message went out in the formative years of India's role in world

---

³ The force commanders include Maj. Gen. P. S. Gyani, Brigadier Indar Jit Rikhye, Gen. Thimayya, Lt. Gen. Dewan Prem Chand, Lt. Gen. Satish Nambiar, Maj. Gen. Vijay Jetley, Maj. Gen. L. M. Tewari, Brigadier Shiva Kumar, Maj. Gen. Rajender Singh, Lt. Gen. Chander Prakash, Lt. Gen. J. S. Lidder, Lt. Gen. Iqbal Singh Singha and Lt. Gen. Shailesh Tinalkar. The two military advisors to the Secretary General were Maj. Gen. Indar Jit Rikhye (1960–1964) and Lt. Gen. Randhir Mehta (2005–2007). Besides, two senior police officers, viz. O. P. Rathor and Kiran Bedi served as chief police advisors in the Department of Peacekeeping Operations. For a detailed biographical sketch of many of them, see Nambiar (2009: 19–59).

affairs that its stand on every peace and security question would be guided first by its national interests and next by the merits involved.

It may be interesting that the UN did not have a prior design of peacekeeping, before it ventured into action. The Charter has no reference to peacekeeping at all, but it would not be incorrect to say the activity is very much in line with the spirit of the Charter. It combined the function of Chapter VI on peaceful settlement of problems and the form of Chapter VII on use of military force, as Dag Hammarskjold famously described it 'Chapter six-and-half' activity. It was a result of a series of *ad hoc* responses given suiting the peculiarity of particular circumstances. The technique of peacekeeping by the UN evolved on a case-by-case basis marked by a series of improvisations made over a long period (Saksena 1977). As a natural corollary, India's policy too towards UN peacekeeping operations did not emerge suddenly one day. Arguably, the origins of the evolutionary policy can be traced to India's experience during the Korean conflict in the early 1950s. The mistakes committed both by major member countries and the world organization pointed to the limitations of the great power mode of maintaining peace (i.e. by using coercive force as a sequel to the stage-managed collective authorization). This, in turn, vindicated the alternative, non-coercive mode articulated by India in the deliberations.

The quest for such a mode of organized action for peace took a dramatic turn with the establishment of the UNEF in 1956 as an *ad hoc* and limited measure to reverse the Israeli invasion against Egypt. India supported the initiative on the weight of the following considerations. First, the UNEF was not designed as a successor force to replace the invading troops, and as such it posed no threat to the sovereignty and territorial integrity of Egypt. Second, Egypt consented to the presence of the new force in its territory. And, finally the composition of the force conformed to the tradition of providing a balanced regional representation, except for the well-advised exclusion of the five permanent members of the Security Council (Parakatil 1975: 81–82). India endorsed two other important guiding principles outlined by Secretary-General, Dag Hammarskjold at that time, viz., the UNEF would not be authorized to use force except in self-defence, and that it would be impartial in its dealings with the conflicting parties.

Although the 1956 guiding principles formed the core of India's traditional approach to UN peacekeeping, the contours of the policy underwent pragmatic adjustments when particular situations demanded. One way of looking at the flexibility of India's approach is to discern the country's willingness to make exceptions to the guiding principles, which essentially highlight respect for sovereignty, deployment with consent of the host country, non-use of offensive force and impartiality. India had always held that peacekeeping was non-military in character, even if military personnel were involved. In general even in the post-Cold War context, India held that 'peacekeeping operations must have the consent of the parties and must not intrude in the internal affairs of governments. Moreover, they must not be a substitute for a negotiated political settlement, and their mandates must be of limited duration' (Chaturvedi 1997: 11).

Respect for the Charter principles of respecting sovereignty, territorial integrity and political independence of member countries has generally been the salient principle governing the establishment and termination of several missions. In 1967, as noted in Chapter 6, India upheld the sovereign right of Egypt as a host state to demand immediate withdrawal of UNEF. In fact, India went as far as to warn that it would pull out its contingent (the largest at that time) from UNEF if the UN ignored Egypt's request for withdrawal (Thant 1978: 225). In the context of the Congo operation in the early 1960s, however, the issue acquired new perspective. In this case, India was inclined to allow to the Security Council authority to overrule the demand of the warring sides for the discontinuation of the peace operation, in the paramount interest of preserving the territorial integrity of the host state of Congo. Basically, similar concern for rehabilitating the state seemed to have prompted India to approve the two UN operations launched in Somalia during the early 1990s, which amounted to bypassing the sovereignty principle. In this instance, India shared the widely held view that collapse of the state structures in Somalia made the sovereignty principle irrelevant, in so far as the need to obtain prior consent was concerned. In another clear case of major departure from the sovereignty principle, India became party to the Council's decision to mount an observer mission, as part of an omnibus scheme of enforcement action against Iraq, after the conclusion of the Gulf War in 1991. India believed that the action of the UN to deploy a mission without securing the consent of Iraq in view of the 'unique situation of which there has been no parallel since the establishment of the United Nations' (Gharekhan 1991d: 72).

Nevertheless, India's anxiety that such exceptions did not undermine the salience of the sovereignty principle accounted for its conservative view on various proposals made in 'An Agenda for Peace' (Boutros-Ghali 1992) to strengthen UN peacekeeping activities. India emphasized in this connection that, in matters of preventive deployment and fact-finding missions, the UN should act only upon the express request of all the state parties concerned and also on the basis of a case-by-case basis (Heptullah 1992b: 50). Again, a few years later, India found fault with the Lakhdar Brahimi Panel (United Nations 2000a; Sharma 2000d: 6) for recommending 'a fundamental change in the principles whereby peacekeepers used force' which would likely lead to new crises, rather than to end them.

The second major issue concerns adjustment of the overarching principle that UN peacekeepers would not use force in their day-to-day operations except to defend themselves when attacked. India supported use of force by the UN mission to remove the foreign mercenaries from Congo and to bring about unity among warring factions in Congo in 1961, after the death of Dag Hammarskjold. However, India preferred to privilege the non-use of force principle by advising caution against taking liberty with the principle while mandating operations in the post-Cold War years. For example, with reference to unfortunate loss of UN peacekeepers in Somalia in 1993 as a consequence of combat operations to disarm Mohammad Aidid's faction in Mogadishu, India cautioned that mixing force (even if for humanitarian purposes) with the concept of peacekeeping would undermine the non-partisan credentials of the peacekeepers (Mukherjee 1994: 15). India was unconvinced about the 'excessive use of force and critical of the use of "Rambo" style of many peacekeeping operations'. A seasoned analyst sums up Indian approach as 'soft' peacekeeping, which stands in contrast to 'pull the trigger' approach (Krishnasamy 2010: 234, 236). Nonetheless, India made exception in the case of Democratic Congo. India became a part of robust peacekeeping in that traumatized country with authorization to use force for stabilizing the delicate security situation there. It has contributed infantry brigade with an aviation contingent equipped to use coercive force under UN instructions to cater to critical needs of the operation in 2005.

Further, India welcomed the active interest of the AU in regional peacekeeping. The AU peacekeeping efforts in many instances have formed the precursor to, and the basis for, several UN peacekeeping efforts, for instance in Liberia, Côte d'Ivoire, Sierra Leone, Burundi, the Central African Republic and Somalia. However, in India's view, regionalization of peacekeeping has its own drawbacks. The primary role of the UN cannot be disowned by subcontracting peacekeeping under regional or sub-regional arrangements in Africa or elsewhere. Such practices may bring impartiality of peacekeepers into question (Bishnoi 2015: 24).

That brings us, finally to the aspect of the composition of UN peacekeeping forces all these decades. Thanks to the interest and commitment by a large number of member countries, UN peacekeeping represented in a big way in the 'non-aligned mode' (James 1987) of maintaining world peace and security. What is remarkable is that the non-aligned character of UN peacekeeping did well by avoiding asking for troops from the permanent members—with only a couple of compelling exceptions in Cyprus and Lebanon. Their support was limited to only logistics and supplies. This arrangement, which was rooted in the Cold War context, should have continued as a time-tested tradition even after the Cold War ended. But, notably many of the second generation peacekeeping operations (like those in Cambodia, Iraq-Kuwait, Somalia and former Yugoslavia) invited participation from the permanent members routinely, not as exception. India was not forthright enough to forewarn the UN against the risks of relying on troop contributions from major powers who were politically biased and had lack of training to avoid heavy fire, unless unavoidable.

Conspicuous Non-participation and Participation in the Cold War Peacekeeping

The political rationale for the UN peacekeeping rests on the Cold War rivalry and the inability of the permanent members to agree on an arrangement regarding the armed forces to be placed at the disposal of the UN for enforcement of international peace and security. Peacekeeping was a limited, pragmatic idea to insulate conflict theatres in Asia and Africa from the Cold War rivalry. In other words, ideationally, peacekeeping was akin to the idea of non-alignment. However, India has taken time to get into the craft of peacekeeping. Indeed, four decades of Cold War era of peacekeeping point to oscillations in India's contribution, indicating an interesting alternation of inertness and enthusiasm. Curiously again, these India-specific characteristics closely correspond to the high and low phases of UN peacekeeping.

During the years 1948–1955, the Security Council launched two military observer missions. This is the UN Truce Supervision Organization (UNTSO), the first and longest operation in existence in the history of UN peacekeeping. India was not approached for contribution of observers at the time of its inception. Given the political polarization prevailing due to the Cold War at that time, the countries invited were only the Western allies. No doubt, after the Cold War ended, its composition underwent some welcome changes, but India has joined much later in 2015. Unlike what many studies tend to include India's engagement in provision of non-combat, medical services during the Korea conflict,[4] the present analysis does not wish to discuss India's role in the resolution of the Korean conflict in the early 1950s as an episode in UN peacekeeping, because the military operations had little or nothing to do with the UN. Of course, this is not to deny the influence of the field experience in Korea India gained on its approach to peacekeeping.

---

[4] The reference here is to several studies. See for example Parakatil (1975), Gupta (1977) and Nambiar (2009).

The years 1956–1963 constitute a break from the previous phase. During those eight years, five peacekeeping operations were mounted by the UN. India participated in all of them except for the small security force the UN sent to West New Guinea (West Irian). Particularly in regard to three missions, India's contribution was both impressive and important. India's chief delegate, Krishna Menon played a key role in the conceptualization and negotiations involving the UNSG, Canada's secretary for foreign affairs, Lester Pearson and Egyptian government in November 1956 (Brecher 1968: 75). As the second largest contributor to the UNEF, India sent one infantry battalion every year on average during the 11 years of its activities; a total of more than 13,000 Indian personnel of all ranks were deployed. Besides, two Indian army officers served as commanders of the Force.

The UN operation in the Congo, during 1960–1964 could be considered as an example of India's stellar contribution. India sent the largest contingent, comprising two brigades with more than 11,000 soldiers of all ranks, and 36 Indian soldiers sacrificed their lives while performing dangerous tasks in that newly freed country from colonial yoke. A distinguished Indian served as the Secretary-General's special representative during the tumultuous developments in Congo during 1960–1961 (Dayal 1976). In all, Indian participation was the most crucial part of major peacekeeping operations launched since 1956 until 1961. No less pertinent is the fact that 66 Indian soldiers laid their lives while working for the two biggest UN missions during this phase.

Then for nearly 25 years, a clear pattern of India avoiding contributing to UN peacekeeping operations occurred. During the years 1964–1987, the UN launched a total of six peacekeeping operations and observer missions, one of which is not relevant to the discussion on India as a peacekeeping participant. Among the remaining five, India as a non-permanent member co-sponsored in the Security Council the proposal for setting up two new operations after the 1973 Arab-Israeli war: one in Sinai area of Egypt (UNEF-II) and the other in Syria's Golan Heights (United Nations Disengagement Observer Force [UNDOF]). Yet Indian troops were conspicuously missing in both these missions. In the missions dispatched to Cyprus (UNFICYP) and Lebanon (UNIFIL) in 1964 and 1978, respectively, India chose to keep away, despite the fact that they belonged to the NAM. Possibly a combination of constraining circumstances might have dissuaded India. One explanation could be that the controversies arising from the first financial crisis in the mid-1960s and the unceremonious withdrawal of UNEF in 1967 turned the Indian political establishment and foreign policy bureaucracy away. Secondly, it could be surmised that India's pragmatism to prioritize management of domestic economic problems after the death of Prime Minister Jawaharlal Nehru and also modernization of defence forces in the light of two wars fought with neighbouring countries in a short span of three years too might have played a role.

Calibrated Activism in Contemporary Peacekeeping

The next twist in India's participation in the UN peace operations roughly coincided with easing of several regional conflicts under the positive impact of the end of the Cold War. Besides, peacekeeping received a morale boost when in 1988 it received the Nobel Peace Prize. It was in this backdrop that the UN peacekeeping witnessed renaissance to facilitate implementation of agreements on cessation of fighting and political reconciliation. Coincidentally, India too became warm towards the UN activity and resumed contributing troops and subsequently police units along with ancillary units. While some regional conflicts eased, new and ferocious conflict theatres emerged across the world, particularly within numerous African countries. The ethnic war leading to disintegration of Yugoslavia posed challenge to the stable European order and to the sustainability of multi-ethnic states, which most countries including India undoubtedly are. These worrisome developments caught the UN virtually off-guard. In the face of increased expectations from the membership, the time-tested technique of peacekeeping came handy to the UN. It had launched a total of 58 operations of varying sizes, the largest being the UNPROFOR with 38,000 personnel of all ranks at the time of its termination in 1995. Further, the UNSC rather liberally took recourse to peacekeeping operations with varying range of astonishingly ambitious mandates—whether it was delivery of humanitarian assistance, protection of civilians and managing safe zones for them, disarmament and demobilization of warring factions, protection of human rights, rehabilitation of refugees, reforming police and armed forces, preparation of electoral rolls and supervision of electoral process or restoration of state authority. In this severely testing process, some major operations were caught in controversies and faced the stigma of failing to deliver what was promised or hoped for (United Nations 1996).

At this moment of challenge and opportunity to the UN, as noted in Chapters 3–4, India had a rather internationally oriented political leadership, conscious of the need to nurture an image of mature and responsible emerging power. With the result, Indian troops, police and other personnel were contributed to 41 operations since 1988. A few shades of India's new, ongoing phase of engagement are worth noting. India has sent observers and other personnel to three old missions—UNTSO, UNDOF and UNIFIL where India stood outside originally. Its presence was noticeable in missions dispatched to locations in four continents: 20 in Africa, nine each in Asia and South/Central America and four in central/eastern Europe. In a far flung country Haiti, Indian police units were sent to as many as six successive UN missions authorized since 1993. Indeed, India sent first female police unit to Liberia in 1997—a first in the history of UN peacekeeping. (In 2019, another all women police unit has been deployed in Democratic Republic of Congo.) At the same time, India has arranged pre-deployment training to prospective peacekeepers from 96 countries; the Centre for UN Peacekeeping organizes training modules, on an average, to 150 and 500 foreign and Indian participants, respectively, each year. Most remarkably, in the years since 1990, India lost 102 personnel—more than half in the missions in Democratic Congo, Somalia and South Sudan. Analysts concluded that the Indian contingents demonstrated their 'staying power' in many difficult situations as in Somalia (Krishnasamy 2003: 269–270), Democratic Republic of Congo and South Sudan (Choedon 2014: 25–26). And for that reason India's contingent was rated as the most effective in Cambodia operation (Berdal 1993: 46–47), whereas in the case of Somalia, it received praise from Somalis for respecting local culture and traditions (Bullion 1997: 104). Secretary-General,

Boutros-Ghali commended the Indian troops for their 'superior training, high standards of discipline... [with] significant contribution in ensuring the early return of peace in Mozambique' (cited in Choedon 2007: 173). As the AU representative put it once in the Security Council thematic debates, India has become an 'exemplary reference point' in the area of peacekeeping (African Union 2011: 23).

The detailed break up of India's contributions for the years 1991–2019 appears in Table 7.2. While troops constitute 90 per cent of the contribution, the military observers are generally in double digits, whose aggregate total is a meagre 1,500. Notably, on the other hand, it emerges that the male and female police component was approximately 10 times more as compared to the strength of military observers.

Table 7.2 India's Troop and Police Contributions, 1991–2019

Year End	Police	Troops	Observers/ Experts	Total (Rank)	Grand Total
1991				35 (25)	11,178
1992	366	1,348	36	1750 (8)	52,154
1993	–	5,876	28	5994 (2)	69,969
1994	75	432	33	540 (36)	69,356
1995	13	2,012	53	2078 (2)	31,031
1996	92	1,081	38	1211 (2)	24,919
1997	180	150	23	353 (17)	14,879
1998	126	778	15	919 (2)	14,347
1999	226	1,745	27	1998 (1)	18,410
2000	617	2,098	23	2738 (3)	37,733
2001	636	2,207	32	2883 (4)	47,108
2002	504	2,203	39	2746 (4)	39,652
2003	307	2,530	45	2882 (4)	45,815
2004	343	3,515	54	3912 (3)	64,720
2005	384	6,810	93	7284 (3)	69,838
2006	361	9,039	83	9483 (3)	80,368
2007	439	8,775	89	9357 (3)	84,309

(continued)

(continued)

Year End	Police	Troops	Observers/ Experts	Total (Rank)	Grand Total
2008	640	7,963	93	8693 (3)	91,712
2009	738	7,942	77	8757 (3)	98,197
2010	1,057	7,550	84	8691 (3)	98,638
2011	1,039	6,997	79	8115 (3)	99,016
2012	1,022	6,744	73	7839 (3)	94,090
2013	984	6,815	50	7849 (3)	98,200
2014	1,002	7,073	64	8139 (2)	104,062
2015	1,011	6,718	89	7798 (3)	107,088
2016	889	6,752	59	7710 (2)	100,376
2017	589	5,982	38 + 88 staff officers	6697 (3)	92,682
2018	430	5,861	49 + 105 staff officers	6445 (4)	89,846
2019	170	5,162	40 + 115 staff officers	5491(5)	83,331

Source: Compiled from UN Website on Peacekeeping Contributions Statistics, https://peacekeeping.un.org/en/troop-and-police-contributors, accessed on 31 March 2020.

A close look at the statistics would reveal that for 25 years, India's contingents rank among the top four and consistently so more than 20 years since 1998. Not only this, for about five years during 1994–1998, a relative slide has occurred, presumably reflecting the overall trend of the decline in the UN peacekeeping activism itself due to the setbacks suffered in Mogadishu, Srebrenica and Kigali during 1993–1995 (Murthy 2001: 224–225).

What also emerges from the table is not just the fact that India has been a key contributor in the UN peacekeeping in *most* missions, but not *all* missions. The question that arises in this connection is how India decides to—or not to—send contingents. In other words, how does one explain the reason why India chose not to send troops to a few operations? The answer to the question whether such decisions were guided by any criteria is indicated for the first time in an address to the General Assembly by India's foreign minister (Gujral 1996: 15):

> Our participation in United Nations peacekeeping does not stem from considerations of narrow gain. We have participated because we have been wanted and because we have been asked, but most of all because of our solidarity and empathy with the affected countries and with the international community, as well as because of our commitment to the United Nations and to the cause of international peace and security.

Among the three considerations hinted, the most important one is the second one—empathy with the affected country—that could explain India's choice of opting in and out of certain missions. In the absence of official explanation, inferences can be made. The decision to join old missions in Golan Heights, Lebanon and the UNTSO or even the new mission in Afghanistan may have been guided by the keenness of the host countries, such as Afghanistan, Lebanon, Syria and even Israel. Contingents were sent to Congo, despite the volatility of the situation, partly due to previous association in the 1960s, and the desire to stand by the UN effort to restore peace in that troubled country. The empathy factor certainly might have guided the country to agree to send troops to South Sudan, a newly independent country. The choice relating to the mission in Sudan might have been guided by India's energy sector investments and the desire not to lose out to China in Africa. On the other side, there were missions in which India was absent. They include missions in Central African Republic, Darfur region, UNPROFOR in former Yugoslavia[5] and the UN Transitional Administration in East Timor. The decision not to contribute troops in those missions, despite the request from UN headquarters, was presumably guided by the uneasiness about the rising violent separatist claims for self-determination and the likely danger

---

[5] Having refused to contribute troops, India yielded to the request to nominate a senior army officer to head the important mission for a year in 1992–1993. This happened, according to the officer concerned, after Secretary-General, Boutros-Ghali made a personal request to the Indian Prime Minister at that time (Nambiar 2009: 42).

to the territorial integrity of friendly countries, such as Yugoslavia and Indonesia. Paradoxically, Pakistan was more active in those missions hoping that the momentum for self-determination might catch up in South Asia soon.[6]

Aggrieved and Indifferent as Host

An understanding of India's association with UN peacekeeping will remain incomplete without its related role as host to peacekeeping operations on its own soil. India's attitude towards the two missions (one of which is operating till date) has been a marked regression from cooperation towards inattention over a long period (Murthy 1998a: 181–182).

The first mission, that is, the UN Military Observer Group in India and Pakistan (UNMOGIP) was stationed in 1949 and was modestly manned to observe adherence to the ceasefire line in Jammu and Kashmir (as agreed to in the Karachi agreement between the two South Asian neighbours). This group of observers is known to belong to the quiet category of peacekeepers, besides being one of the cheapest and fairly safe in terms of low fatality figures. During the period 1949–1971, UNMOGIP went about discharging its duties smoothly with cooperation from both India and Pakistan—only with occasional problems that were overcome. In 1954, for example, in the wake of the military tie-up between the United States and Pakistan, India questioned the suitability of American observers in the group and got them replaced. Another hiccup was the resumption of hostilities between Pakistan and India across the ceasefire line in 1965. India deftly cornered Pakistan at New York by citing the UNMOGIP reports that Pakistan indeed indulged in unprovoked violation of ceasefire line and engineered infiltration into the Indian side of Kashmir. The 1971 war and its aftermath, however, brought a

---

[6] Pakistan foreign minister, Sartaj Aziz (1999: 29) saw lessons from East Timor for UN to help people of Jammu and Kashmir also exercise their right of self-determination.

break and practically froze the relationship between India and the observer group.

As a consequence of the war, India contended that the ceasefire line, as established in 1949, was superseded by what was named as the 'Line of Control' (LoC). In the absence of a fresh mandate to ensure the sanctity of the LoC, according to India, UNMOGIP should cease to function. Disagreeing with India, Pakistan desired the UNMOGIP to continue with its job as before. There was no support to India's viewpoint in New York. Having failed to secure support in the Secure Council to its contention for removal of the vestige of multilateralism in Jammu and Kashmir, so as to reserve the dispute for unfettered bilateral negotiations between India and Pakistan, India took the next logical step. Since 1972 India has ignored UNMOGIP as an operational body. It has stopped lodging complaints with the group about Pakistan's violations even during the Kargil war in 1999.

Further, the period of insurgency and heightened militancy in Kashmir, particularly during the early 1990s, the presence of UNMOGIP had become a source of discomfort to India. In the early 1990s, India sought to oppose firmly the ideas floated at the behest of Pakistan for either augmenting the strength of UNMOGIP or instituting some form of preventive deployment. It was reported at that time that the United States proposed, much to Pakistan's chagrin, disbanding of UNMOGIP by 1999, both as part of the cost-cutting exercise and also in the belief that it no longer served any useful purpose.

The second mission, the UN India–Pakistan Observer Mission (UNIPOM) was sent in the aftermath of the 1965 war to observe and supervise troop withdrawal across the international boundary. Although UNIPOM was a brief and small, but successful enterprise, India was unhappy about the very fact that it was created. In its contention, the 1965 armed hostilities constituted a single process—whether in Kashmir or along the international boundary. And therefore, a single, existing mission, viz. the UNMOGIP should have been entrusted with the task of overseeing the withdrawal to the pre-hostilities positions. On the other hand, Pakistan drew distinction between transgressions of the duly recognized international boundary and violations of the ceasefire line in a disputed territory (Saksena 1974: 292–293). Overruling the Indian objections, the Secretary-General introduced a separate observer group for doing the job on the India–Pakistan international boundary. India was lukewarm in dealing with the new mission and withheld payment of its share of the mission's cost while paying that year's assessed contribution to the UN budget (James 1990: 166).

Perspectives on Operational and Financial Issues

During the past five decades since the early 1960s, several policy questions have cropped up, some of which have threatened the very basis and credibility of UN peacekeeping. They are: whether peacekeeping operations should be deployed in every situation without any discretion, whether the missions are meant to continue indefinitely, the grave consequences of the mismatch between mandates and means, improvement of decision-making procedures on mandate formation, and providing stable and sound funding. It is useful to look at India's take on some of them.

India has been persistently cautioning against results of lack of discretion in acceding to requests for dispatch of peacekeeping operations and equally the consequences of allowing some missions to remain interminably. Perhaps the UN would have profited in the post-Cold War phase of peacekeeping operations if it had paid heed to what India advised quite early on. To quote that important word of caution (Jaipal 1981: 6),

> A peace-keeping operation should be the exception rather than the rule. It had, in fact, been the exception since, out of 88 questions with which the Security Council had had to deal, peace-keeping operations had been established in only two cases. The aim of the United Nations should be to wind up peace-keeping operations as soon as possible by encouraging the countries concerned to keep the peace themselves through bilateral efforts and at the same time helping them to resolve through negotiations the differences that had led to the conflict.

Accordingly, India opined that the Security Council would be erring by renewing without linking it to the desired change in the views of the contending parties in Cyprus. The same approach of prudence continues even in present times, as Prime Minister Narendra Modi reaffirmed at the Summit on Peacekeeping, convened in September 2015 by the UNSG, that 'peacekeeping missions should be deployed prudently, with full recognition of their limitations and in support of political solutions' (Ministry of External Affairs 2015). Aligning prudence with safety of peacekeepers, Indian representatives underlined that there can be no peacekeeping operation when there is no peace to keep. In other words, a durable agreement for peace should precede deployment of peacekeeping mission. Ignoring this has led to increasing loss of lives. Hence safety and security of UN peacekeepers should remain paramount (Sandhu 2009: 34).

In the recent years, mismatch between the mandate and means has emerged as one of the hurdles to the effective management of peacekeeping operations. India pointed out that mandates have become 'too broad and too all encompassing' forcing peacekeepers to face 'situations in which they are more frequently being called upon to use force not just to defend but to enforce mandates' (Puri H.S. 2009a: 13). As India found, too often 'mandates had been ruined and unrealistic, and the resources committed had not been commensurate with the declared objectives' (Tharoor 2010: 7). To buttress the point about the mismatch between the resources and the tasks assigned, India referred to situation in the central sector of the Congo operation where 3,000 peacekeeping troops are responsible for an area of 500,000 square kilometres. It was added,

> If, in such a scenario, we task the troops deployed to enforce the protection of civilians without even providing enabling air assets for rapid reinforcement operations, it is obvious that the size and scale of UN deployments are insufficient for the tasks entrusted to them. The strategy of peacekeepers being required to do more with less is setting us all up for a tragedy. (Akbaruddin 2018b: 23)

As the visibility and importance has grown, India has pressed for recognition of the right to be consulted at the time of mandate formulation, renewal and change. India had demanded trilateral consultations between troop-contributing countries, the Secretariat and the Security Council (Shah 1995: 33). Notwithstanding a few symbolic concessions, including accommodation of top five peace-keeping-contributing countries in the organizing committee of the newly established PBC to nurse societies to normalcy after a conflict is brought to an end in the designated country, the consultation have neither been sustained or substantial. India and other South Asian nations, which together contribute 35 per cent of UN peacekeeping forces, were truly disappointed. India has highlighted the issue in the concept note it circulated as President of the Council before thematic discussion on peacekeeping it initiated in August 2011 (SCOR 2011b). Several contributing countries strongly pleaded for strengthening of the consultation mechanism in the meeting that followed. In the latest thematic debate initiated by Russia too, India pointedly regretted that the suggestion for institutionalization of consultation was mooted 25 years ago, but no substantive improvement has taken place for bringing the Council, the Secretariat and the contributing countries into decision-making process on a regular basis (Akbaruddin 2019d: 28).

The next important issue has a bearing on the ways and means of reducing recurring delays in planning and deployment of peacekeeping operations when mandated. In other words, the proposal for a standby peacekeeping force to which troops committed in advance by willing countries would be available to the UN on demand. When the idea was first mooted in the late 1950s, India sounded sceptical about the practicability of the proposal. Raising constitutional, political and operational objections, India questioned whether the permanent standby troops could be deployed in unspecified locations for unknown purposes (Parakatil 1975: 187). Subsequently, India showed greater accommodation. In the 1960s, India endorsed the outlook of the Scandinavian countries on the question: that standby force would be used as a peacekeeping and not as enforcement mission after being duly authorized by a competent UN organ; and that prior approval of each contributor country regarding participation in an operation should be secured (Menon 1958: 365). In view of the pressing need for more troop requirements in the early post-Cold War years, India announced in 1994 that it would earmark a fully equipped brigade for use as part of the UN peacekeeping standby force when needed in future. Subsequently, it also welcomed the proposal for establishing standing police capacity, but wanted due weightage be given to professionalism, geographical balance and the contributions of troop-contributing countries (Basu 2006: 2).

Similarly, the Indian position on the issue of command and control has been consistent. This question assumed importance as the United States and NATO countries preferred to work outside the control of UN causing unhappy strains to the image of UN peacekeeping (Berdal 1993: 28). India did not share the United States' preference to disallow the American troops to be brought under foreign command and control. India held that each contingent should be commanded by respective national commanders who should be accountable to the force commander named by the Secretary-General after the Security Council's approval.

Yet another salient issue persisting for many decades is the recurring financing crisis faced by managers of UN peace operations. India's conviction that providing sufficient financial wherewithal to UN activities, including peacekeeping activities, is the collective responsibility of member states. In the prolonged debate on the principles of financing UN peacekeeping during the early 1970s, India highlighted the criteria focusing on the special status of the permanent members in the scheme of preservation of peace as also the capacity to pay. This meant that the five permanent members would bear a little more than half of the peacekeeping expenses, thereby providing corresponding discounts to the developing and least-developed countries (Sharma 1988: 11; Sinha 1990: 15). However, as the number of new generation operations and the personnel shot up, the budget requirements grew exponentially from a modest amount of US$300 million exponentially to US$2 billion by 1999. The largest contributor, the United States refused to pay its dues unless the UN agreed to reduce the US share to 25 per cent. Despite protestations from several quarters including the European Union (EU) and under American pressure, the share was brought down in 2000 from 31 to 28.4 per cent. However, as the peacekeeping aggregate budget has grown enormously to approximately US$8 billion in 2019, one-third of the total assessments remain unpaid by the member states in 2018. The issue of financing peacekeeping is not technical, it is fundamentally political. It is not that many advanced countries cannot afford to pay, but they do not want to pay for some reasons. The UN debt to developing countries which provide nearly 80 per cent of human resources has increased monumentally, as the number of peacekeepers shot up. As of October 2019, the UN owed US$285 million to the troop/police contributing countries (GAOR 2019). On its part, India has been meticulously meeting its funding obligation to the tune of US$1.2 million by paying its share in full and in time. India often reminds that the expense incurred on peacekeeping is only 0.5 per cent of the total military expenditure across the world. At the height of the UN peacekeeping in the mid-1990s the dues India was owed ranged between US$60–70 million, although the amount was brought down to US$38 million in 2019. But the fact is that this remains the largest outstanding amount owed.

Push and Pull Factors

There are clearly political and military expectations that explain India's active participation in the UN peacekeeping. Between the two arms of government involved in the decision-making, the Indian Army seems to be more enthusiastic than the External Affairs Ministry. Over the years, India's military capabilities have grown in terms of manpower, training and the inventory of advanced equipment. Despite the combat experience gained in wars with external enemy forces and also in controlling armed insurgencies internally, the Indian army tends to believe that participation in peace operations is an opportunity to enhance professional exposure to combat and non-combat situations while learning how to use new equipment. The encomiums the Indian contingents received from the host countries as well as those at the helm of managing operations at the UN headquarters reinforce their capability to deliver high levels of performance. To refer to just one of them, the force commander of Rwanda Mission at the time of its closure in 1996 paid rich tributes by acknowledging that the Indian troops 'demonstrated what it is to be good soldier and you brought also a sense of professionalism in everything that we have to do for the Rwandese. I say this without any reservation, you are probably one of the best soldiers in the world at this time (cited in Choedon 2007: 174), exceptional episode of Sierra Leone apart.[7] Conversely, a few analysts characterized India's mixed record as 'weight of history and lack of strategy' (Gowan and Singh 2013: 177–196).

From the vantage point of army and the individual personnel, huge economic gains from a peacekeeping assignment are a motivating factor. The army would get attractive reimbursements on account of equipment costs, which partly can be used for purchase of newer equipment (Murthy 2007b: 163). The subsistence and other allowances that a soldier below the rank of an officer may get are considered a windfall, given modest salary levels in India. It needs to be highlighted, however, that the payments are not made inflation-adjusted on a regular basis. In the midst of demands to enhance the 18-year-old allowance of US$1028 to $1762 in tune with the inflation rates, it was only moderately increased to US$1428 in 2014.

The Western media carried negative stories that the peacekeepers had spread human immunodeficiency virus/acquired immunodeficiency syndrome (HIV/AIDS) and indulged in sexual misconduct in countries such as Cambodia (Murthy 2007b: 164) and Democratic Republic of Congo. At best it could be considered as an unintended consequence of peacekeeping. India on its part objected to the negative image against the troop-contributing countries' services. Indian representatives asserted:

> Not one Indian peacekeeper has either arrived in the theatre in Africa with HIV/AIDS or left with it. Our soldiers have died in Africa and elsewhere of diseases ... most recently in Sierra Leone

---

[7] The professional conduct of Indian officers has received praise with rare exceptions. Adverse comments were made that the Sierra Leone Force commander, Major General Vijay Jetley was 'high handed and aloof, often acting without consultation with close colleagues' and he 'surrounded himself with an inner circle of Indian officers' (Bullion 2001: 78, 81). Jetley blamed Nigeria's interference in the functioning of the force operations (Choedon 2007: 159).

from particularly virulent form of cerebral malaria—but no one has died of AIDS (Sharma 2001b: 13).

On establishing a code for ensuring individual culpability, India fully endorsed the UN policy of zero tolerance towards sexual abuse and exploitation by peacekeepers (Mahajan 2005: 11).

As regards foreign policy motivations for undertaking active peacekeeping responsibilities, the Ministry of External Affairs (MEA) possibly looks at peacekeeping as a window to build empathetic partnership in addressing the problems of the people of Asia, Africa and South America and promoting future economic, commercial and cultural ties with them. Its activism and reliability as peacekeeper country helps in the campaign for permanent membership in the UNSC for which the support of the countries that have hosted Indian contingents would be of great help. As against these motivations, reference may be made to a couple of interesting outcomes of positive nature in the wide spectrum of bilateral relations. Cooperation on peacekeeping matters appeared prominently in the high-level meetings between India and the United States. The two countries have established a joint working group to review twice a year the problems of UN peacekeeping and to draw appropriate lessons for joint action. The United Kingdom and other countries too have entered into similar arrangements with India (Murthy 2007b: 160–161). Again, peacekeeping has meant healthy and cordial relationship between the contingents of India and Pakistan wherever they are deployed together, setting aside perennial distrust between the two nations. Furthermore, an element of positive competition has also been noticed between the two countries. India's sudden withdrawal from the Sierra Leone mission prompted Pakistan too to do likewise (Murthy 2007b: 161).

The negative comments in Parliament and outside about the need to put lives of Indian soldiers in harm's way have apparently made the External Affairs Ministry more cautious than the Indian army.[8] Again,

---

[8] Questions were raised in Indian Parliament about the need to keep soldiers in dangerous conflict theatres like Somalia or Sierra Leone, or in far-away Haiti where no national interests are at stake (Murthy 2007b: 162).

the Sierra Leone withdrawal decision was linked to the strong disquiet expressed by Indian political parties and parliamentarians over the hostage crisis involving 500 personnel belonging to contingents from India and other countries, and the negative publicity about the role of the force commander, General Jetley (Bullion 2001).

Way Forward

Any attempt to redefine India's approach to UN peacekeeping as a major troop-contributing country may have to take into account the following aspects: the different kinds of peace operations the UN has so far launched in relation to lessons drawn from the past and present patterns of the country's participation, and also the interests and motivations driving the country to take part.

While it is true that for many years, India has taken decisions on a case-by-case basis, it is time to define the broad parameters of a policy framework with sufficient scope for flexibility. On the one hand, the official rhetoric protests that our participation in UN peacekeeping eschews 'considerations of narrow gain', on the other hand, it is open to question if participation would be justifiable when the country's foreign policy interests are not furthered. Notably, the governments at different points of time have been guided by a blend of apparent common interest and latent national interest. For instance, given the geopolitical importance of regions like West Asia and South East Asia, presence of Indian troops as peacekeepers conformed to the country's foreign policy principles and purposes. Equally worth mentioning is the secondary interest of stabilizing the sovereign state system by managing threats emanating from the intrastate conflict situations, hence participation in a number of African operations. Moreover, India has earned goodwill for building economic partnerships in several countries, including Sudan.

In this connection, one or two policy options may be outlined here for further deliberations. Instead of too thinly spreading its presence in numerous operations launched by the UN, India could become backbone of an operation suiting its larger and narrow interests and capabilities. Such contribution could make qualitative difference to an operation while India might be able to showcase its effectiveness and professionalism. Second, pooling of South Asian peacekeeping capabilities between India, Pakistan and Bangladesh is a possibility worth exploring with a view to bargaining better in respect of determination of mandates, matching of means/powers with mandate, reimbursement and compensation rates and so on. Unlike the AU, Economic Community of West African Countries (ECOWAS), Commonwealth of Independent States (CIS) and Organization of American States (OAS), the South Asian regional capacity for peacekeeping is not meant for peacekeeping within South Asia. It has to serve the purpose of projecting cumulative and complementary capabilities for undertaking peacekeeping outside of South Asia, on the lines the EU is doing in the Democratic Republic of Congo. As India's ambassador told the Security Council lately, a worthwhile consideration while serving in UN peacekeeping 'is to keep incentivizing change, institutionalizing best practices and placing a premium on innovation' (Akbaruddin 2019d: 28).

CHAPTER 8

India–Pakistan Conflict
A Test Case for the UN

India–Pakistan conflict belongs to that category, which often frustrates all efforts to conceive a just solution (de Reuck 1984). India and Pakistan have been in conflict ever since they became independent more than seven decades ago. The width and breadth of the conflict envelops the political, territorial, historical, ideological, psychological and other dimensions. And each dimension intersects with others, thereby complicating any purposeful problem-solving effort. Moreover, new issues are added to compound the old problems. Gains and losses are seen in absolute, exclusive terms. The domestic opinion is aroused for jingoist purposes to obviate any dramatic compromise. The fractious political climate in the outside world, involving especially the major powers, had only sharpened the mutual mistrust between India and Pakistan. They resorted to major military hostilities four times so far—in 1947, 1965, 1971 and 1999. On each of those occasions, much of the global community, as organized in the UN, was gravely concerned over the adverse consequences to the larger domain of international peace and security. That is perhaps the reason why it may not be wide off the mark to suggest that, except for the Arab-Israeli conflict it would be difficult to cite a more protracted and multifaceted conflict than the one involving India and Pakistan (Brines 1968; Ganguly 2002; Paul 2005). To cite specific statistics, the UNSC held

151 meetings (including the two closed door meetings held after revocation of Article 370 in the Indian Constitution in August 2019) and adopted 19 resolutions on particular aspects of the India–Pakistan conflict so far. The UN involvement in defusing the conflict has been rather sporadic, depending on the seriousness perceived about an emergent situation. For instance, the UN was grimly watching the rising tensions between India and Pakistan particularly regarding Jammu and Kashmir in the 1990s. When these tensions threatened to reach a nuclear flash point in May 1998 in the wake of the surprise nuclear tests by the two countries, UN expressed 'grave concern' at the danger posed to peace and stability in the region (Security Council 1998a; Security Council 1998b).

How unique is the India–Pakistan conflict to the UN in terms of the challenges to its role so far? Which factors have the defining influence on the UN role in this conflict over the years? How does each of these two countries perceive the relevance of the UN to their respective objectives and interests? What role is the UN likely to play in this conflict in the foreseeable future? Will the UN be able to force a solution to the India–Pakistan conflict? Is it true that bilateralism and multilateralism are mutually exclusive approaches vis-à-vis the India–Pakistan conflict? This chapter examines these questions.

There seems to be a striking attitudinal incongruity between the outlooks of India and Pakistan towards the UN. Whereas Pakistan views the UN as a protective shield against India, India has traditionally sought to project its potential to play a larger role in global affairs. While professing 'complete and consistent' support to the UN purposes and principles, India asserted during the early years that its voice could not be dismissed as that of 'a little nation somewhere in Asia'. Years later, on the occasion of the 50th anniversary of the UN, India announced that it would be too willing to join the right thinking nations and peoples' to make the world body 'truly and effectively a global repository of human aspirations' (Rao 1995: 45).On the other hand, Pakistan's outlook towards the UN role in maintaining world peace has had a strong India-related tinge. Then or now, Pakistan constantly reminds the UN about its duty to set right the excesses committed by India. In the early years, its theme was the aggression committed by a 'powerful' India against a 'weak and peaceful' Hyderabad (Khan 1949: 57), whereas since the beginning of the 1990s the salient issue has been Jammu and Kashmir whose 'noble people [are] committed to the right of self-determination, committed to the ideals of the UN, placing their hopes on the United Nations' (Bhutto 1995: 24). In short, the expectations of both India and Pakistan from the UN turn out to be mutually exclusive in the context of their conflict. They want the UN to promote their respective foreign policy objectives. For Pakistan, the UN should compensate for the military, economic shortcomings it suffers in comparison with India; it would also like to use the global forum to check India's 'hegemonic' tendencies. On the other hand, India thinks that the UN forum is meant to address common and global problems and not for pursuit of narrow, short-sighted goals. India perceived that forces not very sympathetic to India's concerns and sentiments are trying to misuse the UN forum.

Pakistan and India have indulged themselves liberally in an action–reaction process to give the desired twist to the deliberative agenda before various organs of the UN over the years. The patterns of these countries' articulation of their perceptions have by now become familiar and repetitive, therefore predictable. In the process, many representatives of the two countries have come to be highly regarded for their skills in parliamentary diplomacy. As a matter of practice and tradition, it may be noted, the UN offers to parties concerned with opportunities where they are expected to express their viewpoints, paint the conduct of the adversaries as inconsistent with the accepted principles or norms of interstate behaviour, offer defence against the charges made by the adversaries, and seek endorsement of one's own positions. These opportunities are particularly attractive to the parties which otherwise are weak in negotiating directly with the relatively stronger adversary for a fair deal. With the help of the UN, they hope to boost their bargaining power vis-à-vis the stronger side. If successful, the stronger side may be compelled to yield more ground to the weaker side to ensure some sort of damage control at the UN. These general propositions apply aptly to the patterns of diplomatic conduct of Pakistan and India within the UN forums. A related aspect of this deliberative process is the spillover effect on India–Pakistan differences. Numerous questions have often acquired strong India–Pakistan dimension. The debates on the question of a zone of peace in the Indian Ocean, the issue of right of self-determination, observance of human rights, and expansion of the Security Council testify to this trend. As it transpires often, the India–Pakistan altercation contributed to deflection of attention from the main issues of a question to the advantage or relief of the targeted major power.

The experiences of the UN in the context of the conflict between India and Pakistan cannot be viewed independent of the influence of various factors. A brief reference has to be made to two important factors, viz. the perceptions of India and Pakistan as the parties directly concerned, and the political calculations of the outside powers that have a major say in the decision-making dynamics of the UN bodies.

Given the fact that issues in the India–Pakistan conflict touch the core of the national interests of both countries, it is only natural for them to bring to bear suitable diplomatic strategies in the UN. Moreover, the domestic opinion in these countries is often made strongly sensitive to the developments in the zero-sum equations between the two countries. As such, each country can ill-afford an outright rejection of its viewpoint and endorsement of the opponent's contentions. Who started the armed hostilities, whether events in the immediate background should be linked to the deep seated, long-drawn-out circumstances, or even whether the UN should discuss a particular development are treated by both parties as prestige questions. A recent example is the high profile legal battle India successfully waged at the World Court during 2017–2019 against Pakistan for denying consular access to Kulbhushan Jadhav, sentenced to death on charges of espionage and terrorism for India. This is hardly the kind of the backdrop against which the UN needs to find a solution acceptable to both sides. But the UN being an institution of political nature has to engage in an exercise of diplomatic engineering to harmonize the conflicting interests and positions, and work out face-saving solutions, rather than taking one-sided view.

The mainstay of the political processes at the UN is the interplay of interests of not only the parties directly involved, but also those of the major players in the UN decision-making processes. Particularly the role of the permanent members has had a great bearing on the UN initiatives in the India–Pakistan conflict. On many occasions, the positions taken by the then Soviet Union and the United States—the two giants among the five permanent members in the UNSC—were largely guided by the Cold War considerations, extraneous to the issues involved. For example, the Western interest in Kashmir, owing to its strategic location contiguous both to the Soviet Union and China, was defined by the desire to stem any expansion of the Communist influence. Pakistan made the task of the Western countries easier by offering its cooperation to this end in return to their political support in its conflict with India. The former Soviet Union launched counter diplomatic offensive to win over India, and promised political and diplomatic cover against any unwelcome UN resolution in the Security Council. The divergence of perceptions between the United States and the former Soviet Union—except for the brief break in the mid-1960s—chiefly accounts for the role or non-role of the UN in this conflict. The deliberations at the UN before and during the 1971 war aptly depict how the US-China combine and the Soviet Union severely impacted on the UN role (Murthy 1993: 58–75). The end of the Cold War has not completely wiped out the divergence, although it has brought about some fluidity in the political equations between the major powers and the two South Asian neighbours. With the result, neither India nor Pakistan could take the American or the Russian support for granted. Regardless of the continuity or end of the Cold War, China remained an important factor to be reckoned with in the UN decision-making. Its postures, both during the time of the Nationalist China and also since the time People's China occupied the Security Council seat, were intended to favour India or Pakistan, respectively, because it suited its specific national interests. All in all, the interests of the permanent members have been an important influence on the UN ability to perform the necessary role in managing the conflict between India and Pakistan. Moreover, because of the much improved relations with India and decline of Pakistan's importance to it, the United States has refused to mechanically support Pakistan's attempts to bring up the Kashmir question on occasions in the changed context. Pakistan complains that India's huge markets are compelling the United States to turn soft towards India. On the other hand, the Russian equations with Pakistan have signalled positive change, as India no longer depends solely on the Russian support. At the same time China has become 'all-weather friend' to stand by Pakistan inside and outside the UN. All in all, interests of the permanent members have been an important influence on the UN ability to perform the necessary role in managing the conflict between India and Pakistan.

In view of the above governing factors, the UN had to be wary in applying mechanically the Charter framework for addressing the issues in the India–Pakistan conflict from time to time. It may be noted here that under the various provisions of the Charter, the General Assembly and the Security Council in particular are equipped with an array of both persuasive and coercive powers to tackle the diverse manifestations of differences between states. In responding to numerous situations of interstate conflict, the UN bodies have tended to rely more on the spirit rather than the letter of the Charter mandate. The flexible and pragmatic approach stands for resorting to the best possible mix of moral and political measures suiting the peculiarities of a situation. These included a gentle request for show of restraint, emphasis on the negotiations as a route for conflict resolution, a nudge for an early end to an armed action without naming the wrongdoer, plea for restoration of the situation that existed before the outbreak of armed conflict, warning of strict action in case of non-compliance by a stubborn state party to a conflict, imposition of economic sanctions and rarely authorization of military action for restoration of status quo ante. Obviously, some of these actions gave rise to controversies and are said to have proved at times counter-productive to the world body's stated objectives. The Korea, Cyprus, Kuwait or even the Kosovo situations amply attest to one or the other components of this general characterization of the UN role in managing international conflicts. The conflict between India and Pakistan is one of them.

Dimensions of the UN's Role

In terms of the past experience and future options, the UN role in the India–Pakistan conflict can be analysed under three broad but intermixed dimensions. They relate to (a) pacifying the parties in the wake of actual or likely armed conflict through different techniques of moderation; (b) helping the parties narrow down their existing differences through mediation and other acceptable measures; and (c) eschewing any temptation to force a solution. The detailed analysis of each of these three dimensions follows.

Pacify on Priority

The UN's approach to the India–Pakistan conflict is characterized foremost by its efforts to keep the two countries peacefully apart, by either restraining them from doing anything that might endanger peace in the region, or prevailing on them to stop fighting if it had already started. The UN bodies have always held the view that the threat or actual use of force in the subcontinent could seriously undermine international peace and security – one of its very founding purposes. Therefore, it was imperative for the UN to take up the more pressing and urgent issues, such as war than other long-standing facets of the India–Pakistan conflict. Accordingly, for the UN, pacifying Pakistan and India became an immediate and urgent concern, without entertaining the demands to first redress all the pending and partisan grievances before stopping the battle field confrontation. In doing so, the UN hoped to make its task of ending or averting breach of peace easy to handle.

Each time Pakistan and India were engaged in war, they advised the UN to place the onset of military conflict in proper perspective, that is, to say that military confrontation was a consequence of lack of sufficient and urgent attention from the world community to resolve the political, territorial and other problems to their partisan satisfaction. Accordingly, they exhorted that commitment from the UN to resolve the outstanding disputes urgently was as important as the immediate aim of stopping a military fight in the subcontinent. However, the UN did not wish to make its task unmanageable, by linking the two aspects. It focused its attention only on the immediate task of fire-fighting, rather than submerging it under an array of long-standing grievances that might have led to the conflict. Indeed, this has become a time-tested and well-established practice the UN evolved right from the early days (Saksena 1974: 78–81). In 1948, the Security Council gave priority consideration to the Kashmir problem setting aside complaints of Pakistan in regard to accession of Junagadh to the Indian Union, communal violence after partition, and so on. In 1965, the UN ignored Pakistan's contention that cessation of military operations against India could not be agreed to without an undertaking about a favourable solution to the Jammu and Kashmir problem through implementation of the previous UN resolutions adopted in the late 1940s.[1] In 1971 too, the UN did not share India's contention that the Pakistan–India war could not be ended without putting an end to the genocide perpetrated by the Pakistani troops in East Bengal and the resultant exodus of the East Pakistanis in unprecedented numbers to India (Sen 1971: 17).

The question may be raised whether the approach of isolating the outbreak of armed conflict from the deep-rooted causes was advisable or effective enough. It may be argued that, by adopting a limited, short-sighted approach, the UN was helping perpetuation of an unjust situation; and resort to force to remove such injustices was necessitated by the UN failure to bring about the desired changes through diplomatic and peaceful methods. Indeed, in a situation where a country with substantial territorial and political advantage blocks the negotiations apprehending loss of its present advantage, the UN's limited, short-sighted approach of confining only to ending a fight was indeed tantamount to encouraging one side's posture of obstructionism. On the other hand, it may be pointed out that the UN could not be expected to endorse use of force by member states as a means of redressing grievances. The piecemeal approach of the UN did not imply in any way that the root causes of the India–Pakistan conflict should be ignored forever. It only implied that priority be given to the immediate and manageable task of exercising pacifying influence whenever India and Pakistan tensions escalated.

---

[1] President Ayub Khan of Pakistan wrote to the UN Secretary-General, U Thant, expressing his reservations on unconditional ceasefire without a 'durable and honourable settlement' of the Kashmir dispute (Secretary-General 1965).

The pacifying approach of the UN appears to have manifested in three inter-related strategies, viz. not blaming or condemning either country for infringement of the international obligations, calling for cessation of fighting or restraint in the battle zone, and dispatch of military observers to the field to ensure adherence to the ceasefire arrangements as also to supervise withdrawal of armed forces to the positions held by parties before the hostilities began.

Non-condemnation

As an integral element of its moderation approach to international conflicts, the UN considered that blaming or condemning any country in a conflict would not only alienate that country but also further precipitate the environment. Accordingly, the UN refrained from blaming India or Pakistan explicitly for initiating hostilities even when evidence might have warranted it. To put the record straight, the question did not arise in 1948–1949, as India did not desire any condemnation of Pakistan for its complicity in the tribal invasion of Kashmir. However, in 1965 India wanted Pakistan to be named as an aggressor for organizing armed intrusions across the ceasefire line in Kashmir, and later Pakistan demanded condemnation of India's invasion of Pakistan across the international boundary. But the UN chose to skirt the issue. In 1971, a similar scenario arose. Pakistan desired the denunciation of the Indian army's entry into Pakistan's territory before the declaration of war, while India pressed for condemnation of Pakistan for its genocidal activities against the innocent people of East Pakistan. Nevertheless, the UN response was on the familiar lines of avoiding any apportionment of blame between the contending sides. Although the Council did not hesitate to condemn some countries for their actions unacceptable under international law, one would not know for sure how the Security Council would have reacted if India went to the UN with a demand for the condemnation of the Pakistan-sponsored intrusion into Kargil and other areas in the summer of 1999. As a consequence of its policy to keep Kashmir outside the rubric of multilateral forums, India did not approach the UN. Nor could Pakistan approach the world body, because of the definitive disapproval of its action already made known across the globe.

A couple of departures from the non-condemnation posture would be worth referring to. In the wake of the multiple underground nuclear tests carried out first by India in Pokhran and then by Pakistan in Chagai in May 1998, the UNSC condemned those nuclear tests (SCOR 1998). To be clear, the condemnation was not aimed against India or Pakistan directly and exclusively, but the actions of the two countries were clubbed together. It may be pertinent to note here that the UN condemnation conformed to a pattern of the UN responses to events challenging the major features of the post-Cold War order. Non-aggression and non-proliferation are important norms of that order. The tests were widely perceived as a dangerous twist to the India–Pakistan rivalry, and at the same time a disquieting challenge to the nuclear non-proliferation regime sought to be institutionalized and legitimized through the NPT as well as the Comprehensive Test Ban Treaty (CTBT). Interestingly, Pakistan's statement in the Security Council in June 1998 was directed as much against the discriminatory policies of some of the nuclear weapon powers, as understandably against India.[2] Indeed there was much that India would have stated to reinforce Pakistan's arguments against the nuclear weapon countries if it had participated in the Council's deliberations on the issue.

Another instance of recourse to condemnation occurred 10 years later in the aftermath of the Mumbai terror attacks in November 2008. Without explicitly referring to the Mumbai attacks and without naming Pakistan directly, the Council's President issued a statement to 'condemn in the strongest terms the incitement of terrorist acts and [it] repudiates attempts at the justification or glorification of terrorist acts that may incite further terrorist acts' (Security Council 2008).

---

[2] Criticizing the Security Council's 'extremely short-sighted' approach, Pakistan's representative stated that the resolution adopted was 'in fact a transparent exercise in self-assurance by the official nuclear five to seek legitimacy for their possession of lethal arsenals of weapons of mass destruction'. Furthermore, 'any attempt at imposition of NPT obligations on non-parties is, by its very nature, unequal and unsustainable' (Kamal 1998: 29).

Cessation of Hostilities

In the wake of India's complaint against Pakistan in 1948, the very first response of the Security Council and its President was to appeal to India and Pakistan to 'refrain from making any statements and from doing or causing to be done or permitting any such acts, which might aggravate the situation'. The UN has sought to prevail upon India and Pakistan in agreeing to an immediate ceasefire, as a first essential step, each time military conflict erupted in the past. In August 1948, the UN in a resolution desired the governments of India and Pakistan to 'issue separately and simultaneously a cease-fire order to apply to all forces under their control' in Jammu and Kashmir 'as of the earliest practicable date' (UNCIP 1948). A ceasefire was agreed upon subsequently. In September 1965, the Council called upon the two countries to 'take forthwith all steps for an immediate ceasefire and respect the ceasefire line' (SCOR 1965a). Showing displeasure with both the warring countries that showed reluctance to promptly and unconditionally accept the plea for a ceasefire, the UN 'demanded that the delayed ceasefire should take effect by a particular deadline set for the purpose (SCOR 1965b). Six years later in December 1971, as the Security Council was unable to discharge its primary responsibility owing to lack of agreement among the permanent members, the General Assembly stepped in to call upon India and Pakistan 'forthwith to take all measures for an immediate ceasefire' (GAOR 1971). When this call did not produce the desired results immediately and consequent to India's announcement of a unilateral ceasefire a week later, the reconvened Council 'demanded' a 'durable ceasefire in all areas of conflict' (SCOR 1971). The wording implicitly took cognizance of the dismemberment of Pakistan and the emergence of independent Bangladesh. This was followed by the Shimla agreement between Pakistan and India to establish a Line of Control (LoC) in place of the UN established ceasefire. Since then the theme of the sanctity of the LoC recurred in all the formal positions taken by the UN. Years later in the summer of 1999, in wake of the large-scale infiltration of the Pakistani armed men into the northern parts of the LoC existing since the 1971 war, the UN did not get involved except through the appeal from the Secretary-General to the parties to scrupulously respect the sanctity of the LoC.

Alongside, the UN underlined two other aspects: first, restoration of the ceasefire line or the international boundary as the case may be, and secondly, a call of restraint to all sides from doing anything that might further worsen an already delicate situation in the subcontinent. This has happened in 1948, 1965 and 1971 episodes. Interestingly, such a plea addressed to 'all' states during the 1965 war (SCOR 1965b) carried special significance in view of the threat of the Chinese intervention in the war.

Field Observation

Observing the adherence by India and Pakistan to their ceasefire commitment became equally important task of the world body. To perform this job of observing truce on the ground, the UN relied on the well-known technique of peacekeeping and deployed with the consent of both countries, unarmed or lightly armed military personnel borrowed from willing member countries. The UN dispatched two observer missions—UNMOGIP and the UN India–Pakistan Observer Mission (UNIPOM) —at different points in time with the consent of both countries.

The latter mission, UNIPOM worked briefly for a period of six months in 1965–1966 to observe cessation of fighting and to supervise troop withdrawals to their respective pre-hostilities positions along the India–Pakistan international border. Although its purpose was accomplished smoothly and swiftly, the very idea of the UNIPOM was a subject of contention. India opposed the inception of a new observer mission, arguing that the two sectors of India–Pakistan fighting, viz. in Jammu and Kashmir and across the international boundary, constituted a single whole and, therefore, the job of observing cessation of fighting and supervision of troop withdrawals could be undertaken in a unified fashion effectively by the observer mission already in place, that is, UNMOGIP. Nevertheless, the UN went ahead with the proposal to send the UNIPOM, accepting the Pakistani contention that a qualitative difference existed between the situations, one arising from violations of the internationally recognized boundary and the other in the then ceasefire line in Kashmir.

The experience of the other mission, the UNMOGIP, is different. It has the distinction of being the most long-lasting peacekeeping mission, next only to the UNTSO in the Palestine (Shucksmith and White 2015). It has been on duty in Jammu and Kashmir ever since it was incepted in 1949 to observe adherence to the ceasefire line (LoC since 1972). The professional integrity and impartiality of the observers was beyond question, except in the 1950s when the US observers were replaced at India's request after Pakistan and the Western countries entered into a military alliance, the Central Treaty Organization, in 1954. That the ceasefire line remained largely respected during 1949–1965 is a testimony to the usefulness of the mission. The mission investigated violations of the line and reported its findings to the UN headquarters. For instance, the UNMOGIP chief observer, R. H. Nimmo reported to the Security Council through the Secretary-General about the sustained ceasefire line crossing from the Pakistan side into the Indian side in August 1965 prior to the outbreak of the war. Indeed, these reports had influenced the proceedings and their outcomes in the Council at that time. However, the aftermath of the 1971 war marked a stressful chapter in the history of the UNMOGIP. After the conversion of ceasefire line into LoC, India saw no reason for continuation of the UNMOGIP, but it did not find support in the Council. Therefore, the UN observers continued to observe the situation on the LoC. On its part, however, India stopped field-level relationship with the UNMOGIP by choosing not to lodge complaints about violations by the Pakistani side (James 1990: 161–163). On the other hand, Pakistan continues to view the work of UNMOGIP as a symbol of international community's engagement with the Kashmir issue. In 2018 alone, the UNMOGIP received 229 complaints from Pakistan about violations of LoC from the Indian side.

It is notable that the UNMOGIP was not allowed any say in the events associated with India's successful repelling of the armed infiltrations from the Pakistani side in 1999. The situation across LoC witnessed anxious moments in the recent years. In September 2016, the Indian army launched surgical strikes to destroy terrorist launch pads across the LoC on the Pakistani side of Kashmir in retaliation to the killing of 18 soldiers in Uri. Again, in February 2019, the Indian Air Force went deep into the Pakistan territory and struck Balakot in retaliation to the killing of 40 paramilitary personnel by the terrorists trained in Pakistan.

In the late 1990s, a proposal was reportedly initiated in the UN Secretariat to close the UNMOGIP for cutting down peacekeeping expenses, but Pakistan lobbied successfully against it. Moreover, the changing character of the South Asian security scenario after the acquisition of nuclear weapon capability by India and Pakistan and the growing tensions caused by the cross-border terror attacks launched in several cities in India with Pakistan's active complicity for more than two decades rule out any option to disband the mission. All said and done, the UNMOGIP with a total of 44 military personnel from 10 countries is one of the most cost-effective among the UN missions; its budget estimate for 2019–2020 stands at US$10.4 million.

Roadblocks to Resolution

Conflict resolution is an important dimension of the UN involvement in the India–Pakistan conflict. The UN took up two tracks of the problem-solving with a view to addressing some of the intricate causes of the conflict. They are mediation and holding of a free and fair plebiscite on the future status of Jammu and Kashmir. Both the tracks initially showed promise of a breakthrough. But in the course of time, they reached a dead end.

Mediation

The UN attempted mediation to bring about an agreement between India and Pakistan on different aspects of their conflicting claims during the years 1948–1957. The idea of the UN undertaking mediation emerged in the early stages of the consideration of India's complaint against Pakistan in 1948. A five-member mediation team, known as the UN Commission on India and Pakistan (UNCIP) was set up with mutual agreement in April 1948 to conduct negotiations with the two countries. The UNCIP attempted to work out the modalities towards operationalizing the willingness of India and Pakistan to let the future status of Jammu and Kashmir be decided by means of an impartially supervised reference to the people of Kashmir. Having facilitated a ceasefire, the Commission brought the two parties around to agree hesitantly to important measures, such as withdrawals (first of all the Pakistani troops completely followed by the bulk of the Indian forces), exit of all outsiders, including the invading tribesmen, disarmament of the local forces in Pakistan-occupied Kashmir, return of the uprooted Kashmiris to homes and so on. The implementation of these measures was essential for creating conditions suitable for ascertaining the wishes of the people in a free and fair manner. The UNCIP also obtained India's agreement on the modalities of appointment of a plebiscite administrator and his powers.[3] It was actively at work for nearly two years during 1948–1949 and submitted three interim reports to the Security Council. But unfortunately, the differing interpretations by India and Pakistan to their own and the other side's commitments proved insurmountable to the Commission. Also, the Commission was not free from differences within.[4] Under these circumstances, it was disbanded and succeeded by four single mediators—General A. G. L. McNaughton of Canada, Owen Dixon from Australia, Frank Graham from the US and Gunnar Jarring from Sweden—who sought to pick up the threads from where the Commission left the job, including the question of the number of forces each side would be allowed to retain pending the conduct of the plebiscite. There was no trace of agreement between India and Pakistan (Brecher 1953; Bailey 1982: 59–150). A suggestion to refer the differences for arbitration was not acceptable to India. The suggestion to adopt a fresh approach to resolve the problem (meaning partition with part or no plebiscite) (Dixon 1950: 44–45) was cold-shouldered by Pakistan. One of the mediators saw no point in continuing the UN

---

[3] These steps were outlined in two resolutions of the Commission, adopted on 13 August 1948 and 5 January respectively, and both India and Pakistan accepted these resolutions while reiterating some of their apprehensions and reservations (Doc. S/995 and S/1196).

[4] The third interim report of the Commission had a minority report penned by the lone dissenting member, Oldrich Chyle of Czechoslovakia. See Addendum to UN Doc. S/1430, 16 December 1949 (Deora and Grover 1991: 312–325).

mediation and in fact recommended leaving the problem to be tackled directly between India and Pakistan. The Security Council members did not favour the recommendation, but slowly by 1957, the UN mediation reached a dead end and was abandoned.

The UN third party role was lost out to the Soviet Union after the 1965 war. As per the Tashkent agreement signed in January 1966 in the presence of the Soviet prime minister, India and Pakistan re-affirmed their obligation under the UN Charter 'not to have recourse to force and settle their disputes through peaceful means'. The Soviet mediation was useful for the moment and was notably not institutionalized. That there was no room for the UN mediation or even a third country role was a clear message, which came out of the 1971 war. After the war, India and Pakistan got together in Shimla in July 1972 and solemnly articulated their resolve to 'settle their disputes by peaceful means through bilateral negotiations' and agreed that pending their final settlement neither side would unilaterally alter the situation. The agreement ensured that the UN would not meddle without the consent of India and Pakistan. In the post-Cold War years, successful resolution of regional conflicts in Namibia, Cambodia, Mozambique, El Salvador and others by the UN seems to have fuelled hopes for re-engaging the world body in the India–Pakistan conflict. In 1993, Secretary-General, Boutros-Ghali offered to help in search for a 'lasting solution' if both parties so request (United Nations 1993: 44). But India did not approve of any such suggestions. Similarly, of late, the American President, Donald Trump claimed that Prime Minister Modi sought his help to resolve the issue with Pakistan. These claims were strongly denied by officials of India's MEA as well as the US State Department (NDTV 2019).

In retrospect, the UN mediation failed to fructify for two interplaying reasons. The foremost was the unwillingness of the parties to cooperate with the UN, for doing so might put at risk their claims on the disputed territory. Pakistan could not afford to vacate its part of Kashmir and squander away its bargaining lever in the face of the apprehension that India might turn truant in meeting its part of the deal. Likewise, India could not afford to take any risk by unilaterally withdrawing the bulk of its forces first, leaving its part of Kashmir vulnerable to the activities of the forces raised and armed by Pakistan. Neither could over-rely on the UN to check against the rival party's mischief-making potential. Gains and losses have come to be seen in zero-sum terms, leaving little scope for give-and-take process. Any unfavourable change in the Kashmir status quo, even in honourable circumstances, was feared to shake off the roots of the losing country's political and ideological identity. Hence, respective national positions hardened on both sides. The climate of suspicion and insecurity led to a search for support from countries outside the region. It is in this background that the role of major powers assumed significance. From the beginning, the United Kingdom, by virtue of being the erstwhile colonial master, and the United States hoped to prevail on India through a UN-sponsored face-saving formula so that the disputed princely state could join Pakistan and eventually help the free world in defending against the expansionist designs of the Soviet Communism. The British-declassified documents show the attempts by Great Britain and its Western partners to influence and interfere with the mediation activities of the UN (Murthy 1989). The Soviet delegates were unhappy that the West was fanning tensions and fishing in the troubled waters, but it did not block adoption of UN resolutions on the subject for some time. But the formation of the military alliances in Central Asia and South East Asia in 1954 to make Pakistan an ally triggered a change in the Soviet approach. As a consequence, the Soviet Union not only tended to show open sympathy to India, but also did not hesitate to veto a proposal in February 1957 to send a UN force to Kashmir to prepare ground for holding a plebiscite (SCOR 1957b: 29).

Plebiscite

The India–Pakistan dispute over Kashmir provided the UN with an opportunity to explore a problem-solving role through the conduct of a 'plebiscite' to ascertain the wishes of the people of Kashmir as to whether they wanted to remain with India or join Pakistan. The rationale for the UN role of that nature rested on the readiness of India and Pakistan to repose confidence in the ability of the UN to organize a free and fair plebiscite.

The UN adopted some general principles for the conduct of the plebiscite. A plebiscite administrator was designated in 1949 with the concurrence of India and Pakistan. But he could not carry on with the responsibility to make arrangements for plebiscite, as disagreement continued over the methodology of the troop withdrawals or compliance with other requirements. Besides, both parties started nursing doubts about the suitability of the incumbent, Fleet Admiral Chester Nimitz, a war hero from the United States. He quit the office in 1953 in disappointment, and no successor was appointed. A few years later, V.K. Krishna Menon elaborately attempted to redefine in the Security Council the Indian commitment on the plebiscite. According to him, India's 'offer' of plebiscite under the UN auspices was not meant to be binding infinitely without regard to the change in circumstances; it was no more than a 'wish' to refer the issue of accession to the people of Kashmir; and the reference could not necessarily mean only the plebiscite, indeed it could mean 'anything' from a general election to a Gallup Poll (Menon 1957: 38). (It is pertinent to note here two domestic developments: framing of a constitution by the Constituent Assembly, which reaffirmed the instrument of accession, and subsequent Nehru–Sheikh Abdulla fall out leading to the dismissal of his government and latter's prolonged imprisonment.) However, the Council did not buy India's claim and reaffirmed that the UN-supervised plebiscite remained the only acceptable mode of deciding the future status of Kashmir (SCOR 1957a), although the UN mediator conceded the argument about the change of circumstances (Jarring 1957). The Soviet Union merely abstained on the text. Thereafter the UN never had an occasion to take up the question of conducting a plebiscite.

Is it that the parties did not let the UN conduct the plebiscite because they were not convinced that the UN had requisite experience and expertise? It is true that the UN did not have previous experience of conducting or even supervising polls of any kind and, therefore, the project would have run into problems given the magnitude and complexity of the task. However, the argument of lack of experience does not seem to stand to reason in the years since the end of the Cold War. In the years since the successful work in Namibia, the UN has acquired rich experience as also a reasonable reputation in the conduct or supervision of electoral processes in more than 100 countries. Besides, the UN is associated with the conduct of referendum to ascertain the preferences of the people of Namibia and Eritrea, which culminated in their independence from South Africa and Ethiopia in 1990 and 1993, respectively. A similar exercise was undertaken in East Timor in 1999, and the referendum contemplated for Western Sahara has been long held up due to procedural disagreements.

Whether UN experience in the above democratic process is relevant to resolving the India–Pakistan conflict over Jammu and Kashmir is a relevant question to ask. Two contrasting models deserve attention in this connection. One model represents the experience in Eritrea, Namibia and East Timor and the other in Western Sahara. In the case of Namibia and Eritrea, the UN played a facilitating role because there was no doubt about the popular preference in favour of freedom from colonial occupation. Second, the occupier countries (South Africa and Ethiopia, respectively) cooperated with the UN with a conviction that they could be better off without these territories under their continued occupation. And third, the exercise did not involve a triangular relationship, that is, two member countries claiming allegiance of the population in question. All these considerations would apply to the case of East Timor too. Therefore, notwithstanding the Pakistani attempt to project the successful UN-conducted process of 'popular consultation' in East Timor as a forerunner of a plebiscite in Kashmir, this model is of little help in so far as the India–Pakistan conflict is concerned. On the other hand, the Western Sahara situation presents a different picture and may be somewhat relevant to the India–Pakistan dispute. Though an agreement in principle was reached in 1990 between Morocco and Polisario (the liberation movement with international status in the Organization of African Union and the UN), subsequent disagreement has put off indefinitely the referendum scheduled initially for 1992.

Unlikelihood of Imposing Sanctions

In view of the failure to resolve peacefully the India–Pakistan conflict even after many decades, should the UN force a solution through invocation of its coercive authority under Chapter VII of the Charter by imposing economic sanctions? To the extent the India–Pakistan dispute is concerned, the UN was able to arrest the armed hostilities without resorting to enforcement powers, notwithstanding the fact that the idea of adopting this approach was reportedly entertained on one or two occasions in the past. In 1951, the United Kingdom and the United States prepared a contingency plan to seek UN sanctions if India and Pakistan went to war. In 1965, the initial reluctance of the warring parties to agree to UN calls for immediate and unconditional ceasefire made the Secretary-General weigh the option of urging the Security Council to order a ceasefire under the terms of Chapter VII. But, notably these plans did not become necessary as events followed in the desired direction. In any case, such a drastic response from the UN would not have been easy to be authorized in the Cold War climate.

The era of the unipolar phase of the post-Cold War period prevailed in the Security Council for about 12 years. During this period the United States held sway in the decision-making of the Council that accounts for a series of Chapter VII decisions to impose varying sets of sanctions and authorizations for military action under Chapter VII. Somalia, Haiti, and other episodes represent that trend. The situation has changed ever since the United States misadventure in Iraq in 2003. The Council is often a divided house, as deliberations on Iran, Libya and Syria have brought out. On these questions, the three Western permanent members are opposed by the combine of China and Russia. Neither China's growing footprint in Pakistan nor the rise of India as one of the fastest growing economies in the era of globalization will make any reckless punitive action acceptable and therefore workable in the new century. Moreover, the sanctions announced (outside the UN framework) by the industrially advanced countries against India and Pakistan after their nuclear tests in 1998 hurt the imposing countries as much as the target countries; hence, they were gradually eased.

Assessment

What emerges from the discussion is that the dominant aspects of the UN role in the India–Pakistan conflict are by no means unique or exceptional. The UN responses to issues from time to time had to factor the extent of intersection between the interests of the parties to the conflict and the preferences of the major powers at whose behest the UN decisions are invariably made. The UN has stuck to a pragmatic approach of responding with caution and in piecemeal fashion. That approach was translated into taking up the urgent task, such as cessation of fighting for priority action, identifying areas of agreement between the contending parties so as to create a workable basis for peace and allowing the differences to be narrowed in a slow motion, if not sporadic process of negotiation and mediation. Accordingly, the UN cooled off the tensions by securing immediate and unconditional cessation of fighting between India and Pakistan each time they resorted to large-scale use of force. Simultaneously, it pressed for prompt withdrawal of troops to the territories held previously. The significant dimension of the UN role that made a great deal of difference to the situation on the ground is the deployment of two observer missions to facilitate voluntary adherence to the parties' commitment on ceasefire or troop withdrawals. As a high watermark of its moderation approach, the UN scrupulously avoided naming either of the countries as a violator in the interest of not vitiating the prospects of playing a role of an honest broker between India and Pakistan. The liberal strategy of the UN in conflict containment between the two countries has generally paid off in the sense that the intended results were achieved.

These actions towards conflict management by the UN were not conceived to be end-all responses; they were only preliminary steps to help create an atmosphere suitable to a meaningful exercise aimed at resolution of the deep-seated causes of the India–Pakistan tussle. The mediation exercises undertaken by the UN as part of its conflict resolution strategy were long drawn out, given the nature of the complexity of the issues at stake. As the UN mediators realized, working on long-term solutions in a fast changing situation was no way to succeed. The UN might have succeeded if there were will on the part of the parties to yield some ground to each other. The UN could not force a solution; it could only engage the parties in reconciliation process. Hence, for the parties wanting to play safe, the UN mediation became a convenient scapegoat. With the failure of the UN mediation to make any progress, the hopes for a 'free and fair plebiscite' in Kashmir collapsed concomitantly. At large, even the mediation strategy was mainly concentrated on making necessary arrangements for the plebiscite. It would be plausible to ask whether the UN was really equipped or experienced to hold a plebiscite of the magnitude required for Jammu and Kashmir in the early days. The rich experience the UN acquired in conducting referendum in the early post-Cold War years does not seem to be of much relevance to the India–Pakistan problem.

The tendency in the UN after the Cold War to use stick against the countries obstructing implementation of a conflict resolution drive may not be viable in the case of India and Pakistan dispute. It might create more problems than resolving, as experience in different conflict theatres confirms. As such, the role of the UN may not go beyond expressing concern about deteriorating human rights situation, appealing for India–Pakistan restraint along the LoC and encouraging resumption of the frequently halted bilateral talks. The UN role is likely to be of this nature, no matter how hard Pakistan may try to involve the world organization on its behalf in the conflict. This became pretty clear in August 2019 as also in January 2020 when Pakistan desperately tried in vain to have a formal meeting of the Security Council with the help of the Chinese delegation to get India's action to revoke the special constitutional status of Jammu and Kashmir denounced.

In sum, expecting that the UN will be able to exercise its coercive authority to force a particular mode of settlement (such as the internationally supervised plebiscite) or actually enforce a settlement is unrealistic in the foreseeable future. A realistic appreciation of the relevance of the UN to the management of conflict between India and Pakistan would show that its effectiveness may have to be seen less in terms of helping these countries settle their intractable disputes, but more in terms of assisting them to settle down with their intractable problems.

CHAPTER 9

India against International Terrorism at the UN

One of the most important priorities in India's participation in the UN during the past two or three decades is to combat collectively the Frankenstein monster of international terror and its varied manifestations. This issue area, without a doubt, caters to the concerns of India's national security as well as the larger interests of the interstate system itself. As India's Nirupam Sen aptly observed once, terror

> knows no border or boundary; it observes no codes of conduct or constraints of religious ideology; nor is it restrained by humanity or the bounds of civility. Its objective is, inter alia, to provoke a state of terror in the general public or in a group of persons or particular persons, intimidate a population or compel a government or an international organization to do or to abstain from doing any act. It dictates its terms through death and destruction, fear and confusion. It is indiscriminate in its wrath. (Sen 2004d: 25)

Among various diplomatic and political levels at which India approaches the battle against international terror, the UN forums occupy crucial place. While the international community has made some progress in evolving a rule-based order for managing the economic and commercial dimensions of globalization, the absence of an effective, rule-based order is acutely felt in addressing contemporary security threats, such as terrorism and proliferation of weapons of mass destruction' (Sen 2005d: 27). As such, the UN is uniquely placed to provide the multilateral platform necessary for real global cooperation and coordination in the common fight against terrorism and the proliferation of WMDs. As India rightly points out, states tend to think only nationally not globally as terrorists do, the role of the UN is imperative to promote cooperation (Akbaruddin 2017: 13). As such, India actively took part in all possible forums to highlight the problem and build a common position.

India is party to 14 of the 19 international counterterrorism treaties. In line with its obligations under those instruments, India has enacted scores of domestic laws in line with its obligations and the imperatives of internal and external security[1]—the latest being the amendment in 2019 to the Unlawful Activities Prevention Act 1968 to empower designation of individuals (not just organizations) as terrorists for appropriate prosecution and punishment. India informs, 'Our laws incorporate provisions dealing with all aspects of terrorism including conspiracy and incitement to terrorism. Our laws criminalize the raising of funds for terrorist activities, the holding of the proceeds of terrorism, the harbouring of terrorists, and the unauthorized possession or use of any bomb, dynamite or hazardous explosive substance or other lethal weapons' (Mukerji 2014a: 18).

The chapter will examine the subject from historical, moral, legal and diplomatic perspectives to the issues addressed during India's participation on the subject at the Plenary and subsidiary bodies of both the General Assembly and the Security Council. An analysis will be made about the issues articulated, initiatives pursued, positions

---

[1] Reference may be made to a few legislations and executive orders issued over the years. To prevent and punish incitement of terrorism, the Unlawful Activities Prevention Act (1967) was amended in 2004 and 2019. While Prevention of Terrorist Activities was repealed, the illicit financial transactions are sought to be controlled through the Directorate of Enforcement under the provisions of the Foreign Exchange Management Act (Yadav 2014: 83).

defended and contributions made for the strengthening of the organizational capacity to counter the menace of international terrorism since the beginning of the 1990s. Before this, a brief overview of the engagement of the UN since the beginning of the 1990s would be useful.

UN Action against Terrorism

A few years before the onset of the Nineties, India suffered a major terror attack when Air India Flight Kanishk exploded mid-air over the Atlantic Ocean in June 1985. The UN had little to do with the investigation or trial, as the trial and conviction of the accused Sikh terrorists took place in Canada. The 1990s began when the first meeting of the Security Council was held at the level of heads of state or government to emphasize that all terror attacks will be effectively dealt with (Security Council 1992: 144). India, as a newly elected non-permanent member, was a party to that presidential statement. Soon thereafter, India supported the Security Council resolution (SCOR 1992) to strongly deplore Libya's refusal to hand over two of its nationals indicted in the Western countries for bombing a Pan Am aircraft over Lockerbie in 1988 for trial. Further, to demonstrate its seriousness, the Council mounted mandatory travel and diplomatic restrictions against Libya. This time of course, it was not a unanimous decision (Murthy 1992).

Whereas the Security Council was paying attention to specific situations, the General Assembly started deliberating on building global consensus on a normative framework against terrorism. In the early 1990s, member states represented in the Legal Committee of the General Assembly deliberated on the ways of forging international cooperation to prevent and eliminate terrorism. The outcome of those deliberations was the Declaration on Measures to Eliminate International Terrorism in December 1994 (GAOR 1994). The Declaration denounced all forms of terrorism without any exceptions. It was a significant step forward in that no country opposed such formal stigmatization of terror actions. Two years later in 1996, the Assembly set up an *ad hoc* committee which delivered two important legislations—the international convention for the suppression of terrorist bombings followed by finalization of the international convention for the suppression of the financing of terrorism in 1997 and 1999 respectively.

At the *ad hoc* committee, the Russian Federation had proposed in 1998 a convention to combat acts of nuclear terrorism to extend the definition of nuclear material (contained in the 1980 Convention) to include objects and materials for military use, as well as the provision of a clearer definition of the crime of illegal acquisition of nuclear materials for terrorist purposes and the inclusion of terrorist acts against nuclear power plants, vessels with nuclear power sources and the use of automatic nuclear devices. After protracted negotiations to iron out differences on such issues as exemption to be provided to the activities of the armed forces of a State from its scope, the draft convention received the General Assembly approval in 2005.

Following the recommendation made by the Secretary-General's High-Level Panel on Threats, Challenges and Change (GAOR 2004b), the Assembly unanimously agreed in 2006 (GAOR 2006b) and renewed 10 years later in 2016) on Global Counter-Terrorism Strategy outlining a range of measures to prevent, contain and eradicate terrorism at national, regional and global levels, through capacity-building and full respect for human rights. This has been regularly reviewed by the General Assembly biennially since then.

The Security Council's engagement in the concerted action against terrorism was in fits and starts in the 1990s (Boulden and Weiss 2004). After Libya in 1992, the next major episode in the Security Council's action was imposition of aviation, financial sanctions against the Taliban rulers of Afghanistan on 15 October 1999 for continuing to train and shelter terrorists and terror camps and for refusing to turn in Al-Qaida's head, Osama bin Laden (SCOR 1999a), which put in place one of the toughest implementation and monitoring mechanism against the individuals named from time to time. Four days later, in a notable departure from the practice of responding to specific terror groups and moving towards delegitimizing terrorism as a legitimate tool for achieving political ends, the Security Council in a resolution (SCOR 1999b), unequivocally condemned 'all acts, methods and practices of terrorism as criminal, unjustifiable, regardless of their motivation, in all their forms and manifestations, wherever and by whomever committed, in particular those which could threaten international peace and security'.

The most significant turning point in the Security Council's sustained and strong action occurred in the wake of the terror attacks on 11 September 2001 planned and executed by the Al-Qaida against the commercial and government buildings in New York, Washington DC and Pennsylvania. The Security Council launched a series of path-breaking measures under Chapter VII of the Charter, beginning with the omnibus requirement from all states to (a) criminalize the wilful provision or collection of funds in support of terrorism in their territorial jurisdiction; (b) refrain from any form of overt or covert support to entities or persons involved in terrorist acts, (c) prevent commission of terrorist acts, (d) deny safe havens to those who plan, commit terror acts or help in collecting funds, (e) prevent movement of terrorists or their groups through effective border control measures, and (f) extend support to cooperation bilaterally and multilaterally through exchange of information in accordance with domestic and international legal measures. The reference here is to Security Council omnibus resolution (SCOR 2001), unanimously adopted in September 2001. Furthermore, member states are to report to the Counter-Terrorism Committee (CTC) set up to monitor compliance through periodical reports and also site visits (Murthy 2007c; SCOR 2004b). Subsequently in 2004, the Council mandated all countries not to provide support to develop, acquire, manufacture, possess, transport, transfer or use nuclear, chemical or biological weapons and their means of delivery (SCOR 2004a).

One of the recent phenomena that emerged as a troubling manifestation of international terrorism is the recruitment of foreign terrorist fighters. This theme has found mention in various reports of the Secretary-General, in the documents relating to the review of the Global Strategy, and in the Security Council deliberations too. According to the UN estimates in 2019, approximately 30,000 terrorists originating from nearly 100 countries are actively part of terrorist acts under the stewardship of, among others, the Al-Qaida and the Islamic State (Da'esh) in conflict theatres of Iraq, Libya, Mali,

Somalia, Syria and Yemen. The Security Council took cognizance of the problem in the recent few years by adopting two resolutions SCOR 2014; SCOR 2017) to suppress the recruitment, training and engagement of foreigners turning into terrorist fighters. India too has remained deeply concerned about this.[2]

At the Secretariat, a Counter-Terrorism Implementation Task Force (CTITF) was created in 2009 followed by the UN Counter Terrorism Centre in 2011 to coordinate the activities of different UN organs and sub-organs. At the same time, the UN has been criticized on grounds of overlap among the activities and lack of effective coordination in view of the acknowledged fact that there are as many as 38 separate entities dealing with one or the other aspect of counterterrorism. The core tasks of the UN Office on Drugs and Crime, INTERPOL, the International Civil Aviation Organization, the International Maritime Organization and others are necessary to be made mutually reinforcing to counterterrorism. For long, there is no single point or coordinator accountable to the States Members of the United Nations for the activities of these various entities. As part of the continuing UN managerial reforms, Secretary-General, Antonio Guterres announced creation of UN office on counterterrorism under the leadership of an under-secretary general in June 2017 by bringing the Counter-Terrorism Implementation Task Force (CTITF) and other bodies under the direction of the new office. The new administrative structure is aimed to (a) provide leadership to the General Assembly counterterrorism mandates entrusted across agencies of the UN system through enhanced coordination and coherence, particularly for balanced implementation of the Global Counter-Terrorism Strategy, (b) strengthen the delivery of UN counterterrorism capacity-building assistance to member states and (c) improve visibility, advocacy and resource mobilization for UN counterterrorism efforts. Member States widely welcomed the move and pledged necessary support.[3] To keep

---

[2] Indian representative cited the case of the UNDOF, which faced attacks from foreign terrorist fighters affiliated to the Al-Nusra Front, a terrorist group proscribed by the Security Council (Mukerji 2014b: 29).

[3] For example, India announced a voluntary contribution of US$550,000.

up the momentum, the Secretary-General convened a high-level conference of heads of counterterrorism agencies of member states in June 2018.

The preceding brief discussion on the UN structural and monitoring architecture against terrorism would help locate the four focal features of India's approach on the subject. As the analysis below brings out, much of India's effort was devoted to push for early acceptance of Comprehensive Convention on International Terrorism (CCIT) it proposed initially in 1996. Simultaneously, India painted itself as a major open, democratic society suffering for long from the inhuman terrorist activity propped up from across the border, thereby blaming its neighbour as the epicentre of international terrorism. The consequential feature relates to Pakistan's counter to India in painting itself as a victim of terror—not perpetrator. The third element of India's approach relates to its persistence to make the Security Council sanctions regime effective and transparent in its conception and implementation for better results. Finally, India's perspectives bring out the positives and pitfalls of the Global Counter-Terrorism Strategy (GCTS), adopted by the General Assembly. The foregoing analysis takes up each of these major aspects.

Prioritization of Comprehensive Convention

India sensed that the legal framework for tackling multiple and growing manifestations of terrorism is segmented and fragmented, much before the attacks took place against the United States in September 2001. India was convinced more than any other country that the time has long arrived to adopt a more comprehensive legal framework, incorporating very many elements of the existing sectoral conventions. Accordingly, in one of its few early initiatives during the post-Cold War years, India submitted in November 1996 a draft CCIT for the consideration of the General Assembly (GAOR 1996). Describing the CCIT as the 'capstone of the structure of conventions' against terrorism, the Indian permanent representative (Sharma 2001c: 27) referred to the nature of 11 September 2001 attacks and explained the rationale thus:

[T]he cluster of conventions on hijacking provides for action only against the hijackers; on 11 September, they killed themselves with their victims.... [T]he conventions on terrorist bombings have precise definitions of what constitutes an explosive; no one thought that a plane would ever be used as an explosive. Therefore, as experts on international law now realize and our citizens will find hard to believe, under the framework of the existing conventions on terrorism the international community could not take action against those who recruited, trained, ordered, supported, instigated or harboured the terrorists who committed the most horrendous act of terrorism the world has ever seen.

Nevertheless, it was not paid the kind of desired attention leading to circulation of a much revised version in August 2000 (see Box 9.1 below). It may be noted that the revision exercise was enabled particularly by two UN conventions adopted during the years 1997–1999, relating to suppression of terrorist bombings and the suppression of financing of terrorism. Part of the accepted phraseology from those texts was borrowed to garner greater support. The operative part of the revised draft added 11 Articles with more than 1,600 words to the 1996 text to define the terms, to elaborate and strengthen various provisions and procedures. Furthermore, the revised version appended three annexures to the draft convention, detailing the list of political offences, the procedures for mutual legal assistance as well as extradition.

Box 9.1: Salient Features of India's Revised Draft Counter-Terror Convention

Article 2: 1. Any person commits an offence within the meaning of this Convention if that person, by any means, unlawfully and intentionally, does an act intended to cause:

(a) Death or serious bodily injury to any person; or (b) Serious damage to a State or government facility, a public transportation system, communication system or infrastructure facility with the intent to cause extensive destruction of such a place, facility or system, or where such destruction results or is likely to result in major economic loss; when the purpose of such act, by its nature or context, is to intimidate a population, or to compel a government or an international organization to do or abstain from doing any act.

Article 3: This Convention shall not apply where the offence is committed within a single State, the alleged offender is a national of that State and is present in the territory of that State and no other State has a basis under Article 6.

Article 12: Any person who is taken into custody or regarding whom any other measures are taken or proceedings are carried out pursuant to this Convention shall be guaranteed fair treatment, including enjoyment of all rights and guarantees in conformity with the law of the State in the territory of which that person is present and applicable provisions of international law, including international human rights law.

Article 15: Nothing in this Convention shall be interpreted as imposing an obligation to extradite or to afford mutual legal assistance, if the requested State Party has substantial grounds for believing that the request for extradition for offences set forth in Article 2 or for mutual legal assistance with respect to such offences has been made for the purpose of prosecuting or punishing a person on account of that person's race, religion, nationality, ethnic origin or political opinion or that compliance with the request would cause prejudice to that person's position for any of these reasons.

Article 16: 1. A person who is being detained or is serving a sentence in the territory of one State Party whose presence in another State Party is requested for purposes of identification, testimony or otherwise providing assistance in obtaining evidence for the investigation or prosecution of offences under this Convention may be transferred if the following conditions are met: (a) the person freely gives his or her informed consent; and (b) the competent authorities of both States Parties agree, subject to such conditions as those States Parties may deem appropriate.

Article 18: 2. The activities of armed forces during an armed conflict, as those terms are understood under international law, which are governed by that law, are not governed by this Convention, and the activities undertaken by the military forces of a State in the exercise of their official duties, inasmuch as they are governed by other rules of international law, are not governed by this Convention.

Source: GAOR 2000

It would be instructive to underscore a few new notable additions or improvements. First, the revised draft text, unlike the original one, attempted an operational definition of terrorism covering a range of specific unlawful, criminal acts committed with terrorist intent to intimidate or cause death and/or serious bodily injury to any person, serious damage to public or private property and/or compel a government or an international organization to do or abstain from doing any act. Also, notably, the revised draft excluded crimes committed within the territorial limits of one country and when the offender is a resident of that country. Moreover, the accused are afforded guarantee of fair trial with enjoyment of all basic rights, safeguards against forced extradition in case of suspicion that prosecution or punishment by the requesting country would be on the basis of race, religion, ethnicity or political opinion. And finally, a provision was inserted to keep explicitly the operations of the armed forces during an armed conflict out of the purview of the Convention, since they would be governed by the UN Charter and other rules of international (humanitarian) law. India actively appealed to countries during bilateral meetings and in multilateral organizations for support to the CCIT. In 2003, the Working Group of the Assembly's Legal Committee cleared three articles pertaining to extra-territorial jurisdiction of the victim state, blocking safe havens/asylum to perpetrators of violence and state responsibility for suppression of terrorism (Yadav 2014: 83). Subsequently in 2007, a 'compromise package' on Article 18 relating to the activities of armed forces was presented, with India's support, which tried to meet these concerns by carving out the scope of application of the comprehensive convention from other specific legal regimes, and to avoid the politically sensitive attempt to distinguish between acts of terrorism and acts committed during an armed struggle for national liberation (Singh N. 2017: 4). Although progress had been made, more remained to be done, especially to address the root causes of terrorism and eliminating its breeding grounds. Indian representatives urged all delegations to work to resolve the outstanding issues and reach a compromise that would satisfy all parties, since a comprehensive convention would provide a solid legal basis for the fight against terrorism (Sen 2007b: 15).

The prolonged delay to agree on the CCIT even after deliberations and revisions during the past nearly two decades has been a source of genuine disappointment to India. The lack of progress occurred despite the recommendation by the 2005 World Summit in favour of early adoption of the convention. Referring to the inability of the Assembly to clinch the protracted process, India tellingly noted that 'one cannot say that the General Assembly is the law-making body and should make laws, and that the Security Council should not, and yet we are unable to make laws ourselves' (Sen 2008a: 3).

Political Delegitimization of Terror as a National Instrument

While law as a tool appeared to be an important part of India's counterterror approach at the UN, India also sought to make a political point by denouncing the claims of any legitimacy or justification put forward by sympathizers and supporters of terror on any count.

India suffered hugely at the hands of the terrorist groups sponsored from across the border from the onset of the 1990s. The targets were innocent people and public property not just in Jammu and Kashmir, but also outside. Targets in cities, such as Ahmedabad, Bangalore, Delhi, Hyderabad and Jaipur, besides the Indian diplomatic offices in Kabul were attacked causing loss to lives and property. In less than 25 years, over 60,000 were killed in various parts of India as a direct result of terrorism, quite apart from the concomitant impact upon economy (Sen 2008b: 21). In India, a few weeks after September 2001 attacks against the United States, two major attacks occurred against the Legislative Assembly of Jammu and Kashmir in Srinagar and the Indian Parliament in New Delhi in October and December 2001, respectively. The responsibility for these two dastardly attacks was claimed by Masood Azhar, leader of the terrorist group Jaish-e-Mohammed and another group, Lashkar-e-Tayyiba, based in Pakistan. India stated that it was not aware whether Pakistan took any action against those outfits whose activities are an affront to the provisions of Security Council Resolution 1373 (2001) (Sharma 2002: 21).

In the wake of a series of bomb attacks in different parts of the country in July 2006, the Security Council in a presidential statement, condemned them 'in the strongest terms' and expressed its deepest sympathy and condolences to the victims, as well as their families, and to the Government of India (Security Council 2006). Hoping that the solidarity the international community demonstrated with the United States in the wake of the Al-Qaida attacks would continue in respect of other incidents too, it was stated, 'Without it, countries that have been preyed upon by a global network of terrorism simply cannot cope with the challenge alone. We therefore hope that the solidarity... will not be confined to a hunt for an individual or a group, or to dealing with the symptoms alone; we must destroy terrorism as a system' (Sharma 2001c: 25).

India rebutted the argument that freedom fighters are not to be construed as terrorists. In its view, nothing can ever justify the targeted killing of innocent men, women and children (Malhotra 2005: 11). Clearly one could see a shift from India's approach articulated in the 1970s towards sympathizing with armed struggles for liberation of Palestine and in Southern Africa, because of the changes in the international situation. India rests its view on the newly emerged norm that there can be no impunity for crimes that constitute a grave violation of human rights. In the words of India's permanent representative,

> When political office, and bureaucratic or diplomatic immunity, have not protected some who have committed grave violations and have now been brought to justice, it cannot be admissible to argue that freedom fighters or any other group would be the only individuals who would be above the law. Terrorism is defined by the act, not by a description of the perpetrator. Secondly, while the cynical view might be that the end justifies the means, in all worthwhile political enterprises, the means are as important as the ends. (Sharma 2001c: 26)

The scale and suffering of the attacks in November 2008 against several public places in Mumbai by terrorists trained, funded and monitored by their masters in Pakistan attracted all-round shock and condemnation. India characterized the systematic targeting of a hospital, a railway station and hotels aimed to produce crippling effect not just on daily life in a bustling metropolis, but on an entire country of a billion people. Welcoming the Council's strong condemnation of the Mumbai attacks, India's junior minister for external affairs demanded banning of and tough sanctions against the terrorist groups responsible, especially Jamaat-ud-Dawa operating from Pakistan. Pointing finger at Pakistan, it was suggested that the terror group's country of origin should take urgent steps to stop further attacks (Ahamed 2008: 24). India continued to press its assessment that neither Pakistan's commitment to terrorism as an instrument of official policy nor its practice of hypocrisy has abated one bit. Unlike the killers of 11 September 2001 who met their fate, the mastermind of 2008 Mumbai attacks, Hafiz Saeed, continues to roam the streets of Pakistan with impunity (Swaraj 2018: 10), despite the fact that he was UN-designated terrorist and his repeated appeals were rejected by the Security Council.

It may be argued that the 2008 attacks helped India push Pakistan to an unenviable position. The tame denials carried no credibility. Hence, it increasingly painted itself as a victim of terror activities and therefore strong supporter of global effort against terrorism. While partaking in the Security Council deliberations on Mumbai attacks, Pakistan's foreign affairs minister empathized with India's pain over the tragic and indiscriminate killings of innocent civilians, but in the same vein referred to the brutal terror attacks against school children in Pakistan's Peshawar (Haroon 2008: 31). In its counter-terror operations, Pakistan's prime minster claimed once that it lost more than 27,000 citizens, including 6,500 military and law-enforcement personnel, besides the economic losses at more than US$120 billion (Abbasi 2017: 9). Pakistan's diplomatic representatives struggled hard to demonstrate that their government condemned terrorism in all its forms and manifestations. Further it rued the fact that terrorism 'had become ever more brutal and lethal, and continued to exploit sensitive political, ethnic and sectarian fault lines', despite the range of counterterrorism measures taken by the UN in the new century (Lodhi 2015: 8).

India took a dim view of Pakistan's attempts to paint itself as a sincere partner in the global fight against terror. Pakistan was accused of constructing narratives based on 'distortion, deception and deceit'. Just as Pakistan sheltered Osama bin Laden for 10 years until he was killed in a daring operation by the American strike force in 2011, it became a 'terroristan' (Gambhir 2017: 41) by virtue of the existence of a 'flourishing industry that produces and exports global terrorism' as exemplified by the legitimization of the notorious activities of Hafiz Muhammad Saeed, leader of a UN-designated terrorist organization, Lashkar-e-Tayeeba. Referring to the Pakistani claim of huge costs it was incurring due to terror activities inside its territory, India described Pakistan as a polluter and therefore was paying a heavy price.

Indeed, the General Assembly in its seventy-second regular session witnessed a series of interjections by both India and Pakistan diplomats in response to comments made by one country about the conduct of the other. India's external affairs minister commented that Pakistan produced terrorists and terrorist camps in contrast to scientists and scholars produced by India (Swaraj 2017: 21). To this Pakistan retaliated to paint India's democracy as 'the world's largest hypocrisy' employing spy agencies to destabilize its neighbour (Lodhi 2017: 14).

Caveats and Consensus on Global Counterterrorism Strategy

For India, the 2006 UN GCTS (GAOR 2006b) is a 'unique and universally agreed strategic framework' for guiding counterterrorism efforts undertaken at the global, regional, sub-regional and national levels comprehensively covering all its four pillars (Puri, M. 2012b: 20). India has laid emphasis on the radicalization of youth attempted by terrorist groups in different groups through various channels misusing latest communication technologies of Internet and social media, which should be addressed through appropriate education and by mainstreaming the youth into the socio-economic milieus. 'Moderate views can be spread effectively through the education system, civil society, opinion-makers and domestic political leadership.... [to encourage] positive and balanced narratives about the fallacies of extremist ideologies and the successes of peaceful coexistence need to be disseminated more widely' (Akbaruddin 2016b: 49).

Though member countries have reached a consensus that a comprehensive approach would be appropriate to counterterrorism, close scrutiny of statements reveal some measure of divergence in terms of emphasis placed. It would be suffice to highlight an important issue here. Whereas India's focus is on non-state actors, Pakistan has chosen to focus on state-sponsored terrorism. Pakistan's prime minster rued the silence in the Strategy on the need to prohibit and punish state-sponsored terrorism which was described as the 'instrument of choice of the agents of chaos and aspiring hegemons' (Abbasi 2017: 10). Pakistan's understanding of comprehensive approach is based on three Ds, namely, deterrence, development and dialogue. As such, in its conviction, the Strategy should have acknowledged the root causes of terrorism which go beyond poverty and ignorance, since terrorism is 'an extreme response to real or perceived political and/or other grievances, including foreign intervention, oppression and injustice' (Rabbani 2013: 14).

Equally important is the fact that Pakistan desires that the Global Strategy should sharpen its focus on countering the unjust defamation of certain religions and communities in the context of combating terrorism. The unfair and biased portrayal of Islam and Islamic beliefs was unacceptable. In its perspective, 'acts of incitement and hate speech against Muslims, which fostered misperceptions between the Islamic world and the West, must be addressed through political, normative and legal measures, as well as through dialogue and diplomacy' (Lodhi 2015: 9). India concurs that terrorism should not be associated with any religion, but it questions any 'distinction drawn between acceptable and unacceptable or good and bad terrorism' (Rao 2015: 11).

On respecting human rights in countering terrorism, a much accepted, in principle, pillar of the Global Strategy, India has a slightly different take. India has pointed out that democratic societies, which have become vulnerable to terrorism, must necessarily take steps to defend their citizens as against threats to their lives from terrorists. In that direction, it notes that the state apparatus, unable to cope with the security challenge posed by terrorism, is forced to take draconian measures to counter it, with an inevitable impact on civic and human rights (Sharma 2001: 27). As such, in its considered view, disproportionate attention on member states' actions restrictive of rights would provide 'a handle for non-State actors who seek to evade responsibility for their own action', besides placing 'rule-abiding Member States and lawless terrorist outfits on the same plane' (Nambiar 2003c: 23–24). Just to buttress its position that terrorists commit the most egregious violations of human rights, India cited the remarks of the High Commissioner for Human Rights in the Commission on Human Rights a few weeks after the September 2001 attacks that the terrorists deprived victims of their foremost right, the right to life (Sharma 2001c: 26). Understandably, therefore, India opposed and voted against paragraphs 10 and 11 of draft resolution (GAOR 2003), which made no reference to violation of human rights by terrorists in 2003.[4]

Again, there were moments of dissatisfaction during the review process undertaken every two years. During the latest review of the Global Strategy review process in 2018, India was not happy that the resolution adopted by consensus did not denote substantive modification from the original version. 'It is disappointing to see the lack of meaningful progress even in the Global Counter-Terrorism Strategy resolution language, which continues to reflect the inability of Member States to act collectively to tackle threats from non-State actors' (Lal 2018: 18).

Engaging with the Security Council Counter-Terrorism Committee

Fully convinced that terrorism is the most important threat to international peace and security and given the powerful role the Security

---

[4] India has co-sponsored a resolution in the Human Rights Council for observing international day of remembrance and tribute to victims of terrorism (UNHRC 2011).

Council has come to play in tackling the emerging threats, India took active interest in its thematic debates held at regular intervals, particularly since 2001, even when it was not serving as an elected member of the Council. It extended unstinted support to all decisions of the Council; in fact, it wanted more effective implementation of the measures taken. India enthusiastically welcomed Security Council Resolution 1373 (2001) as a far-reaching measure that, in its expectation, could provide a framework for collective and individual action, laying down a permanent obligation on all members (Sharma 2001c: 27). In the words of the head of India's Permanent Mission, 'the adoption of resolution 1373 (2001) by the Council sent an inflexible and unambiguous signal that the world community will admit no space for terrorists or their sponsors. It conveyed the resolve that henceforth there would be zero tolerance for the perpetrators and instigators of terror' (Sharma 2002: 19). Further, satisfaction was derived from the institutionalization of resolution 1373:

> The dispatch with which the Council adopted resolution 1373 (2001) and set up the Counter-Terrorism Committee, under the Permanent Representative of the United Kingdom, underlines the importance and the urgency with which the international community has decided to combat terrorism collectively and unitedly. The Committee has worked tirelessly and with energy in the short period of its existence to mount a counter-offensive on international terrorism.

India drew attention to the areas where the CTC should address certain areas of concern in the interest of more effective checks against terror networks. Some of the points raised in 2003 were (Nambiar 2003a: 3–4):

- The CTC could consider the question of how to deal with a situation in which a member state is not enforcing effective compliance by concrete actions, even while professing to do so in its responses to the committee.
- The key task would be to ensure that the committee would receive relevant information and assistance from member states, without

breaching the secrecy of information and procedures followed in counterterrorism measures by member states.

- As a complement to the international standards developed by the Financial Action Task Force on money laundering, the CTC may forge suitable arrangements acceptable to all member states.
- While it is understood that the CTC does not need to move at the speed of the slowest member, it needs to consider whether it is desirable to move at the speed of the fastest. It may be advisable that the committee could avoid a situation in which the majority of states from the developed regions fulfilled their obligations, while those striving to comply with the requirements are those that represent the developing world.
- Another concern is to examine whether the bilateral assistance offered by one or two countries is truly representative of the entire gamut of bilateral assistance, with reference to the matrix of assistance devised by the CTC.

While noting the increase in the number of tours to states to enhance coordination and information exchanges, India advised that such visits should be carefully coordinated between the 1373 and 1267 committees and the Counter-Terrorism Executive Directorate (CTED), in the context of greater cooperation envisaged with these bodies so as to ensure less duplication and optimal coherence (Sen 2004b: 28). Besides this, it was suggested, the Council could profitably look at lists of terrorist organizations announced by member countries as part of their national anti-terrorist legislation. Reports that accounts are being frozen after allowing the terrorist organizations to withdraw funds or transfer assets to organizations which have not been named in the lists, and reports of banned terrorist organizations mutating into other bodies need to be looked into critically (Sharma 2002: 20).

India urged the subsidiary bodies of the Council with counterterrorism mandates to engage donors and beneficiaries on the facilitation of technical assistance for capacity building at the national, subregional and regional levels (Puri H.S. 2012e: 17). A writer notes with interest that India politely refused to take assistance from the CTED, as India considered that it had considerable expertise suited to its own peculiar requirements. Rather India has offered to provide technical assistance to other countries in the training of immigration officials, computerization of immigration systems, setting up of financial intelligence units, analysis of intelligence related to money-laundering and terrorist financing, technology for analysis of financial information, and the like (Yadav 2014: 84).

For a country that continues to be a victim of terrorist attacks, it was but natural for it to prioritize counterterrorism efforts in its agenda during its 2011–2012 UNSC non-permanent membership tenure. During this tenure, its permanent representative was elected as the chair of the CTC, established as a sub-organ of the Security Council on 28 September 2001 under the terms of Resolution 1373, for a period of two years. It was a rare opportunity for India, as, in addition to chairing the CTC, it was also chosen as the chairman of the Working Group of the UNSC on individuals, groups or entities involved in or associated with terrorist activities and to recommend compensation for their victims, established by Resolution 1566 (2004). Delivering on the Indian promise to be active, the committee adopted its programme of work on an annual rather than biennual basis to streamline its functioning and held meetings more frequently than the normal practice.

During the two years of its chairmanship of the CTC, three special meetings of the committee were held, with the participation of the wider UN membership and international, regional and sub-regional organizations. The committee held a special meeting in New York in September 2011 to commemorate the 10th anniversary of the adoption of Resolution 1373 (2001) and the establishment of the committee, and at that meeting it unanimously endorsed zero-tolerance approach towards terrorism in its outcome document. The committee organized another special meeting at New York in November 2012 that focused on prevention and suppression of terrorist financing, with the participation of International Monetary Fund and the World Bank. It was reported that the meeting was immensely helpful in putting a spotlight on the issue of terrorist financing, which lies at the heart of Resolution 1373 (2001) (Puri H.S. 2013: 14).

Pleading for Transparent and Effective Implementation of Sanctions

Traditionally India's approach to coercive steps like non-military and military sanctions is cautious, and remarkably this cautious approach witnessed change in respect of countering terrorism effectively. To begin with, on questions of terrorism too, India was unenthusiastic about sanctions, and this was clearly evident when diplomatic and travel sanctions were imposed against Libya in 1992 and thereafter.[5]

As terrorism has acquired internationally dangerous dimension, particularly in its immediate neighbourhood in the late 1990s, India came on board to extend full support to the imposition of non-military sanctions against the Taliban leaders, extension of those measures to the Al-Qaida and later on to the Islamic State. Again it strongly endorsed the action taken by the Council to prohibit access of WMDs to terrorists. However, India referred to the acknowledgement of the limited impact of sanctions in the reports of the monitoring team with a sense of disappointment. The Indian officials repeatedly referred to the continuing ability of Al-Qaida to finance its activities, the ineffectiveness of the travel ban, the continued use of small arms and light weapons and the nexus between drug smuggling and terrorism (Sen 2004b: 27).

By way of stressing the point, India expressed serious concern over the ineffectiveness of the travel ban on members of Al-Qaida and on the continued use of small arms and light weapons and the possible flow of illegal weapons across states, resulting in increased attacks on coalition forces in Afghanistan and the use of heavy-calibre weapons in the Afghan region bordering Pakistan—raising questions as to how and by whom such weapons and ammunition are being supplied.

---

[5] As recalled sometime later, India's abstention in the vote on Resolution 748 (1992) was based on three valid reasons – viz. the judicial process before the World Court initiated by Libya was yet to conclude, secondly, there was ambiguity about the circumstances under which the sanctions either would be eased or lifted, and finally, more importantly, there was no commitment on the efforts to mitigate the suffering of the third countries affected by sanctions, as mandated in Article 50 of the Charter (Sharma 1998: 68).

The nexus between drug smuggling and terrorism, the organized flow of arms across Afghanistan's borders and the increasing attacks on coalition forces would tell their own tale of complicity and deceit (Nambiar 2003b: 26). Therefore, India's permanent representative highlighted the need for the UN counter-terror machinery to take cognizance of the 'increasingly sophisticated tactics and use of systems and equipment by terrorists, coupled with their continuing ability to elude the restrictions placed by Governments on their movements and their access to arms and financing' so as to come up with effective new counter-strategies to combat international terrorism (Nambiar 2004b: 24). India has expressed its readiness to share information with other relevant UN mechanisms, besides its assistance to other countries through bilateral and multilateral channels to tackle the growing proportion of the menace (Sen 2008c: 27).

India took active interest in the Taliban/Al-Qaida Sanctions Committee (also known as the 1267 Committee), which listed numerous entities and individuals for freezing of bank accounts.[6] Equally it showed active interest in the work of the Analytical Support and Monitoring Team, established in 2004. On the question of anomalies in the listing procedure, it was pointed out that listing of individuals tends to be coloured by extraneous considerations and political perspectives, thereby not only delaying but also discouraging states from making genuine recommendations. Therefore, it becomes necessary to revise procedures so as to enable states to communicate their views on the proposed listing within defined period of time (Nambiar 2004b: 26). Referring to the 1267 Committee's mandate to identify those individuals and entities, India hoped that the procedure would be followed without fear or favour. However, as the experience showed, the Consolidated List suffered from practical and technical problems. In its view, the first priority of the committee and the Monitoring Team should be to convince member states to be more forthcoming with information, particularly with regard to the Taliban, on individuals and entities in territories under their control. Simultaneously states

---

[6] As of 2019, 708 individuals and 305 entities appear in the Consolidated List of the Security Council.

that harbour such listed individuals or entities should be held accountable for non-compliance (Sen 2004b: 27).

India has had disappointing experience in getting Masood Azhar, the chief of Jaish-e-Mohammad the already banned organization active in Pakistan, listed by the 1267 Committee. A prompt designation would have subjected Azhar to an assets freeze, travel ban and an arms embargo. But in the closed door proceedings of the committee, China had blocked the attempts for nearly a decade since 2009—a delaying tactic employed as much to annoy India as to protect its all-weather ally, Pakistan. The Chinese obstinacy stood in sharp contrast to the positive response from the rest of the members in the committee. India has sharply criticized the 'anonymity and unanimity' procedure followed in the committee without any transparency (Akbaruddin 2016a: 32). The pressure on China greatly mounted in the wake of the killing—for which Masood Azhar claimed responsibility—of 40 paramilitary personnel near Pulwama in Jammu and Kashmir in February 2019. It was finally in May 2019 that China lifted its objections to listing Masood Azhar as a global terrorist after the United States, France and the United Kingdom jointly mooted a proposal to take the matter straight to the Security Council for a vote in an open meeting. Of course, China secured a significant concession in favour of Pakistan that there appeared no reference to Pulwama attack as a trigger for the instant action (Economic Times, 2 May 2019). As analysts commented, China's counterterrorism diplomacy sometimes prioritizes bilateral cooperation with Pakistan over the larger interests of the global struggle against terrorism and contradicts its stated goal of giving the UN a leading role in counterterror efforts (Duchatel 2016: 5).

Recapitulation

Terrorism is an issue area India has shown deep interest in. As India's current Prime Minister, Narendra Modi, asserted in his latest address to the UNGA in September 2019, the lack of unity in countering terrorism, one of the world's biggest challenges, would dent those very principles that are the basis for the creation of the UN. The most significant outcome of India's engagement on the issue of international terrorism at the UN since the 1990s is the progressive support it garnered in denouncing and delegitimizing terror in all its manifestations, so much so that Pakistan, which India accuses of sponsoring cross-border terror, is also pushed to the corner to paint itself as one of the major victims of terror. The international response to the 2008 Mumbai attacks can be said to be the turning point in the process. True, India is disappointed with the inability of the General Assembly to reach a consensus on its draft CCIT, particularly with reference to the definition and scope issues. Again, although India is largely satisfied with the comprehensive approach of Global Counter-Terrorism Strategy adopted by the General Assembly in 2006, India seemingly has had difficulty in accepting that human rights should be protected while fighting against terror. Its argument is that states have primary duty to protect its citizens from the terror threats emanating from the non-state groups.

In contrast to the General Assembly, in India's assessment, the Security Council has performed better through its mandatory measures requiring all states to take all legal and administrative steps to proscribe and punish terror acts, maintain consolidated list of entities and individuals associated with the Taliban, the Al-Qaida and the Da'esh who are subjected to freezing of funds and travel embargo. India took active interest in the work of various sanctions committees, particularly the Taliban/Al-Qaida Committee and the CTC and in the improvement of their working methods. India chaired the CTC for two years during its seventh term as a non-permanent member.

On the one hand, India sincerely saw it as an obligation to implementing the Security Council mandatory resolutions because it was in its own vital security interests. On the other hand, it is so confident about the efficacy of its administrative mechanism, India chose not to avail any UN or multilateral assistance. Instead, it offered assistance both bilaterally and multilaterally. At a complementary level, India has developed wide network of bilateral and regional arrangements, including with all the five permanent members of the Security Council. To that extent, one could say that India did not wish to risk putting all its eggs in the UN basket, because of its mixed feelings about the protracted delays on its CCIT initiative.

Finally, it emerges that India brought about two notable shifts in its traditional positions. First, by unequivocally rejecting any distinction between terrorists and freedom fighters, India has moved away from its position in the 1970s to support armed struggles for liberation and self-determination. Equally notable is the demand India makes in favour of effective coercive measures against non-state actors indulging in terrorism, signifying adjustment of its traditionally cautious stand on rushing with imposition of sanctions.

CHAPTER 10

Contemporary Development Discourse and Diplomacy of India at the UN

In line with the general orientation of its foreign policy, India's multilateral diplomacy has taken a pronouncedly economic turn in the 21st century. As such, development as central theme has clearly assumed salience in India's economic diplomacy at the UN and outside. The primacy of economic and social development is evident in the opening statements made by India's dignitaries in the UNGA.[1] Economic diplomacy at the UN remains a vital tool to pursue India's aspirations to shape a rule-based equitable order and this objective cannot be furthered at major economic and financial organizations, such as the Bretton Woods

---

[1] The Indian Prime Ministers opened statements at both the Millennium Summit (2000) and the 60th anniversary World Summit (2005) by dwelling on economic and development issues. Besides, India opened its interventions in the general debate of General Assembly annual sessions with economic/development issues on most occasions during the years 2005–2019, Speeches available at the Website of the Permanent Mission of India to the UN in New York. Available at: https://www.pminewyork.org/statement.php?id=19, accessed on 8 October 2019.

Institutions because of the latter's inherent ideological and institutional bias favouring the Western advanced countries.

The new features of India's economic diplomacy at the UN in the 21st century are manifested in four ways: strong, but critical, support to the UN's advocacy of MDGs, which are now refashioned into the SDGs; targeting the financial and trade policies of developed countries that principally account for the setbacks to the implementation of the UN-set development agenda; recasting of group negotiation strategy through small issue-based, regional, cross-regional coalitions; and increase in financial contributions to select UN operational bodies. In a sense, India's economic diplomacy at the UN is demonstrated by the remarkable growth in its yearly contributions to international organizations — from IN ₹32.27 to 912.10 crores during the period 2000–2019.[2] Presumably, this kind of economic investments for aiding the cause of developing world would bring political dividends, in terms of garnering greater support to its campaign for a permanent seat in the enlarged Security Council at a future opportunity.

The dynamics of India's economic diplomacy is dialectically related to the changing priorities, opportunities and challenges facing the country in the increasingly globalized economic order. Liberalization of India's economy in the early 1990s has brought investments from foreign companies along with remittances from non-resident Indians abroad, with the result that its foreign exchange reserves have reached comfortable levels thanks to its edge in information and communication technologies—which together helped the economy to grow at an enviable rate of nearly 7–8 per cent during the first decade of 2000s. At the same time, the crisis in rural farming communities and the growing income gaps both among rural and urban populations is attributed to the dark side of India's new economic policy.[3] As such,

---

[2] See especially the Annual Reports of the Ministry of External Affairs for the years 2000–2001 and 2018–2019 at pages 161 and 376, respectively. Available at: http://mea.gov.in/Uploads/PublicationDocs/163_Annual-Report.pdf, accessed on 1 November 2019.

[3] Critics like Chimni (2010: 164) note that India's new economic policy meant in multilateral negotiation settings moving away from the Non-Aligned Movement and the G-77, and closer to G-20 and the like.

while India's current global economic diplomacy reflects the impressive economic rise it has achieved, the imperative of harnessing economic and social development—with a particular focus on poverty alleviation for countries and communities alike—remains the central concern of India's policy articulations and negotiating positions at the UN. It is India's conviction that 'just as prosperity cannot be sustained by being walled in, poverty cannot be banished to some invisible periphery. Development, therefore, must return to the centre of the global discourse' (Singh M. 2004: 14).

What do we understand as enduring as well as emerging features of India's economic diplomacy at the UN in the 21st century? How does growing economic clout of India account for new dynamism in India's economic diplomacy at the UN? Does ongoing transition of India from recipient to donor of funds help the political goal of securing a permanent seat in the UNSC? What could be challenges to India at the UN in the domain of development diplomacy? These are some of the questions that this chapter will explore by dwelling on India's sustained belief in the vitality of the UN for coordinating international economic relations, the progress and problems associated with development goals launched since the onset of the 21st century, the patterns in India's development assistance through the UN, and the new strategies India is adopting to pursue group negotiations to better effect.

Reaffirming the Relevance of UN Instrumentality

Ever since India became a founding member of the UN in 1945—two years before attaining independence—India played a key role in underlining need to work for solution of international economic problems through cooperation. India's active support at the San Francisco Conference for making ECOSOC a principal organ of UN perhaps helped the election of India's representative, Sir Ramaswamy Mudaliar, as the first president of that body (Jha 1987).[4] India's strong

---

[4] Unlike other delegations, such as Australia and Canada, Indian delegation was inactive in the UN deliberations at San Francisco on international economic cooperation proposals. Critics point out that the initiative taken by India to convene the first UN conference on trade and development in 1964 should have come in the formative years of the UN (see Tawale 1975: 41–43).

commitment to and engagement with the UN since its inception was built on the belief that the UN and its economic agencies held the promise in transforming economic conditions of the developing world (ICWA 1957).

In particular, India's support for the larger goals of the UN builds on its own experience since independence in three different areas (Saksena 1995). First, as a newly independent country, India was convinced that its hard-won political independence could only be sustained through strengthening economic foundations and supporting these ideas at the UN. This reflected a more universal belief that international peace was of little meaning without strengthening the economic and social roots of peace. Second, India has long believed that any policy initiative to help economic growth in poor countries would be beneficial also to the advanced economies due to growing economic interdependence between the developed and developing countries. Hence, India argued since early years at the UN that a more farsighted approach to the problems of poor countries would be very much in the interest of developed world because it would create sustained demand for goods produced in the donor countries. Third, India's economic diplomacy recognized the limitations of newly formed countries to address their economic and social concerns alone. Hence, India has strived to mobilize, maintain and strengthen the unity and solidarity of economically less developed countries from Asia, Africa and Latin America at the UN, in order to pressurize rich countries to consider the pressing demands of the developing world for urgent remedial action (Mathur 1995: 66). India's role in the formation of both the NAM, the Group of 77 (G77) and UNCTAD since the early 1960s particularly in the articulation of common positions of these countries on a range of economic issues—be it on assured prices for raw materials produced, tariff concessions to enable exports from developing markets, concessional aid flows or regulation of multinational corporations—during consultations at the UN-sponsored conferences has been already extensively analysed (Murthy 2013: 131–132; Dubey 2014: 23–26).

India has believed that the UN deserves greater role in the management of economic flows among member countries, although in reality it is not the case (Singh M. 2013: 22). As per 2017–2018 figures, the UN along with its funds and programmes spent approximately US$33.6 billion on account of operational activities for development, providing policy advice, technical assistance and support to major sectors, such as health, education, water, sanitation, population and social integration (United Nations 2019). It is about 23 per cent of the total ODA, although it is admittedly one-third of what (US$63.9 billion) is provided by the World Bank group in 2018. As per the widely shared criticism, the Fund and the Bank have achieved notoriety in interfering in the economic affairs of the debtor countries, thereby fuelling political and economic instability in those countries. India trusted the UN and other non-financial organizations comprising the UN system as sources of assistance, because unlike the International Monetary Fund (IMF) and the World Bank, the UN is committed to the Charter principles of non-intervention in internal affairs and respect for sovereignty of recipient (developing) countries. Therefore, India has insisted that aid to developing countries through the UN would be more welcome, as it would be multilateral, devoid of the intrusive conditions at times imposed through bilateral channels (ICWA 1957: 37–38). The point is not that the development assistance India received from the UN is huge. According to officials and experts who were in the know of the trends prevailing up to the 1980s, the assistance was in the range of US$200–250 million a year (Jha 1987: 23).

Indian diplomats at the UN have also increasingly spoken out on the decreasing contributions of developed countries towards the development activities of the UN. Indeed, the 21st century has not augured well for the funding of UN development activities, particularly as assessed (other than voluntary) contributions to UN activities remained stagnant. According to UN official sources, in 2003–2017, the core funding for UN development activities experienced steadily sharp decline from 39 to 19.4 per cent (United Nations 2019 5–6). It is possible that if funding situation for operational activities fails to reach critical minimum level, the relevance of the UN to cater to long-term development needs of the poor may suffer. Unfortunately, the trends do not seem to provide any reassurance. For instance, the actual contributions made available to the UN development work in 2000 were only US$634 million as against the requirement of US$1.1 billion (Rangachari 2001). Similarly, the resources of the United Nations Children's Fund (UNICEF), at US$563 million in 2000, were much less than expected (Ravi 2004: 12). Indian representatives cautioned the fellow delegates at the General Assembly in 2001 that the situation, if not rectified, could compromise the role of the UN system in development, and would only take away the incentive for further reform (Rangachari 2001).

Pursuing Unfinished Business: MDGs and the Post-2015 Agenda

At the turn of the new century, human concerns regarding security and development have come to occupy the centre stage of economic diplomacy at the UN (Jolly 2007). As former Secretary-General, Kofi Annan puts, the challenge for the UN in the era of globalization ultimately involves 'meeting the needs of peoples. It is in their name that the Charter was written; realizing their aspirations remains our vision for the twenty-first century' (United Nations 2000b: 14). In its response, the UNGA took major initiative towards human development and launched the MDGs, which stressed eight inter-related areas, including halving extreme poverty in the world, halting the rate of deaths among children under age of five, providing universal primary education, controlling HIV/AIDS and other major health issues affecting women and children, by 2015 (United Nations 2000c; Ziai 2011).

India joined the rest of the international community in endorsing the UN initiative on MDGs. As foreign minister, Yashwant Sinha, noted, 'the Millennium Development Goals may not by themselves constitute a comprehensive development plan, they are a measurable set of benchmarks which could provide indications of whether the world is moving towards a more inclusive and equitable globalization' (Sinha 2003). The challenge of implementing MDGs was undoubtedly enormous. As UN reported, nearly 2.8 billion people earn less than two dollars a day and 1.2 billion live on less than a dollar a day; most of them are concentrated in Africa and South Asia (United Nations 2000b: 19). Therefore, in the words of a senior Indian diplomat, 'we need to work collectively to reverse this trend of increasing disparities to ensure that globalization works for all—all nations and all segments of society' (Sharma 2001d: 6). The free movement of global capital unsettled economies across the world leading to impoverishment of millions even in the rich countries. Participating in a high-level meeting on MDGs, India's foreign affairs minister cited the fact that 60 million slipped into poverty in just a year after the economic crisis in 2008 (Krishna 2010). Poverty levels are reportedly on rise in the United States, even as unemployment levels reached a peak at 10–12 per cent in advanced countries, such as France and Italy, in 2014. As per the International Labour Organization, unemployment rates in the United States and Europe are falling, though the quality of employment is a concern (ILO 2019).

Despite the claim that the number of people living under extreme poverty had fallen from 1.9 billion in 1990 to 836 million in 2015, progress on MDGs has been admittedly uneven across regions and countries, leaving significant gaps in terms of gender inequality, growing income gaps between rich and poor, rural and urban people, and so on (United Nations 2015: 4–9). According to analysts, whatever the MDGs achieved was by-product of rapid economic growth of China and India (Poku and Whitman 2011: 186), although India is nowhere near achieving many of those goals relating to reducing child and maternal mortality (Venkat 2015). Of course, India has used the tools of economic diplomacy to showcase some of its domestic socio-economic welfare schemes relating to the national rural employment guarantee, wireless local loop technologies, *sarvashiksha abhiyan*, universal elementary education programme, and progress in controlling spread of HIV/AIDS and maternal mortality rates (Krishna 2010: 20–21).

Prime Minister, Manmohan Singh, told the General Assembly that the international community viewed the UN was 'generous in setting goals, but parsimonious in pursuing them' (Singh M. 2005: 29). Reflecting on the imperfections of MDGs, India has criticized the idea on three counts (Singh M. 2013). For one, however noble the intentions could be, the MDGs did not emerge out of an intergovernmental negotiation process. The MDGs were inspired by a technocratic approach to development and were handed down to governments. Second, they were focused only on responsibilities of developing countries, while the developed countries had, at best, undefined obligations to facilitate their achievement. Thirdly, domestic resources rather than genuine international collaboration were highlighted as vehicle for actualizing MDGs (Singh S. 2013). In other words, global partnership was regrettably not taken seriously enough.

India sought to ensure that such shortcomings do not afflict the process of negotiating the updated set of goals (known as Sustainable Development Goals) and the formulation of the post-2015 development agenda. While hoping that the post-2015 development agenda would carry forward the 'unfinished business' of MDGs (Khurshid 2013), Indian delegates at the UN have strongly suggested that the post-2015 development agenda should be duly deliberated and agreed by consensus among all member government in a constructive framework, with priority attached to the challenges of poverty, employment, food and energy, water, health, environmental sustainability, unsustainable lifestyles, and above all, economic growth (Krishna 2012: 11). In essence, the post-2015 development agenda should be 'transformational rather than transactional in nature and the one that enables genuine international collaboration to create a better future for our world and our people' (Singh S. 2013). Guided by this approach, India served as member of the Open Working Group that finally framed SDGs comprising a set of 17 goals spreading across social, economic, environmental dimensions of sustainable development with poverty eradication as a central goal.[5] Prime Minister Modi lauded the 'lofty and equally comprehensive vision' of the 2030 Agenda for Sustainable Development with particular focus on social, economic and environmental issues (Modi 2015: 17). India used the occasion to reaffirm its continued commitment to fulfil its responsibilities as a development partner of sister-developing countries, as well as small island states

---

[5] Former Planning Commission member, N.C. Saxena, is quoted as stating that India has only 5 per cent of funds required to implement SDGs. It is only by improving its tax-to-GDP ratio from the current 17 per cent and by plugging the erosion of tax revenues at home through international cooperation that the resource gap could be narrowed (see Venkat 2015).

from the Pacific to the Atlantic. After two years, India's foreign affairs minister delivered a note of urgency to make timely progress in SDGs else 'we will be in danger of losing control' (Swaraj 2017: 20).

Faulting the Policies of Developed Countries

One of the central elements of the Millennium Declaration was the responsibility the developed countries held in partnering with poor countries by meeting the commitments made earlier on ODA targets. At the UN, India faulted the developed countries for not honouring the norms regarding ODA targets as a percentage of gross national income, for not being proactive in providing the adequate debt relief and for inflexible positions on demands of developing countries regarding world trade issues.

Table 10.1 below captures the grim trends during the period 2000–2018 regarding gross official development aid from the advanced countries, along with the indications on the aid received by the UN agencies as also the least developed countries. Though there has been increase of ODA in terms of dollars transferred, it was a far cry from the original target of 0.7 per cent of gross national income; it was in

Table 10.1 Aid Flows from OECD DAC Countries, 2000–2018 (in Billion US Dollars)

Years	Gross ODA	Multilateral Institutions	UN Agencies	To Least Developed Countries
2000	53.7	17.6	Not available	19
2001	57.4	17.4	Not available	23
2002	58.6	17.6	Not available	Not available
2003	69.6	19.5	4.9	16.5
2004	80.1	25.4	5.2	16.0
2005	108.3	25.2	5.5	15.9
2006	105.4	27.9	5.3	17.3

(continued)

(continued)

Years	Gross ODA	Multilateral Institutions	UN Agencies	To Least Developed Countries
2007	105.0	31.3	5.9	19.7
2008	122.9	35.8	5.9	23.5
2009	120.7	36.7	6.2	24.3
2010	128.5	37.8	6.5	28.2
2011	135.1	40.3	6.5	30.7
2012	127.0	38.6	6.6	27/4
2013	134.8	41.4	6.9	30.0
2014	137.6	42.8	6.8	26.4
2015	131.6	37.3	6.1	25.0
2016	142.6	41.8	5.9	24.6
2017	147.16	41.7	7.2	48.6
2018	131.6	37.2	7.6	-

Source: The data compiled from the tables in the United Nations annual publication, World Economic Situation. See for latest table A16 in United Nations (2020: 199).

fact no more than 0.32 per cent. Furthermore, the 2008 economic crisis in the United States and the Euro zone crisis redirected the attention of advanced countries toward reviving their domestic economies rather than complying with ODA commitments. The gap in commitments and disbursement of ODA reached US$167 billion in 2011 (Singh S. 2013), and it further widened to US$192 billion in 2014. Little wonder, only four (Cape Verde, Equatorial Guinea, Maldives and Samoa) among 48 least-developed countries (LDCs) could move out of that category during 2007–2017.

In India's view, development cannot rely on aid alone; trade has to become engine of growth and development. The UN continues to remain important to India as a venue for advocating the position of developing countries on trade issues. As India's Minister for External Affairs complained once at the UN:

Protectionist tendencies in developed countries, a lack of political will to implement commitments undertaken regarding development finance, tardy amelioration of the debt burden of developing countries aggravate the situation. Special and differential treatment for developing countries guaranteed under WTO provisions must be translated into operational reality. Developed countries should not seek to restrict market access to goods and services and free movement of natural persons, especially at a time when developing countries are being asked to open up their economies and compete in the international economic domain. (Singh J. 2000)

Unfortunately, the existing global trade regime dominated by the Western countries is far from being helpful. Economists have calculated that protectionism of the developed countries actually costs the developing countries US$700 billion in export income, which is 14 times what they receive as ODA. India has used the UN forums to highlight the unfair trade policies and practices, which continue even after the WTO was established. One of the main grievances India has articulated is that WTO is not brought into coordinating relationship with the UN (Murthy 2010: 215–217). At the UNGA, India has pleaded for removal of trade barriers and for greater inclusivity in the construction of the international trade regime. As a member of WTO, India has continued to push for the principles of fair trade to manage global trade in commodities and investment flows. At the Millennium Summit, India projected economic multi-polarity as a critical factor of the 21st century world order and asserted that the tendency of some countries to rely on non-tariff barriers to preserve markets and perpetuate current balance of trade should be resisted. The WTO Doha Development Agenda, which was originally launched in 2001 to make trade rules in agriculture and manufacture sectors fair for the developing and LDCs was successfully torpedoed in a decade's time by the rich countries. The multilateral WTO regime has presently come under severe strain, as the United States complains that a few developing countries, such as China and India, have taken advantage of the developing country status at the cost of the American economic interests.

The other issue India's economic diplomacy at the UN paid attention to is the debt burden of developing countries, which stood at

4 trillion dollars in 2010 (*Global Development Finance* 2012). Many countries in Africa are unable to service these debts. Hence, India supported the Highly Indebted Poor Countries (HIPC) Initiative to cancel some of the loans to enable them to invest in social sectors. In 2006, India cancelled the debt of seven HIPC countries. It opened concessional lines of credit for Africa to worth US$5 billion as a mark of its intention for a long-term partnership with Africa. The lines of credit to African countries from India grew from US$300 million in 2004 to US$8 billion by 2017 (Mishra 2018) and is targeted to reach US$28 billion in 2018–2019. In many ways, India has also actively promoted the idea of South–South cooperation. However, in India's conviction, South–South cooperation does not nullify the responsibilities of the rich countries of the Global North (UNCTAD 2014). It has asserted further that sustainable economic and social development will require cooperation between the Global North and the Global South.

Growing Profile as a Resource Provider to UN Development Activities

A particularly positive facet of India's economic diplomacy at the UN is its growing profile as a resource provider to the development-oriented operational activities of the UN. India's net contribution (i.e.

Table 10.2 *India's Assessed Contributions to the UN Regular Budget (2001–2019)*

Year	Percentage of the UN Regular Budget	Gross Amount in US$ (in Millions)
2001	0.343	4.161
2006	0.421	8.103
2011	0.534	14.143
2015	0.66	19.821
2019	0.834	25.558

Source: Available at http://www.un.org/en/ga/contributions/budget.shtml, accessed on 14 February 2020.

Note: UN Secretariat documents (ST/ADM/SER.B/568, 668, 824, 910, 992 for the relevant years).

exclusive of credit accrued from staff assessment) to the assessed budget of the UN is nearly US$25.5 million in 2018–2019, making it the 25th largest contributor. Table 10.2 shows that India's contribution to the UN regular budget quadrupled primarily because of its impressive economic indicators, which are taken into account for apportioning the UN budget requirements among member states. In fact, as things presently stand, India's contribution to the UN regular budget is larger than some OECD member countries, such as Belgium, Denmark, Finland, Greece and New Zealand.

Equally notable is the fact that India has transitioned from being a major recipient to being a major contributor to UN funds and programmes, such as UNDP and UNICEF, at least among the countries of Global South. Its voluntary contributions to the funds and programmes of the UN signify its commitment to multilateralism and to international solidarity for poverty alleviation.[6] In fact, India's commitment to funding the UN and ideals of multilateralism has a long history, with India providing financial contributions to UN funds and programmes soon after independence. For example, for the first five years of the UN Special Fund, founded in 1958, India provided 36 per cent of the total contribution of all developing countries.

In 2017, India in association with the UN Office for South–South Cooperation, established the India–UN Development Partnership Fund, a US$100 million development finance facility. In November 2018, India pledged a sum of US$13.3 million to various UN funds and programmes (Kumar 2018). India has announced five-fold increase in its contribution to the relief agency for Palestinian refugees as a political gesture. Similarly, India enhanced its contribution to the Technical Cooperation Voluntary Fund from US$100,000 to US$200,000 in 2018. Also notable is India's pledged payment of fifth largest sum for combating the Ebola emergency in African countries in 2014. There is more to it. As seen in Table 10.3, India's financial contributions to major development and operational organs of the UN,

---

[6] India's voluntary contribution to the UNDP, UNICEF and World Food Programme (WFP) was highest (US$6 million) among the developing countries (Bishnoi 2001).

Table 10.3 India's Voluntary Contributions Pledged to UN Funds and Programmes, 2002–2019 (in million US Dollars)

	2002	2005	2007	2012	2013	2014	2019
UNDP	4.5	4.5			4.5	4.5	4.5
WFP	1.92	1.92			1.92	1.92	1.92
UNICEF	₹31	0.9			0.9	0.9	0.9
UNFPA	₹0.9	0.2	0.5		0.5	0.5	0.5
UNEP	0.1	0.1			0.1	0.1	0.1
UNHABITAT	80,000	80,000		0.1	0.1	0.1	0.15
UNODC	60,000	60,000	0.3		0.3	0.1	0.1
UNRWA	225,000	20,000		0.1	1.0	1.0	5.0
UNV	15,000	15,000			15,000	15,000	
UN-Women			–	–	5.0 for 5 years		
Voluntary Fund for Tech Coop				0.1	0.1	0.1	0.2
UNMEER						12.5	

Source: Compiled on the basis of the statements made by the Indian officials on regular occasions in the UN bodies.

such as the UNDP, UNEP and the WFP have remained constant since the turn of the century. Nevertheless, the profile of India as a provider of funds to UN development activities appears modest when compared to India's assistance through bilateral channels.[7] One explanation for India's reluctance to privilege UN channel over bilateral channels (see Table 10.4) is the perception among Indian officials that the UN humanitarian activities are geared to the interests of Western

---

[7] The largest allocation in the External Affairs Ministry's latest budget was for Technical and Economic Cooperation (TEC) with foreign countries through grants and loans. In FY 2018–2019, of the total budget of ₹15,011 crores, the TEC outlay was 41.53 per cent or ₹6,235.05 crores, of which ₹5,398.55 crores (35.96%) was for grant programmes and ₹836.50 crores (5.57%) was for loans (MEA 2019: 377).

Table 10.4 India's Grants and Loans to Foreign Countries (2008–2019; in ₹Crores)

2000–2001	2004–2005	2008–2009	2010–2011	2013–2014	2015–2016	2017–2018	2019–2020
12	17	2,699.93	3,053.85	6,910.37	8,726.58	5,890.29	9,069.34

Source: *The Wire* (2019).

donor countries (Meier and Murthy 2011: 27). The two notable examples of India routing through the UN its disaster relief were in the aftermath of the 2008 earthquake in Haiti and the floods in Pakistan in 2010. Whether bilateral or multilateral, India's growing profile as aid provider may also be linked to its efforts to explore the potential for economic relationship and secure greatest possible support among the developing countries for realizing its ambition to become a permanent member of an expanded Security Council.

Reworking Group Strategy

There have been interesting developments in India's economic diplomacy in terms of using group negotiations as a strategy at the UN in the 21st century. On a few key issues of larger interest, India continued to join G77 efforts to resist reform measures that were seen adversely affecting the development apparatus of the UN. India has held, for example, that revitalization of the role of UN organs, such as ECOSOC and the General Assembly, in guiding and monitoring the world economy would be essential for safeguarding the interests of the developing countries. In the words of a seasoned Indian representative,

> Quite clearly, ECOSOC has to recover its function of oversight of specialized agencies and the UN its role of being the planetary system that sets the international economic agenda. Only through such a reform would developing countries have a voice in decision-making on international trade, monetary and financial questions (Sen 2004a).

However, despite India's long-standing support to the cause of promoting solidarity with developing countries, a major challenge the Indian economic diplomacy experienced at the economic and financial organizations and at the UN, in particular, is to refashion old ways of group negotiation strategies in tune with the changing needs and demands of the new century. The relative decline of the Third World-oriented UNCTAD right from the early 1990s was a major setback to the effective pursuit of group negotiations across the UN system. Furthermore, growing power of liberalization and globalization has cast its shadow on the collective identity of the Global South. It is open secret that the G77 was too diverse to be effective on a wide and divisive issue areas, such as trade in agriculture, greenhouse gas (GHG) emissions, and so on. The anti-climax witnessed at the UN-sponsored Copenhagen Summit on Climate Change where many of the G77 rejected the agreement secretly negotiated by the United States, China and India is yet another case in point. In one of the recent developments, G77 could not admittedly negotiate as a group the SDGs and the post-2015 development agenda.

As part of related developments, it may be noted that the high growth rates registered by the emerging economies, such as India, China and Brazil, not merely bestowed new stature but also required them to redefine their negotiation strategies distinct from the previous ones. On the one hand, India extended financial support through the UN for holding of conferences of small-island developing countries and the landlocked-developing countries.[8] On the other hand, India actively joined hands to form smaller, informal or semi-formal issue-based coalitions of a few relevant states ranging from the IBSA coalition to the increasingly formalized BRICS (Brazil, Russia, India, China and South Africa). They have become active at the UN on specific issues of interest. For example, these countries vigorously raised demands at the UN for review of quotas in the IMF. Notably again, India has drawn satisfaction from being invited to join 'economic high table' of rich advanced countries. India's joining G20 (an

---

[8] India provided financial assistance of US$250,000 for the organization of third conference of small-island countries and second UN conference of landlocked-developing countries.

expanded club of G7 countries, formed in the aftermath of 2008 global financial crisis) has sharpened divisions within G77.

At the centre of these dynamics lies India's dilemma of striking a balance between the growing imperative of acting as a responsible economic power for reaching negotiated outcomes with advanced countries on the one hand and the need to adopt a confrontationist approach and reject any flexibility on major issues of global economic wellbeing. Indeed, some commentators contend that while India's economic strength has grown, it is reluctant to accept commensurate responsibilities in fields, such as climate change and global trade regime (Mukherjee and Malone 2011). The issue of emission cuts exemplifies how India has tried to do a tight rope walk to resist the attempts by the United States and EU to force it to accept binding commitments and then realized the need to show some flexibility to meet the expectations from the climate change-threatened small developing countries.

From a hard line position adopted initially, India has evolved a more flexible strategy on the issue at the UN. From a maximalist assertion that 'all development cannot be sacrificed at the absolutist altar of environmental preservation', India has acknowledged that 'sustainability of growth strategy and environmental conservation cannot and should not imply sustenance of poverty' (Singh J. 2000: 19). India has softened its stance by explaining that its per capita GHG emissions would at no stage exceed the per capita GHG emissions of developed countries (Chidambaram 2007). Though it is presently one of the top four CO_2 emitting nations, its per capita emissions were only around one tonne of CO_2 equivalent per annum, which is a quarter of the global average and half that of the developed countries as a whole. India steadily mellowed partly because of the perception problems it encountered in the international community and partly because of the growing environmentalism within the country. In 2014, Indian minister for environment announced in the General Assembly the acceptance of voluntary goals for reducing emission intensity of its GDP by 20–25 per cent by 2020 over 2005 levels (Javadekar 2014). As a well-known scholar noted in a broader context, India has 'consistently used integrative bargaining strategies, formed southern factions and shown willingness to share the burden of international responsibility with smaller actors.... India is perhaps not reluctant to be responsible power per se, but... it seeks itself as owing its responsibility to different constituencies' (Narlikar 2013b: 571).

Concluding Observations

The UN has long served the aims of India's development-centred economic diplomacy. Through the UN, India has pursued its central goals of framing an inclusive and equitable global economic agenda and creating consensus on specific action programmes. This is exemplified by India's sustained focus on the dwindling levels of development finance and its pursuit of human development goals to bring the benefits of globalization to all peoples and nations. The discussion in the chapter has demonstrated how India has sought to make the best out of the challenges arising in the 21st century world economy. India has resorted to a mix of intricate strategies in order to achieve competing objectives, viz. to enhance the role of the UN as a conscience keeper of the developing countries' interests, to extract from the advanced countries enhanced contributions for improvement of economies of poor countries, and to be regarded as a responsible economic power for sharing its financial resources selectively while at the same time pursuing particularistic specific interests through smaller elite groups. On the other hand, it is quite possible that there could be political dividends by way of support on critical questions at the UN from the small island, landlocked and least-developed recipients of India's development assistance. This is the style of a 'canny negotiator' (Mukherjee and Malone 2011: 321) that could deftly traverse across traditional fault lines in the terrain of existing global political economy.

CHAPTER 11

India's Human Rights Record at the UN

India's interest in international human rights, as also from the side of the international community in India's human rights record, is natural for many important reasons. First and foremost is the fact that India is admired for its well-earned reputation as world's largest and long-standing electoral democracy. The human rights architecture has evolved around the constitutional guarantees for fundamental freedoms, jealously protected by independent judiciary, free media and active civil society groups, apart from an array of public institutions created to cater to the status of rights of various vulnerable groups. In that sense, what India states and does in fact remains a source of inspiration for especially many countries in Global South. This is true in the midst of the redefined priorities on global agenda that highlight human rights as one of the principal pillars of global peace and justice. For years many developing countries of Asia and Africa have been targeted on account of human rights abuses. India too has received adverse attention on account of discrimination against minorities, women, occurrence of forced labour and child labour, torture by law-enforcement personnel, fake encounters and victimization of human rights defenders. At the same time, India garnered some goodwill by actively participating in the deliberations of various UN agencies and carefully picking up some normative instruments for domestic legislation and implementation.

This chapter will trace first the early signs of India's short-lived internationalism during negotiations at the UN on common framework of human rights standards, and follows up with an account on how a definitive shift towards statist discourse has taken place. The major part of the analysis in the chapter is devoted to the UN Human Rights Council and India's role therein with reference particularly to the issues raised in the three cycles of the UPR so far and the response strategies India has devised to defend its record.

Glimpses of Short-Lived Internationalism

Promotion and protection of human rights as a principal priority for intergovernmental conduct remained close to India's heart from the beginning of emergence of independent India and the UN. One of the handful of amendments India proposed to the Charter at the founding conference at San Francisco was to Article 1 to include promotion of human rights as a purpose of the UN (Rajan 1973: 445). Based on its strengths of democratic polity along with an array of flourishing human rights institutions, India has claimed to nurture a climate of promotion and protection of human rights.[1]

Parallel to India's active interest in collectively mitigating problems of international security, India played its role in setting an agenda for the furtherance of human rights in the formative years of the UN. The eventually successful campaign against the apartheid system of South Africa was India's initiative in the very first session of the General Assembly. The wartime horrors about the crime of genocide also impelled India to join Cuba and Panama in 1946 to propose a draft resolution to declare genocide as an international crime (Schabas 2007: 381). India played an active role during the drafting stage of the Universal Declaration of Human Rights (UDHR), which outlines a range of human, civil, economic and social rights as 'foundation of freedom, justice and peace in the world' and urges member nations to

---

[1] See website of the Permanent Mission of India (PMI) to UN, Geneva. Available at: https://www.pmindiaun.gov.in/adminpart/uploadpdf/50545Statement-General-Segment-1March12.pdf, accessed on 11 September 2018.

promote all of them. With the debates about fundamental rights in the Constitution fresh in mind, the Indian delegation succeeded in securing insertion into the text references about freedom of movement within a country, non-discrimination without regard to race, religion and political opinion, just and favourable conditions of work as part of right to work, and indivisibility and universality of human rights (Kothari 2018).

Also, more interestingly, India proposed that human rights should be made 'actionable' and 'justiceable' at the international level—taking cue from what the framers of the Indian Constitution were contemplating to do at that time. The Indian delegate, Hansa Mehta, proposed an implementation mechanism—either in the form of a specially mandated body to adjudicate complaints filed by individuals about rights violations against their own governments or referral to the Security Council. India's proposal to make human rights on international plane 'actionable' or 'justiceable' was cleared at the sub-committee level, but was voted down in the Commission on Human Rights (Bhagavan 2010: 329–332). The point here is not about the unsuccessful attempt, but the fact that such an initiative was made by India which was perhaps emblematic of 'idealism' or international orientation that drove Indian leaders at that time.[2] It would be unthinkable for a 'pragmatic' India now to propose or even support such an intrusive approach to international promotion of human rights.

Sustained Shift towards Statism

Traces of retraction from advocacy of international mechanisms to ensure human rights protection to a definitive disinclination to allow any initiative that might weaken status quo of post-colonial sovereign statehood is very much evident to discerning observers from the mid-1960s onwards when the UDHR had begun to be transformed into twin covenants on civil, political as well as economic, social and cultural

---

[2] Even in the case of 1951 Refugee Convention, India tried to put itself above the Euro-centric normative obligations by citing existence of longstanding historical and cultural ethos known for warmly welcoming those who sought refuge for political reasons (Chimni 2003: 445).

rights and when the pitch for assertion of right of self-determination reached its peak. At the behest of the newly independent Afro-Asian anti-colonial lobby, the right of self-determination was provided privileged place over and above all other rights in both the covenants. India's apprehension was that the right of self-determination might be misused by Pakistan to buttress its claim over India's Jammu and Kashmir. That is why India introduced a caveat to its instrument of ratification of both these covenants that it understands that the right of self-determination enshrined in Article 1 would apply only to the people under foreign domination and not to sovereign independent states.

Further, the conservative (or nationalist) approach is sustained in different forms in later years. India is yet to become a party to any of the optional protocols of the International Covenant on Civil and Political Rights (ICCPR).[3] It is also noteworthy that P. N. Bhagwati, former Chief Justice of India, served as an independent expert member of the Human Rights Committee tasked to ensure adherence of the parties to the obligations under the covenant on civil and political rights during 1995–2010. Similarly, India has been extremely selective and cautious in choosing to join the core human rights treaties negotiated in the UN. Table 11.1 shows that, on the one hand, there has been delay for long decades in ratifying, for example the International Convention against Torture (which it signed in 1997), on the other hand, India was among the first to ratify the Convention on the Rights of Persons with Disability. As regards meeting reporting responsibilities under the ratified conventions, the records show long delays by India in submitting its periodical reports to the treaty bodies concerned. The reporting pattern noticed in respect of the International Covenant on Economic, Social and Cultural Rights (ICESCR) is a case in point.[4]

---

[3] The first optional protocol to the ICCPR allows individual citizens to complain against their government to the Human Rights Committee, while the second one deals with putting an end to capital punishment.

[4] The reports that were due on 1991, 1996 and 2001 were submitted in 2006 after several reminders (Vijapur and Savitri 2006: 29). The report due in 2011 is not yet submitted. See https://tbinternet.ohchr.org/_layouts/TreatyBodyExternal/countries.aspx?CountryCode=IND&Lang=EN, accessed on 5 May 2019.

Table 11.1 Status on India and Core Human Rights Instruments

Treaty	Signature	Ratification
Convention on the Prevention and Punishment of the Crime of Genocide	1948	1949
International Covenant on Civil and Political Rights (ICCPR)	1966	1979
International Covenant on Economic Social and Cultural Rights (ICESCR)	1966	1979
International Convention on Elimination of All Forms of Racial Discrimination (CERD)	1967	1968
Convention on the Elimination of All Forms of Discrimination Against Women (CEDAW)	1980	1993
Convention on the Rights of the Child (CRC)	1989	1992
Convention against Torture and Other Cruel, Inhuman or Degrading Treatment or Punishment (CAT)	1997	Not yet
Optional Protocol to the Convention on the Rights of the Child on the involvement of children in armed conflict	2004	2005
Optional Protocol to the Convention on the Rights of the Child on the sale of children, child prostitution and child pornography	2004	2005
Convention for the Protection of All Persons from Enforced Disappearances (CED)	2007	Not yet
Convention on the Rights of Persons with Disabilities (CRPD)	2006	2007

Source: United Nations Office of Human Rights High Commissioner's website https://tbinternet.ohchr.org/_layouts/TreatyBodyExternal/Treaty.aspx?CountryID=79&Lang=EN, accessed on 8 May 2019.

Again, the political divide beginning in the mid-1960s lasting much longer regarding the relative importance of different sets of human rights is a factor that seemed to have refined and reinforced India's cautious approach. The contestation between Western and Socialist perspectives, paralleled by the contradictions between the developed

North and the developing countries largely defined polarized politics over human rights all along. The first axis disagreed on the relative primacy about the political rights of individual rights over the collective economic rights. And the developing countries, having successfully codified the right of self-determination in the 1966 Covenants, moved on to press for recognition of the right to development in the face of objections from the industrially developed, former colonial powers (Saksena 1991). That is why the 1986 Declaration on the Right to Development has not attained the status of a treaty, unlike other declarations on children and disabled persons. Besides, the UNCHR (where India had been a member ever since its creation in 1947 until its disbandment in 2006) was embroiled by the allegations of politicization of human rights and application of double standards in monitoring the human rights record of different countries. To these trends, India's approach was somewhat non-confrontationist. While it joined the group of developing countries to advocate the right to development, implying the responsibility of the rich countries to extend all help for past exploitation, it did not believe that the political and economic rights should be considered mutually exclusive (Shah 1997: 31, 40). While supporting Arab countries' allegations about Israel's violations of rights of Palestinians in occupied territories, India also expressed unhappiness about the double standards applied by the United States and its West European allies in shielding some authoritarian or military regimes.

A major embarrassment to India in the early 1990s was the internationalization of Kashmir problem on the basis of reports about gross violations of human rights by the Indian security forces. After militancy gained prominence in Kashmir since 1990, Pakistan's attempts gained traction with the sympathetic reaction from the Western governments and NGOs. India was accused of using excessive force and enforcing draconian laws against peaceful protesters in Kashmir. During 1993–1994, Pakistan circulated an anti-India resolution in the Commission on Human Rights asking for a visit to Jammu and Kashmir by a UN fact-finding team. Pakistan also tried to get a text adopted in the General Assembly's main committee on international security in 1994. But that attempt did not succeed, although India admittedly experienced some 'anxious moments' owing to Pakistan's energetic campaign (Chandra 2014: 529).[5] Eventually, Pakistan was dissuaded from tabling its text, thanks to the efforts of principally the Chinese delegation; in return, India pledged support to China's objections to resolutions critical of its human rights record (Chandra 2014: 536–537). While the matter was almost entirely handled by the staff of the mission in 1993, the government sent a high-powered bipartisan delegation in 1994.[6]

The end of the Cold War, accompanied by economic and political globalization, brought new importance to human rights in various ways. A look at the reports brought out by two Secretaries-General Boutros Boutros-Ghali and Kofi Annan, bear the point.[7] Besides, the Security Council began taking concrete action to coercively keep peace in response to gross violations of human rights in countries of Global South (Murthy 2001). India was concerned about the tendency of some states claiming to be the champions of human rights and criticizing other, mostly poorer, nations as violators. The World Conference on Human Rights in Vienna in 1993 was a positive development in helping a consensus on ways and means to promote and protect 'all human rights for all people' and on the recommendation in the Final Act for the establishment of the office of high commissioner for human rights for the purpose. It is relevant to note that India abandoned its previous objections (Vijapur 2010: 302) and joined the consensus decision to keep the mandate of the high commissioner modest in conformity with the principles of the Charter and to achieve

---

[5] According to the former chief representative of India at Geneva, the impact of the Pakistani botched attempt was the decision to allow International Committee of the Red Cross (ICRC) and International Commission of Jurists access to prisoners accused of terror attacks in Kashmir and also the establishment of National Human Rights Commission (Chandra and Gupta 2014: 532).

[6] It comprised Leader of the Opposition, Atal Bihari Vajpayee, and Finance Minister, Manmohan Singh, (both of who later became Prime Ministers), Ambassador to UN at New York, Hamid Ansari (who became Vice President subsequently), junior Foreign Minister, Salman Khurshid, Jammu and Kashmir Chief Minister, Farooq Abdullah, and the former foreign service officer who later went on to become the national security advisor, Brajesh Mishra.

[7] The particular reference here is to 'An Agenda for Peace' authored by Boutros-Ghali in 1992, and 'In Larger Freedom' prepared by Kofi Annan in 2005.

administrative coordination and carry on its work as per the instructions of member countries (Sreenivasan 1993: 15–16).

Partly because of the international spotlight on human rights and to pre-empt adverse comments on shortfalls in domestic action, India brought about laws touching upon a range of issues beginning from the Protection of Human Rights Act (1993) that set up the human rights commissions both at national and provincial levels. This was followed by other legislations, such as the Right to Information Act (2005), Mahatma Gandhi National Rural Employment Guarantee Act (2005), Forest Rights Act (2006), Right to Education Act (2009), Prevention, Prohibition and Redressal of Sexual Harassment of Women at Workplace Act (2013) and Rights of Persons with Disabilities Act (2016). Of course, the long delay in the parliamentary approval to the law against torture tells different story. Nevertheless, it is true that the problem is not with the laws, but its fair and efficient implementation.

Later in 2005 World Summit, India went along with consensus to replace the Commission on Human Rights with Human Rights Council with enhanced profile and power. Partly, it did so as it was preoccupied more with the questions of enlargement of permanent membership of the Security Council and the controversy over the concept of RtoP. As discussed in Chapter 4, in the negotiations over the composition and powers of the Human Rights Council, India in a way worked with other developing countries to ensure that the new Council would be reporting only to the General Assembly, and not to the Security Council (GAOR 2006a: 31–32).

India in the Human Rights Council: New Innings, but Old Game

India worked with other countries in the General Assembly in 2006 to ensure that the newly established Human Rights Council is credible and effective with special characteristics and procedures. For example, all the 47 members are to be elected by the General Assembly according to the principle of geographical representation, and no country could contest immediately after two successive three-year terms. Further all member countries, whether represented in the Council or not (unlike the practice in the predecessor commission) would be subjected to peer scrutiny once every four years under what is called the Universal Periodic Review (UPR) (Murthy 2007). Remarkably, India was elected four times so far for a three-year term each, in addition to the one-year term served on the Council in the first year of the inception in 2006. On three occasions, India secured the highest number of votes polled by candidates from all regional groupings in the General Assembly: 173, 185 and 188 in 2006, 2007 and 2018, respectively. India did not do so well on two occasions: 2011 and 2014.[8]

Each time it contested, India made identical pledges: to 'continue' to promote all human rights, including the right to development in conformity with the principles of cooperation and cordial dialogue, promote right to work as also women's empowerment, preserve the autonomy of national human rights commission, support the activities of civil society groups, contribute to strengthening of the working of the Human Rights Council and particularly the UPR system, support the activities of the office of the High Commissioner of Human Rights through voluntary contributions and support the work of various human rights-related UN agencies.[9]

While pledging its 'continued, active and constructive' participation in the newly created Human Rights Council, India underlined its approach thus: 'Our approach in the Council has been guided by the firm belief that promotion and protection of human rights can be best pursued through dialogue and cooperation, while adhering to the principles of objectivity, transparency, non-selectivity, non-politicization and non-confrontation.'[10] These views are complemented

---

[8] Although India secured the highest number (162) of votes in the Asia-Pacific category, the contestants from Africa, Eastern Europe and Western Europe garnered greater voting support. In 2011, other contestants from the Asia-Pacific group (Indonesia and Philippines secured slightly higher number of votes in the General Assembly.

[9] See, for instance, the Note Verbale submitted to the UN Secretary-General on 1 December 2006, Doc. A/61/718. Also similar pledges contained in Doc. A/73/394, 4 October 2018.

[10] Statement in the 16th session, 2 March 2011. Available at: https://www.pmindiaun.gov.in/adminpart/uploadpdf/66381Statement-General%20Segment%20

by what it told lately a seminar on the role of the United Nations Human Rights Council (UNHRC) in preventing human rights violations held in April 2019 in Geneva,[11]

> It is our firm belief that human rights issues cannot be approached in isolation, ignoring the complex and intricate relationship between human rights, development, democracy and international cooperation. A more constructive and non-confrontational approach that is sensitive to the genuine concerns and capacity constraints of countries should be adopted. An aggressive 'naming and shaming' exercise has its limits, is often counter-productive and tends to divide member states into opposing camps.

As a corollary to this, India has continued the cautious approach to oppose any move going against the sovereign powers of states and the principle of non-interference. India asserted on an occasion that the rights of member countries to manage their affairs in the field of human rights must be respected without 'outside intervention':

> We believe that the best approach to prevent human rights violations is strengthening national institutions through capacity building efforts so that they can function consistent with the rule of law and uphold human rights. The human rights situation in a country is more likely to improve by actions taken by the State and its citizens rather than through an outside intervention. This is especially true in the long run as external actors can only provide support for a limited period. State institutions need to be adequately resourced, equipped, sensitized and made aware of human rights language. Familiarity with international human rights laws, treaties,

---

2mar11.pdf. In July 2012, India objected to a text (Doc.A/HRC/20/L.22) that sought to condemn only the Syrian government for violations committed in El-Houleh incident despite the fact that the Commission of Inquiry had not yet found conclusive evidence against the Government's involvement in the incident. And the text chose to ignore the Commission's acknowledgement that violations were committed by the anti-government forces too. See explanation of vote, 20th session, 6 July 2012. Available at: https://www.pmindiaun.gov.in/adminpart/uploadpdf/34241Statement%20on%20Syria%20New.pdf, accessed on 1 June 2019.

[11] Available at: https://www.pmindiaun.gov.in/pages.php?id=1923, accessed on 3 June 2019.

conventions, and agencies must be fostered. This is the most sustainable method for sovereign governments to discharge their responsibility to promote and protect human rights.[12]

Following the same line of thinking, India has not supported what it described as an 'overzealous attempt' in the UN Human Rights Council to turn the national human right institutions (NHRIs) as a subsidiary of the Council, for it would only undermine their independence, integrity operational autonomy. 'It must be borne in mind that the role and nature of NHRIs are clearly defined in national legislations establishing them. The resolution purports to attribute definite roles, including placing NHRIs as an intermediary between Governments and the UN. We should sincerely avoid such attempts keeping in view the unique role of the NHRIs in the national level human rights architecture.'[13] The resolution was adopted by consensus after it was orally revised.

On the role of civil society too, notably India has exhibited a fairly cautious, if not conservative approach to the engagement of civil society in human rights issues. In 2014, for example, it dissociated from the Ireland-sponsored resolution, which attempted to encourage states to enhance the space for civil society organizations by enacting suitable legislations. Clearly, it took the following position after adoption of the text:

> The Resolution is unduly prescriptive on what domestic legislation should do and should not do. This is the prerogative of the citizens of those countries. The Council must exercise caution and avoid overzealousness, which could inadvertently or otherwise lead to undermining national laws that are consistent with international obligations of the concerned state.[14]

---

[12] Statement by India's delegate at the panel discussion on the role of prevention in the promotion and protection of human rights, 18 September 2014 during the 27th session of the UN Human Rights Council. Available at: https://www.pmindiaun.gov.in/pages.php?id=985, accessed on 2 December 2018.

[13] Statement on A/HRC/27/L.25 in the 27th session, 39th meeting, 25 September 2014. Available at: https://www.pmindiaun.gov.in/pages.php?id=990, accessed on 2 December 2018.

[14] See statement on A/HRC/27/L.24 in the 27th session, 40th meeting, 26 September 2014. Available at: https://www.pmindiaun.gov.in/pages.php?id=991, accessed on 11 December 2018.

Continuing Focus on Right to Development

In India's considered view, economic, social and cultural rights are as important as civil and political rights. In fact, India has consistently advocated the salience of right to development as integral to human rights.[15] At the Working Group of the HRC on Right to Development, India noted,

> ... The challenge of guaranteeing human rights becomes nearly impossible to tackle in the face of unmet human needs .... The global development divide of today can trace its origins in an array of historical injustices that have somehow never completely disappeared from the equation. They are evident today in the persisting undemocratic systems of international governance where effective participation of developing countries in international decision-making is paved with all kinds of obstacles. In this regard, our repeated calls for a conducive international environment as well as attempts towards greater acceptance and operationalization of the right to development at the international level have only yielded disappointment and resistance.[16]

To India's regret, despite the supreme importance of the particular right, it continues to be highly misunderstood and given superficial attention by the UN human rights mechanisms. India recognizes that, without a doubt, the process of development needs to be nationally owned and driven by national needs and priorities. But at the same time, there can be no doubt that it needs to be complemented by 'equitable economic relations and a favourable economic environment at the international level'.[17] As such, India has made financial contribution to support the activities of the special rapporteur on right to development.

---

[15] For instance, see statement in 22nd session of the UNHRC, 8 March 2013. Available at: https://www.pmindiaun.gov.in/adminpart/uploadpdf/59194Statement-General%20Debate%208%20mar13.pdf, accessed on 11 December 2018. In fact, an Indian economist, Arjun Sengupta, served as the chair-cum-rapporteur for the working group on right to development.

[16] Statement at Working Group on Right to Development, 17th session, 25 April 2016. Available at: https://www.pmindiaun.gov.in/pages.php?id=1284, accessed on 4 December 2018.

[17] Statement at Working Group on Right to Development, 18th session, 3 April 2017. Available at: https://www.pmindiaun.gov.in/pages.php?id=1456, accessed on 15 December 2018.

Countering Pakistan's Propaganda on Kashmir

The dissolution of the Commission on Human Rights made no difference to Pakistan's persistence to raise the Kashmir issue in the new body, the Human Rights Council, in 2006. India strongly objected to Pakistan's misuse of the forum of the Council to make tendentious accusations on the situation in Jammu and Kashmir, while turning a blind eye to the hardships faced by the people of Pakistan-occupied Kashmir due to sectarian violence and terror attacks.[18] India referred to Pakistan as a 'terror state', citing its failure to fulfil its solemn commitment made in 2004 that use of the territory under its control would not be allowed for terror attacks against India. Furthermore, it was pointed out that Pakistan was using terror against its own people in Balochistan, Sindh, Khyber Pakhtunkhwa, as well as the tribal areas in its northwest. This coupled with the utter disregard for the human rights of religious and sectarian minorities has turned Pakistan into the true 'epicentre of global terror'.[19] Hence, India advised Pakistan to focus its energies on setting its own house in order and acting against the perpetrators of terrorist attacks on its neighbours instead of ritually raking up alleged human rights violations elsewhere.[20]

A landmark development in the relationship between Indian government and the Office of High Commissioner for Human Rights (OHCHR) in regard to Jammu and Kashmir occurred in 2018. The UN human rights high commissioner's office released a first-ever report prepared by the special rapporteur on 'excessive violence' used by the security forces against civilian protesters in Jammu and Kashmir, causing both embarrassment and anger to the MEA. India not only denied the OHCHR team access to Jammu and Kashmir earlier, but also rejected the high commissioner's 'prejudiced' recommendation

---

[18] In exercise of right of reply, 29th session, 22 June 2015. Available at: https://www.pmindiaun.gov.in/pages.php?id=1122, accessed on 15 December 2018.

[19] Statement in exercise of right of reply to Pakistan's statement in 33rd session of HRC, 26 September 2016. Available at: https://www.pmindiaun.gov.in/pages.php?id=1370, accessed on 13 December 2018.

[20] Statement at the HRC's 36th regular session, 11–29 September 2017. Available at: https://www.pmindiaun.gov.in/pages.php?id=1494, accessed on 8 December 2018.

for an international investigation into the matter. India rejected the report for ignoring the disturbing trends in Pakistan-occupied Kashmir and basing its observations on motivated propaganda. Also India objected to the use of the phrase 'Indian administered Kashmir'.[21] Similarly, in national capital, the MEA in a statement rejected the report as 'fallacious, tendentious and motivated' and found it to be 'a selective compilation of largely unverified information.'[22] However, it is particularly important to note that most of the sources for the report came from Indian official bodies, such as the state and national human rights commissions and Indian human rights NGOs. When the high commissioner's office enquired from the Indian authorities about the follow-up to the special rapporteur's report, the permanent representative reiterated its objections to the report and hence it would not entertain any communication on the subject (Haidar 2019).

India's deputy permanent representative expressed concern over the 'politicization of human rights as a foreign policy tool', while addressing the work of the UN and the UNHRC. India sought to highlight the menace from terror attacks to the human rights of victims of terror by urging that 'the global efforts at combating terrorism are not undermined by those who seek to protect the human rights of only the terrorists, and not of the victims of their heinous acts.'[23] However, former diplomat Arun Singh notes that these critical reports must be viewed in light of the fact that except for Pakistan, no other government followed

---

[21] Permanent Representative's statement in 34th session, 9 March 2017. Available at: https://www.pmindiaun.gov.in/pages.php?id=1444, accessed on 5 December 2018. The High Commissioner's Report on 'Situation of Human Rights in Kashmir', 18 June 2018. Available at: https://www.ohchr.org/_layouts/15/WopiFrame.aspx?sourcedoc=/Documents/Countries/IN/DevelopmentsInKashmirJune2016ToApril2018.pdf&action=default&DefaultItemOpen=1, accessed on 2 January 2019.

[22] The statement by the official spokesperson also objected to the description of Indian territory as 'Azad Jammu and Kashmir' and 'Gilgit-Baltistan'. Available at: https://www.pmindiaun.gov.in/pages.php?id=1768, accessed on 5 December 2018.

[23] Statement by Ambassador A. Gopinathan, India's permanent representative, 10th regular session, 4 March 2009. Available at: https://www.pmindiaun.gov.in/adminpart/uploadpdf/17270General%20Segment-%20Speech%20by%20PR%20Gopinathan%204mar09.pdf, accessed on 9 December 2018.

up with statements criticizing India in the Human Rights Council (quoted in Bhardwaj 2018). The sudden changes effected by India in August 2019 to the constitutional special status of Jammu and Kashmir, coupled with the continuing clamp down in the entire state agitated Pakistan to flag the issue as an egregious violation of human rights in the 42nd session of the Council that began in September 2019. The Indian delegation strongly rejected the 'hysterical statements in the false and fabricated narrative' peddled by Pakistan on an internal matter of India (Arya 2019). At the same time, India questioned the moral claim of Pakistan to speak about Jammu and Kashmir situation when its 'gory record' of persecution and elimination of religious minorities is internationally denounced. Nonetheless, it is clear that Indian diplomatic officials and representatives found it hard to ignore the growing international (both governmental and non-governmental) concern about the human rights adverse impact of the steps it had taken in 2019.

Organizational Concerns

India lost no opportunity to put the Council's organizational problems under scanner ranging from the need for better time management as also the working of special procedures and special rapporteurs.

To avoid becoming 'a victim of its own success', India suggested, the Council needs 'to maximize the use of limited time and resources available' and also put 'a cap on the maximum duration of sessions so as not to undermine in any way our commitment to human rights, or our ability to respond to other areas of our work in Geneva that demand our attention, energy and resources constantly.'[24] Particularly what made India uneasy was the growing number of country-specific resolutions in the Council. India apprehended that such resolutions

---

[24] See statements made in 10th regular session, 4 March 2009. Available at: https://www.pmindiaun.gov.in/adminpart/uploadpdf/17270General%20Segment-%20Speech%20by%20PR%20Gopinathan%204mar09.pdf, accessed on 9 December 2018. See also statement in 19th session, 1 March 2012. Available at: https://www.pmindiaun.gov.in/adminpart/uploadpdf/50545Statement-General-Segment-1March12.pdf, accessed on 9 December 2019.

could weaken the constructive dialogue and cooperative approach.[25] Indeed, these concerns have recurred on several occasions in different sessions. For instance, on the 10th anniversary of HRC, India noted 'with particular concern' 'the perpetuation and proliferation of country-specific mandates …, focusing only at developing countries'.[26]

India supported Special Procedures that constitute a key mechanism of the Human Rights Council,[27] but with a caveat. It may be worthwhile to add that the issues which India faced critical comments in the reports of special rapporteur on extra-judicial deaths were with reference to torture during custody, custodial deaths, fake police 'encounters', the abuse of armed forces special powers act, honour killings and crimes against women. Perhaps the most prominent and persistent issue concerned India's rejection of Pakistan's claims about human rights violations in Jammu and Kashmir. According to India, the purpose of special procedures has to be to promote genuine dialogue for strengthening the capacity of the member governments as contained in the Council's relevant resolutions. Reference was also made to the code of conduct that stipulates that the special procedures must 'always seek to establish facts based on objective, reliable information emanating from relevant, credible sources that they have duly cross-checked to the best extent possible'.[28]

The selection and professional background of some 31 special rapporteurs was also problematized by the Indian representatives.

---

[25] Statement at 19th session, 1 March 2012. Available at: https://www.pmindiaun.gov.in/adminpart/uploadpdf/50545Statement-General-Segment-1March12.pdf, accessed on 7 September 2018.

[26] Statement by the Permanente Representative, 31st session, 15 March 2016. Available at: https://www.pmindiaun.gov.in/pages.php?id=1258, accessed on 26 September 2018.

[27] India extended standing invitation to Special Procedures in 2011, as a follow-up to the recommendation in the first cycle of UPR (2008) and commitment made before its election for a second term (2011–2014) in the Council. Since then, visits by special rapporteurs for drinking water, housing, violence against women and for extra-judicial or arbitrary executions have been undertaken.

[28] Intervention in the 20th session, 28 June 2012. Available at: https://www.pmindiaun.gov.in/adminpart/uploadpdf/7868928%20%20June%20Statement-Human_Right_Bodies_and_mechanisms.pdf, 7 September 2018.

It was pointed out that nearly 15 experts hailed from one particular geographical region thereby denying representation to other regions. And as many as 23 (75%) of them had links with the Western countries and had training in law. As a result, India argued, they tended more to be judgmental rather than to engage in cooperative deliberations with the governments concerned.[29]

Another issue India repeatedly raised is related to the regional representation in the High Commissioner's office staff. Quoting reports of the UN watchdog, the Joint Inspection Unit, India pointed out that 47.3 per cent of staff belonged to one region (Western Europe), while many countries from other regions are under-represented.[30] Although the over-representation was brought down from 64 per cent earlier, the situation still remained skewed in favour of developed countries.[31]

Managing Feedback in the UPR Cycles

As noted already, the UPR of the Human Rights Council is a unique procedure. The exercise enables peer review of all 193 member countries' periodical reports on the measures taken to promote and protect human rights once in four years without exception. Its objective is not to name and shame countries but to afford an opportunity for others to offer constructive criticism while responding to the contents of the national reports.

India has welcomed the UPR to be a good mechanism that could make a genuine difference to the situation of human rights on the

---

[29] Statement on agenda item 5 in General Debate, 27th session, 22 September 2014. Available at: https://www.pmindiaun.gov.in/pages.php?id=986, accessed on 7 September 2018.

[30] Statement in 19th session, 2 March 2012. Available at: https://www.pmindiaun.gov.in/adminpart/uploadpdf/76898StatementCompositionStaff-OHCHR19HRC.pdf, accessed on 6 September 20108.

[31] Statement in 21st session, 10–28 September 2012. Available at: https://www.pmindiaun.gov.in/adminpart/uploadpdf/27759Statement-%20General%20Debate%20on%20Update%20with%20High%20Commissioner%2010sep12.pdf, accessed on 8 September 2018.

ground. However, India made a few suggestions for review and improvement of UPR at an inter-sessional seminar organized by the HRC in April 2019. First, more time should be allowed for UPR to facilitate fruitful exchange of views among member states which is presently constrained. Secondly, enhancement of capacity of states through technical assistance and capacity-building measures at the request of the states concerned would contribute to the improvement of human rights situation on the ground. Thirdly, the OHCHR should also prepare a list of best practices shared by member states in their UPR statements, as well as offers of technical assistance.[32]

India had gone through three cycles of the UPR in 2008, 2012 and then in 2017 so far. In the national reports, Indian delegations sought to showcase the legislative and policy measures initiated to improve human rights situation. Notably, the National Human Rights Commission of India fully conforms to the Paris principles on independent national human rights institutions, with the accredited 'A status' in the Global Alliance of NHRIs. India missed no opportunity to highlight the significance to the promotion of human rights arising from the introduction of Right to Information Act, Mahatma Gandhi National Rural Employment Guarantee Act, Right to Education Act, Food Security Act and several other initiatives. All of them are inspired by the constitutional framework of fundamental rights and the directive principles of state policy, which are progressively interpreted and guaranteed by fiercely independent judiciary. Also cited were figures showing the success of mid-day meals programme for school children as a result of which enrolment figures had gone up, while on the other hand poverty levels in urban and rural areas have declined.[33] In the third cycle in 2017, additional welfare-oriented schemes were cited, viz. 'Celebrate

---

[32] Remarks made at inter-sessional seminar organized by the Council on 9 April 2019. Available at: https://www.pmindiaun.gov.in/pages.php?id=1920, accessed on 25 October 2018.

[33] See, for instance, the opening remarks by the Leader of Delegation and the Attorney General, Goolam Vahanvati, in the UPR Working Group, 13th session, 24 May 2012. Available at: https://www.pmindiaun.gov.in/adminpart/uploadpdf/37353Opening%20statement%20by%20Attorney%20General%20of%20India,%20Mr.%20Goolam%20E.%20Vahanvati.pdf, accessed on 25 October 2018.

Table 11.2 India and UPR Cycles*

Cycle Year	No. of Countries Participating in Interactive Dialogue	Recommendations Made in the Working Group Report	Recommendations Accepted	Recommendations Noted
2008	42	18	5	13
2012	80	169	67	102
2017	103	250	152	98

Note: * Table prepared by the author himself.

the Girl Child and Enable her Education', Jan Dhan Yojana-Bank Accounts for All, Digital India, Skill India, Start-up India and Make in India—all designed to mirror the targets of the 17 SDGs for achieving the 2030 Agenda.[34]

As part of building a case for a mechanism for Internet governance, India highlighted the threats to right to privacy arising from digital advances. India does recognize that while advances in information and communication technology further the right to freedom of expression, the misuse of Internet for anti-social and criminal activities must be checked. Therefore, a case is made out for digital surveillance 'in a proportionate and non-arbitrary manner, with legitimate purpose, in accordance with the rule of law and with effective oversight'.[35]

The feedback from member countries was substantial and wide ranging. An overview of the interactive dialogue at the working group along with the nature of India's response to the outcome is attempted in Table 11.2.

[34] Opening statement by the Leader of Delegation and Attorney General, Mukul Rohtagi, UPR Working Group, 27th session, 4 May 2017. Available at: https://www.pmindiaun.gov.in/pages.php?id=1655, accessed on 8 October 2018.

[35] Statement in the panel discussion on the relevant agenda item, 27th session, 12 September 2014. Available at: https://www.pmindiaun.gov.in/pages.php?id=982, accessed on 8 October 2018.

Notably, the number of participants in the interactive dialogue progressively shot up from 42 to 80 and then 103, while the recommendations also went up significantly: from 18 to 169 and then to 250. Correspondingly, India's acceptance rate also progressively grew from a mere 5 in 2008 to 152 in 2017.[36] Notably, a member state can only note the recommendation or accept; it has no option to reject. In the concluding observations, India's delegates acknowledged the challenges, which arise from the diversity of the Indian society, to be overcome in the implementation of some of the recommendations.[37] India appreciated the interest and suggestions by participants and explained the difficulties of implementation in a vast and diverse country with complex federal and administrative structures.

In these three rounds, a very large number of countries urged India to ratify the UN Convention against Torture. Besides, other concerns raised related to the issues, such as abolition of death penalty, banishment of torture, outlawing section 377 of the Indian Penal Code (IPC) to decriminalize same sex partnerships/marriages and criminalization of marital rape. Cancellation of licences issued earlier to more than 20,000 NGOs through inconsistent application of Foreign Contribution Regulation Act rules impinging on the right to freedom of association also came up.

In response to the criticism about not ratifying the UN Convention on Prohibition of Torture and Other forms of Degrading Treatment, India's explanation was that the long delay was caused by the scrutiny of a bill to amend various existing laws by the select committee of Parliament. However, it notes that there are safeguards in the IPC for proper treatment of people in custody, and any violation could be looked into by the NHRC and even the Supreme Court.[38] The Armed

---

[36] Nevertheless, it needs to be clarified that compared to other countries, this is not staggering, for far higher number of recommendations were made in respect of the United States, China and Brazil in the 2012 review (Aravind 2017).

[37] Statement in 36th session, 21 September 2017. Available at: https://www.pmindiaun.gov.in/pages.php?id=1527, accessed on 4 September 2018.

[38] Statement by the official representative in the course of the second round of UPR in 2012. Available at: https://www.pmindiaun.gov.in/adminpart/uploadpdf/48078Interventions%20by%20the%20Indian%20delegation.doc, accessed on 22 September 2018.

Forces Special Powers Act also has come into sharp focus with a strong plea for its withdrawal. The government's defence rested on the argument that there existed safeguards, just as the law was upheld by the Supreme Court. Any complaints about excesses committed by the Army personnel are seriously examined for appropriate action.[39] Responding to the report of special rapporteur on the incidence of extra-judicial or arbitrary executions, based on his visit in March 2012, India stated its unhappiness that many of the clarifications provided to the special rapporteur during his visit were not reflected in the report.[40]

India defended the status of minorities and women by referring to the fundamental rights guaranteed to all citizens without any discrimination as to race, religion, region, caste or gender. Moreover, the minorities enjoy the right to propagate religion, run educational institutions without state interference. And the situation is actively monitored by the separate statutory bodies created both at the central and provincial levels to protect the rights of minorities, women and the disadvantaged sections as well.[41] Similarly, in the light of criticism made by the special rapporteur about the exclusion of lakhs of minorities in Assam and other parts of Northeast India from the National Register of Citizens, the official representatives clarified that the said citizens register was only a draft and before its finalization, care would be taken to afford adequate opportunity to those aggrieved about their exclusion in a 'totally objective, transparent and meticulous' manner, as it was being carried out under the directives and close monitoring of the Supreme Court.[42]

---

[39] Statement by a senior official of Ministry of Home Affairs in the course of the second round of UPR in 2012. See note 38 above.
[40] The Indian representative's statement in the 29th session of the Human Rights Council on 18 June 2015. Available at: https://www.pmindiaun.gov.in/pages.php?id=1125. See Report of the Special Rapporteur in Doc.A/HRC/23/47/Add.1, accessed on 4 September 2018.
[41] See statement in the 40th session, 13 March 2019. Available at: https://www.pmindiaun.gov.in/pages.php?id=1905, accessed on 9 April 2019.
[42] *Ibid.*

Solidarity Strategy: Teaming up with Friendly and Like-Minded Countries

India deployed a variety of tactics in pursuit of its human rights diplomacy in the UN. These include working in collaboration on issues of common interest with diverse group of like-minded countries, such as the BRICS and IBSA, principally on right to development, and supporting Asian and South Asian neighbours, which in turn praised India's submissions. Notably, India and China were on the same page on human rights issues, as they share views regarding non-interference principle while approaching human rights issues and have generally resisted country-specific resolutions. China showered fulsome praise by observing that 'India has not only achieved great progress in the field of human rights but has also accumulated a rich experience to be shared with other countries. As a developing country, China... is faced with many similar challenges and that for this reason it would like to exchange views and experiences with India'.[43] India (along with China) also voted against a resolution that called for moratorium on death penalty (Ferdinand 2014: 385). Interestingly again, the issue linkage between environment and human rights showed India–Pakistan convergence in 2015. A few other examples are cited here.

India spoke on behalf of BRICS countries on mainstreaming of right to development. In another instance, India issued a statement in 31st session (held in March 2016) on behalf of group of 20 like-minded countries that included Bangladesh, Bolivia, China, Cuba, Ecuador, Egypt, Indonesia, Malaysia, Pakistan, Russia, Saudi Arabia, Singapore, Sri Lanka, Uganda and Zimbabwe on issues of technical assistance and capacity building. Similarly India spoke on behalf of 23 like-minded countries on promotion and protection of human rights, including right to development in the 34th session, held on 10 March 2017. Alluding to the funding to the country visits by the special procedures from extra-budgetary sources, India spoke in 2013 on behalf of other countries, such as Algeria, China, Ecuador, Pakistan, Russia, Sri Lanka and Thailand, to question whether the

---

[43] Report of the Working Group on the Universal Periodic Review: India, Doc.A/HRC/8/26, 23 May 2008, para. 33.

selection of the countries to be visited had a connection with the sources of funding.[44]

As for the neighbouring countries, India was quite appreciative of the improvement measures taken by Sri Lanka, Nepal, Bangladesh and Myanmar. In Sri Lanka's case, India seemed to overcome the flip-flop it exhibited in 2013 caused by domestic political compulsions,[45] and came round to appreciate Sri Lanka's efforts to improve the post-conflict reconciliation. It referred to the claim made by the government to hand over 75 per cent of land occupied by the security forces to the original and rightful owners. It partnered with Sri Lanka in rehabilitation, resettlement and reconstruction projects.[46] India lauded Nepal's acceptance of 80 per cent of recommendations made during the UPR in 2016. Similarly welcoming Myanmar's progress in improving human rights situation, India refused to join consensus resolution on sending a fact-finding mission without the consent of Myanmar.[47] India commended the approach adopted by the Government of Bangladesh to provide humanitarian assistance to those who fled from Rakhine province of Myanmar while at the same time welcoming the recommendations made by the Kofi Annan commission for the

---

[44] Available at: https://www.pmindiaun.gov.in/adminpart/uploadpdf/87291Item5-Statement%20-%20GD%20Item%205(Joint%20Statement).pdf, accessed on 1 November 2019.

[45] For two successive years in 2012 and 2013, India supported a resolution that demanded Sri Lankan government to investigate war crimes committed by armed forces against Tamil civilians during the civil war (Lettinga and Troost 2015: 16; Mukherjee 2015: 50). This vote reflected huge political pressure brought about domestically by a key ally of the coalition government in Delhi (the Tamil Nadu-based Dravida Munnetra Kazhagam), which threatened to withdraw support unless India joined the Western countries in denouncing the actions of the Sri Lankan government (Lakshmi 2013). However, next year in 2014, India abstained on the text that demanded independent investigation into the war crimes against the Sri Lankan government (Lettinga and Troost 2015: 16).

[46] Statement made at the Interactive Dialogue on Sri Lanka, 40th session, 20 March 2019. Available at: https://www.pmindiaun.gov.in/pages.php?id=1909, accessed on 6 July 2019.

[47] See statement in the 35th session, 15 June 2017. Available at: https://www.pmindiaun.gov.in/pages.php?id=1737, accessed on 5 August 2018.

resolution of citizenship and issues of the refugees.[48] Incidentally, India provided four tranches of aid totalling US$2 million to the refugees in Bangladesh.

Critical Assessment

According to a scholar who essays the positions taken by India, Brazil and South Africa in the UN Human Rights Council on issues concerning both country-specific situations and a few thematic issues, India's overall record was less forthcoming than Brazil, but somewhat better than South Africa (Jordaan 2015).

In summary, there were divergent views within India on the country's human rights approach in the UN. A section holds the view that the record was tantamount to 'failure of diplomacy' characterized by 'lack of adequate preparedness and evasive replies' in Geneva (Kothari 2018). The contrarian school opines that India did not have to pay much attention to the criticism by foreign countries in the UNHRC; instead, it should demonstrate confidence in its capability to 'come up with its own solutions' to the problems.[49] Other human rights activists desired better response promising reforms and accountability, instead of blaming diplomatic mishandling (Bhardwaj 2018).[50]

In the recent one decade or so, India's situation has become awkward in the eye of international community.

[T]here were 26 critical statements (mostly by UN experts, with some by the UN High Commissioner for Human Rights). Nine were issued in 2018, which was the year that saw the highest number of negative statements on India for the period 2010–2018. The statements have dealt with a number of issues including the

---

[48] Statement by the Permanent Representative in the 36th session, 29 September 2017. Available at: https://www.pmindiaun.gov.in/pages.php?id=1538, accessed on 5 August 2018.

[49] Those who expressed views on these lines were activist and academic Madhu Kishwar and former foreign secretary Kanwal Sibal. See Aravind (2017).

[50] Those who were quoted by the author were Meenakshi Ganguly and Ravi Nair, who represented, respectively, South Asia Human Rights Watch and South Asia Human Rights Documentation Centre.

Assam National Register of Citizens process, online hate speech, the killing of journalist Gauri Lankesh, jailing of human rights defenders, deportation of Rohingya refugees, and excessive police response to protests. (Pillai 2018)[51]

In the Council, India is seen as 'a chronic fence sitter' on key issues while opposing resolutions against specific countries, thereby failing the hopes of playing a leadership role in the promotion of human rights and democracy (Ganguly 2013). Endorsing this critical assessment, another author observes, 'India avoids responsibility for protecting human rights in the rest of the world. Its scepticism of the international human rights regime means that India is likely to continue opposing the expansion of jurisdiction of international human rights institutions and the attenuation of national sovereignty in the process' (Banerjee 2015: 27; Pai 2013: 303–318).

---

[51] Some have linked the UN human rights bureaucracy's assertiveness in publicizing these critical reports to a certain coldness in the US President Trump Administration's approach to Prime Minister Modi. See Jyoti Malhotra's comment in Bhardwaj (2018).

CHAPTER 12

India's Approach to Multilateral Governance of Internet

The chief purpose of this chapter is to analyse India's perspectives on global governance in general and on issues pertaining particularly to Internet governance. It contextualizes this with an exploration of theoretical framings on the nature and purpose of global governance, before weighing factors accounting for the growing salience of global governance and its implications for the relevance of traditional actors, such as intergovernmental organizations (IGOs).

Unlike governance, which is applied to the domain of state activity for long as an analytical tool in administrative science, 'global governance' has entered lately as a buzzword in the discussions involving academic and policymaking circles. All major problems of the day—from environment to Internet, from international security to health and human rights protection—belong to the arena of global governance. Several factors explain this. The increasing complexities associated with the emerging global order and the attendant inadequacies of the existing tools for managing those problems are among principal reasons. Also, the unprecedented pace of advances in technology has not only redefined the nature of political, strategic, economic, social and cultural problems, but also adduced new identities to peoples and groups, thereby privileging the role of certain newly emerged actors, while at the same time diminishing the coping power of established institutions. In other words, governance of common concerns constitutes the central challenge to the emerging global order. And this poses serious crisis of relevance and resilience capability of state and non-state actors alike.

Theoretical Approaches to Global Governance and Order

It is obvious that governance and order are interlinked. As intentional activities designed to regularize the arrangements which sustain world affairs, 'governance obviously shapes the nature of the prevailing global order' (Rosenau 1992: 8). Given the absence of a world government, the concept of global governance refers to the nexus of systems of rule-making, political coordination and problem-solving, which transcend states and societies (Rosenau 2000).

The study of global governance is sometimes referred to as the privatization of global regulation, that is, a redrawing of the boundaries between public authority and private power (Held and McGrew 2002: 10). As Reinicke (1998: 8–9) notes, the 'traditional lines of demarcation between the public and the private spheres are not only being redefined but becoming increasingly blurred'. In that sense, global governance embodies a complex patchwork of overlapping jurisdictions, generating ambiguities about the principal location of authority and political responsibility. Theoretically, global governance is much more than simply a descriptive term: It constitutes a broad analytical approach to addressing the central questions of political life under conditions of globalization, namely 'who rules, in whose interests, by what mechanisms and for what purposes' (Held and McGrew 2002: 8). While some like Falk (1995) make a case for making global governance humane with a call to re-examine the ideas of sovereignty and security, sceptics contend that any talk of global governance substituting the primacy of nation states would be in vain (Gilpin 2001: 22).

Three theoretical perspectives on global governance may be touched upon here. Functionalists portray global governance as sum of formal and informal coordination mechanisms that are beneficial to the actors who create them (Young 1999). Others link rise of global governance to the 'rather messy arena' of world politics after states lost their salience, which propelled continuing efforts to create order through diverse and often novel mechanisms employed by a multitude of actors (Rosenau 1990: 12–16). The third perspective views global governance as a shift from the Westphalian to post-Westphalian governance in the sense that whereas the Westphalian rules originate from international governmental agreements reached without coercion, the post-Westphalian governance acquires legitimacy when decision-making processes become transparent, accountable and inclusive involving all affected parties within and beyond state (Dingwerth and Pattberg 2009: 42–43).

There is little consensus on what normative principles should inform the institutional design of global governance. In the normative literature, global governance is said to be distorted in so far as it promotes the interests of the most powerful states and global social forces, just as it restricts the realization of greater global social justice and human security. Thus, distorted global governance is understood as a product of the mutually reinforcing dynamics of the inequalities of power between states, the structural privileging of the interests and agenda of global capital, and the technocratic nature of the global policy process (Held and McGrew 2002: 13; Latham 1999: 23–53).

In a way, the normative debate about transnational democracy and global social justice is increasingly central to the politics of contemporary global governance (Held and McGrew 2002: 14). These discourses inform the wider academic and political debate concerning the necessary conditions for genuine global governance. Indeed, the official rhetoric of institutional reform, as well as the global politics of protest, characterizes global governance as a significant site 'in which struggles over wealth, power and knowledge are taking place' (Murphy 2000: 799). This understanding is derived from what is seen as the overcasting influence of the neoliberal ideology; global governance is likely to remain inefficient, incapable of shifting resources from the world's wealthy to the world's poor and relatively insensitive to the concerns of labour and rural poor despite the progressive role that it recently may have played in promoting liberal democracy and empowering of women (Murphy 2000: 789).

Global Governance as a Process beyond Governments but Less than Government

Some analysts emphasize that contemporary global governance avoids attacking state sovereignty. It could fill the regulative gap created by economic globalization and the concomitant retreat of the state (Friedrichs 2009: 119). To characterize global governance as 'government-like events that occur in the world of States even in the absence of government' is to emphasize what is done rather than the constitutional basis for doing it (Finkelstein 1995: 363–369). Global governance implies a wide and seemingly ever-growing range of actors in every domain. According to the Commission on Global Governance (1995: 4), global governance does not mean 'a single model, nor even a single structure or set of structures. Instead, it is a broad, dynamic, complex process of interactive decision-making that is constantly evolving and responding to changing circumstances.' Admittedly, global economic and social affairs have traditionally been viewed as concerns basically of intergovernmental relationships, but increasingly they are now framed in comprehensive enough terms to embrace local and international NGOs, grassroots and citizens' movements, multinational corporations and global capital markets (Weiss 2000: 810). Thus, the expansive character of global governance is explained as the 'sum of laws, norms, policies and institutions that define, constitute and mediate relations among citizens, society, markets and the state in the international arena—the wielders and objects of international public power' (Thakur and Weiss 2010: 6). In essence, global governance may be viewed as an enabling tool to allow participation of individuals and groups other than governments and IGOs with the aim to shape solutions to shared aspects of transnational problems. The key point to be noted here in the understanding of global governance is the proliferation of actors ranging from governments, non-governmental and intergovernmental bodies to

Table 12.1 *The Number of IGOs and INGOs during the Years 1981–2018*

Year	IGOs	INGOs
1981	337	4,263
1991	297	4,620
2001	243	6,357
2018	288	9,633

Source: Table 1 in Volume 5 of relevant editions of Yearbook of International Organizations (1981–2019).

the business world and advocacy and expert groups. The moot question about global governance—of, by and for whom—underlines the fundamental issues of representation, legitimacy and accountability of those who take decisions in the name of the 'marginalized majority' (Payne 2010: 729–740).

The role of international organizations in the sustenance of global order focused on interstate relations could also come under new strains. IGOs—which are the creations of states to mitigate cooperative action problems among them (Karns and Mingst 2010: 38–39)—may be seen as some of the settled sites of global governance. As noted already, the primacy of states as principals in world politics is eroding in important ways. As Table 12.1 establishes, the number of international organizations, particularly of the non-governmental character, has doubled since 1991, whereas IGOs have reached a plateau.

The question arises now as to whether the loss of state power infuses new life to the role of these organizations in global governance. There is no simple answer to the question. Some organizations (such as the International Labour Organization) have lost and others (such as the WTO) have relatively gained in the era of globalization. The decline of IMF—a once powerful institution—is an apt example to cite here. Its liquid reserves once estimated at half of world imports have fallen to a level less than 2 per cent of global imports (Weiss 2000: 809). Increasingly as a consequence of neoliberal marketization, the services once provided by public IGOs are now contracted to private, non-governmental and often social movement-style organizations. Today, more than ever before, NGOs run refugee camps, provide disaster relief, design and carry out development projects, monitor and attempt to contain the international spread of diseases and try to save the planet from pollution. Most of them do so primarily with public funds from major donor governments and IGOs (Murphy 2000: 795).

India and Global Governance

India is long known for its strident advocacy of respect for sovereignty as the ordering principle in international relations and is quite wary of any dilution or deviation. India and other rising powers 'display conservative preferences, usually opting for a model of global governance in which national governments serve as essential gatekeepers to global institutions, and IGOs remain the preferred venue for negotiation of international agreements' (Kahler 2013: 719). Conversely, like the United States, India does not seem to want 'very strong global governance' in order more to avoid any constraints on its own behaviour than about establishing global norms that place agreed-upon constraints on stakeholders (Schaffer 2009: 85).

Several observers have noted shifts in India's approach to, as also the country's growing profile in, global policymaking forums. Mohan (2010: 138) notes that 'change might be on the way as India begins to adapt, even if incrementally, to its increased weight in the international system and the responsibilities that come with it'. By way of substantiating this assertion, a reference may be made to the measure of India's enmeshment in international organizations. India is associated with 200 intergovernmental and 3,700 NGOs.[1] India

---

[1] India has been successful in harnessing the support of NGOs for certain types of causes, such as development. In these and other development-oriented efforts, it has been assisted by certain domestic NGOs too, such as Consumer Unity and Trust Society (CUTS). But it is important to bear in mind that such engagement with NGOs is largely state-driven and strategic rather than bottom-up or straightforwardly oriented towards increasing inclusiveness and participation (Narlikar 2013a: 605).

enjoys the 26th position overall. Notably it is the most international organizations-entangled country, next only to Brazil from Global South (leaving China behind). There is one more aspect, according to the information available with the Union of International Associations, 169 organizations have headquarters in India, out of which nearly 110 came up after 1991. This should not in any way brush aside the cautious approach India adopts to the civil society actors in relation to the sovereignty principle. Again, India is associated with numerous regional forums (from Indian Ocean Rim Countries (IORC), Association of Southeast Asian Nations (ASEAN), Shanghai Cooperation Organization (SCO), and so on) as also several issue-focused cross-regional groupings, such as G-20 on global economy, G-4 on Security Council expansion, the caucus of emerging countries (BRICS), in addition to its impending entry into the Nuclear Suppliers Group.[2]

On parallel track, India is engaged in an ambitious mission aimed at recasting important intergovernmental forums, particularly the Bretton Woods Institutions and the UNSC in justification of its newfound importance in global arena (Mohan 2010; Schaffer 2009). Similarly, India contributed in June 2012 US$10 billion to the IMF, with an expectation of timely and comprehensive reform of voting power and reform of quota shares (Narlikar 2013a: 606–608). On its part, the WTO has modified its norms of participation to ensure that India along with other rising powers participates in key consensus-building group negotiations. Indeed, India's refusal to make any trade-offs involving agriculture contributed significantly to the July 2008 deadlock in the Doha Development Round negotiations. This assertive streak in multilateral diplomacy is attributed to the country's impressive economic growth coupled with nuclear weapon state status, besides its strong interest in the issue areas of energy, non-proliferation and disarmament, environment and climate change, development finance, food security and trade in services, and global commons (Kahler 2013; Mohan 2010; Narlikar 2013a). However, this view is contested. A number of scholars

---

[2] On the other hand, some interpret India's engagement with these extra-regional groupings as its 'flight from the region' (Mukherjee and Malone 2011: 324).

are raising the question whether India could be counted as responsible player in global governance. The West-based scholarship regrets that India is more comfortably disposed towards bilateral channels than multilateral ones asserting more often its rights rather than shouldering greater responsibilities for provision of global public good. A recently held panel discussion under the banner of the Brookings Institution concluded that India is relatively successful in bilateral relations with key partners, but not so in maintaining long-term commitments to multilateral relations.[3] Hence, the case is made out for India to assume greater global responsibilities, to help set global governance rules/agenda, so as to use multilateral organizations beyond just defending its interests. India, therefore, finds itself neither able to pull its domestic constituents along on multilateral diplomacy nor able to demonstrate enough weight in the multilateral system to push its domestically determined agenda through without being labelled a spoiler or obstructionist (Mukherjee and Malone, 2011: 323). Further, analysts are not persuaded that India has, as of now, managed the 'difficult transition from international veto player to an agenda setter' (Narlikar 2011: 1609–1612). Others are critical of the stridency in India's policy approaches. For instance, as the proportion of service sector in GDP grew from 28.5 per cent to 54 per cent by 2019, India has become an ardent advocate of liberalization in trade in services, reversing its earlier opposition to inclusion of services in trade negotiations at the WTO (Mukherjee and Malone, 2011: 318). On food security, it chose to fight a lone battle even if it meant losing the company of Brazil and other partners. India dilly-dallied before moving to a more flexible position of being part of solution by voluntarily accepting cuts on greenhouse gas emissions on the eve of the Cancun Conference in 2010 (Ramesh 2014). In a robust criticism of this *ad hoc* approach to issues, a working group recently made a pitch for India to develop the 'power as well as the capacity' to understand the 'complexity across issue areas, anticipate changes, and engage with institutional forums at which to articulate its position and proposals for reforming governance architectures' (Ghosh et al. 2011: 26).

---

[3] Panel Discussion on India and global governance held on 8 January 2014. Retrieved on 5 November 2014, from http://brookings.in/ai1ec_event/india-global-governance/? instance_id=, accessed on 5 July 2019.

India on Contending Models of Global Governance of Internet

The unique characteristics of the Internet—its openness, its global interconnectedness, its decentralized nature and the interrelationships among the layers that comprise it—have made it remarkably resistant to traditional tools of state governance (Waz and Weiser 2012: 331). Increasingly, the governmental interests regarding security and sovereignty, the commercial interests of private corporations (mainly based in the United States and Europe) as also the concerns of civil society and user groups across the world have got entangled in the ongoing debate as to how to devise suitable mechanisms to govern Internet. The chief bone of contention among various stakeholders is about the desirability to treat Internet as global commons, such as oceans and outer space, despite the fact that it is a man-made entity and is owned by private corporations and governments. Occupying the centre stage of the debate is the Internet Corporation for Assigned Names and Numbers (ICANN),[4] a California-based non-profit private enterprise (taken over by the US Federal Administration in 2016) with strong links with the US departments of defence and commerce. And there are by now familiar service provider companies, such as Google, Microsoft and Facebook.[5]

At the other end of the canvas are the IGOs, such as the International Telecommunication Union (ITU), World Intellectual Property Organization and the Organization of Economic Cooperation and Development, all of which are undergoing notable transition either in terms of redefining their international personality or in claiming a prime role in the emerging issue area. While the ITU exists since 1865,

---

[4] In an insightful analysis, Drissel (2006: 110) describes the accusations by the European and the Third World countries that ICANN was furthering American corporate and political interests, and therefore qualifies as 'the lightning rod for global controversy'.

[5] Purkayastha and Bailey (2014: 30) cite the statistics to show that Google enjoyed a global market share of over 80 per cent in May 2013 and has had a share of over 60 per cent of all global searches done since 2007, while Facebook had a global market share of 72.4 per cent in March 2013.

adjusting itself to the demands of advances in communication technologies, the ICANN was established in 1998 as a 'non-profit public benefit corporation' by the United States as a demonstration of antipathy towards the ITU to achieve global as opposed to territorial regulation of the domain name systems (Mueller, Mathiason and Klein 2007: 238–239). While appearing to privatize and internationalize key policymaking functions, the US government at the same time retained considerable authority for itself.

The issues associated with Internet governance on a global scale portray a paradox of the growing Indian power and predicament. The spread of Internet use in India is phenomenal. From 5 million users in 2000, the number has risen to 390 million in 2019, while the broadband connections are estimated to be 600 million. This makes India the third largest Internet user base, after China and the United States (Srivastava 2013). With the estimated contribution to the tune of 5 per cent of the country's GDP, India's Internet economy grew by 23 per cent, making it the second fastest among the G-20 countries. The Digital India Programme, which aimed to bridge the digital divide and empower vulnerable and remote populations, focused on enhancing Internet and mobile connectivity and access, e-governance and e-services information for all electronic manufacturing and information technology related jobs. ICT was also being used for disaster preparedness and early warning and for improving efficiency in transportation and logistics (Dasgupta 2017: 8).

Again, India is associated in different ways with the international deliberations on the issues of Internet governance.[6] India is committed to the free growth of Internet and to the vision, set out in the 2005 Tunis Agenda for multilateral, transparent and democratic Internet governance with the full involvement of governments, the private

---

[6] India's Nitin Desai, in his capacity as Under-Secretary General for Economic and Social Affairs, chaired the meeting of the Internet Governance Forum (IGF; the chief deliberative body on matters of Internet governance) in Athens in 2007 and was later designated as the UN Secretary-General's Special Adviser on Internet Governance. Subsequently Kofi Annan established a Multi-stakeholder Advisory Group under the chairmanship of Desai. Incidentally, the third IGF annual global meeting took place in Hyderabad in 2008.

sector, civil society and international organizations. An appropriate Internet governance system must be flexible, representative and able to keep pace with the ever-changing nature of the Internet and must take regional and national differences and sensitivities into consideration. It must also incorporate a mechanism to deliver justice for cybercrimes in real time without being limited by political boundaries (Jaiswal 2013: 8).

And yet, some of the positions taken by India have puzzled observers. This requires some discussion on the broader issues of policy under contestation. According to experts, a global regime to govern Internet should embody two cardinal norms, namely (a) Internet as the commons should neither be privatized, nor should it be overregulated; and (b) multi-stakeholder framework of Internet governance should be collectively legitimized and be maintained with adequate safeguards (Mueller, Mathiason and Klein 2007). Essentially there are four areas in Internet governance that are of concern: cyber security, intellectual property, content regulation and the control of critical Internet resources [domain names and Internet protocol (IP) addresses].[7]

Given its complexity, diversity and international nature, how should the Internet be governed? Some assert that a multi-stakeholder model of governance is appropriate, where all stakeholders (both public and private sectors) arrive at a consensus, through a transparent bottom-up process. Others argue that a greater role for national governments is necessary, either through increased influence through the multi-stakeholder model or under the auspices of an international body, exerting intergovernmental control.

India has actively joined developing countries in advocating the multilateral model to strengthen the role of the ITU and the UN. India prefers that the ITU be entrusted with the Internet governance too, keeping in view its long experience in the regulation of telecommunications network. While the United States has been arguing for content

---

[7] Perri 6 (2002: 149) elaborates that there exist conflict between freedom of expression and libel, privacy or obscenity, conflict between commercial freedom and universal service obligation, conflict between freedom of expression and the rights of law-enforcement authorities.

on Internet to be free from censorship by states, it wants all content that violates the intellectual property rights of US companies to be stopped and even seized from hundreds of such domains. The view of the United States and a number of those propagating an Internet independent of nation-states (or any form of multilateral control) is that the Internet should be governed by contracts amongst parties and organizations and run under a multi-stakeholder model. That is the so-called bottom-up approach to Internet governance (Purkayastha and Bailey 2014: 31). However, there are two problems with contract-based Internet governance. One is that it leads to privatization and corporatization of the Internet. The other is that contracts do not and cannot incorporate 'human rights' or 'sovereign rights'—the rights either of individuals or of nations. A bottom-up Internet governance, as distinct from developing technical standards and protocols, has no legal mechanism to enforce rights of people, corporations or sovereign rights of countries (Purkayastha and Bailey 2014: 32). The political overtones of the issue have assumed domestic significance in the wake of revelations about the motivated violations of privacy norms committed by the American intelligence agencies. The extent of illegal monitoring of mails and conversations involving not just elected officials but also rights activists in India, Brazil and Germany has exposed the huge gaps in making global Internet governance free from state control.

The global deliberations held in the recent years mirror the contestation between multi-stakeholder (signifying rejection of state regulation) and multilateral (invoking the sovereignty principle of states) approaches on the subject. The former is spearheaded, most ironically, by the United States and the latter by non-Western countries, including India, Brazil, China and Russia. In the 2005 World Summit on the Information Society (WSIS) held in Tunis, four models of Internet governance, of which three would have involved an intergovernmental body to oversee the Internet and the domain names system, were floated. At the summit, the United States and its allies have fought to keep Internet completely out of the purview of the International Telecommunication Union (ITU). Since the WSIS ultimately decided not to pursue an intergovernmental model in 2005, some nations have persisted with advocacy of intergovernmental approach. In September 2011, India, Brazil and South Africa suggested that a suitable body was urgently needed within the UN system to 'coordinate and evolve coherent and integrated global public policies pertaining to the Internet'. India followed it up with a proposal to the UNGA for the establishment of the UN Committee for Internet-Related Policies (UN-CIRP) to 'integrate and oversee the bodies responsible for technical and operational functioning of the Internet, including global standards setting' (Purkayastha and Bailey 2014).

Expectedly, the issue of creating appropriate governance mechanism for Internet came up at the World Conference on International Telecommunications (WCIT) held in Dubai in December 2012 at the initiative of the ITU to revise the International Telecommunication Regulations (ITRs). As the existing 24-year-old ITRs predated the Internet, one of the key policy questions in the WCIT was how and to what extent the updated ITRs should address Internet traffic and Internet governance. The US administration and Congress took the position that the new ITRs should continue to address only traditional international telecommunications traffic, while a multi-stakeholder model of Internet governance (such as ICANN) should continue, and that the ITU should not take any action that could extend its jurisdiction or authority over the Internet (Kruger 2016: 13). The intricate and inconclusive negotiations led to adoption (by a vote of 89–55) of a weak and non-binding resolution, which stated that 'all governments should have an equal role and responsibility for international Internet governance' while requesting them to 'elaborate on their respective positions on international Internet-related technical, development and public policy issues within the mandate of ITU at various ITU forums'. The United States walked out in protest against the resolution and declined to accept the new ITRs relating to spam and cyber security (Purkayastha and Bailey 2014: 32). The leader of the US delegation stated:

> The Internet has given the world unimaginable economic and social benefits during these past 24 years—all without UN regulation. We candidly cannot support an ITU treaty that is inconsistent with a multi-stakeholder model of Internet governance.... [T]he United States continues to believe that internet policy must be multi-stakeholder driven. Internet policy should not

be determined by member states but by citizens, communities, and broader society, and such consultation from the private sector and civil society is paramount. (quoted in Kruger 2016: 14)

Although India supported bringing Internet governance under ITRs, it refrained from supporting the revised ITRs with an observation that it needed time to consider the ramifications of the changes. At the Global Multistakeholder Meeting on the future of Internet governance, held at Sao Paulo (Brazil) in April 2014, India laid out broad outline of its views on political, technical, security, social, legal and governance issues.[8] These may be summarized in the form of 10 bullet points.

- Open access to Internet should be 'stable, secure, universal, unhindered and accessible' as it 'is crucial to global connectivity, innovation and economic development'.

- Communities must reap the benefits of the digital dividend by putting an end to the existing digital divide. To that end, a transformational shift from the Internet of today to the 'Equinet' of tomorrow would be necessary.

- Given that the core infrastructure of the Internet is not protected by any international legal regime, it is important to shape a globally acceptable legal regime to maintain the openness, security and international trust in the Internet.

- Although the management of Internet should involve all stakeholders and relevant intergovernmental and international non-governmental organizations, the policy authority for Internet-related public policy issues should rest with sovereign states.

- The 'foundational principle' of Internet governance is that it should be 'multilateral, transparent, democratic, and representative, with the participation of governments, private sector, civil society, and international organizations, in their respective roles'. In that

---

[8] The Government of India's initial submission to the Global Multi-stakeholder Meeting on the Future of Internet Governance; Sao Paulo, Brazil on 23–24 April 2014. Available at: http://www.mea.gov.in/Images/pdf/official_submission_to_the_conference.pdf, accessed on 28 February 2015.

sense, the Internet must be 'owned by the global community for mutual benefit and be rendered impervious to possible manipulation or misuse by any particular stake holder whether State or non-State'.

- Compliance with international law, and in particular the Charter of the UN, is essential for maintaining security and stability and promoting an open, secure, peaceful and accessible ICT environment. Given the pace of ICT development and the scope of the threat, states need to intensify practical cooperation through regular institutional dialogue under auspices of the UN, as well as regular dialogue through bilateral, regional and multilateral fora, and other international organizations.

- A mechanism for accountability should be put in place in respect of crimes committed in cyberspace, such that the Internet is a free and secure space for universal gain. 'New cyber jurisprudence' needs to be evolved to deal with cybercrime, without being limited by political boundaries and cyber-justice can be delivered in near real time.

- All stakeholders need to facilitate the transfer of information technology and capacity building to developing countries, in order to 'help them to take measures to improve cyber security, develop technical skill and appropriate legislation, strategies and regulatory frameworks to fulfil their responsibilities, and bridge the divide in the security of ICTs and their use'.

- The same rights that people have offline must also be protected online, in particular freedom of expression, which is applicable regardless of frontiers and through any media of one's choice in accordance with Article 19 of the UDHR and the International Covenant on Civil and Political Rights.

- The governance of the Internet should also be sensitive to the cultures and national interests of all nations. All stakeholders should work earnestly towards multi-lingualization of Internet in areas, including domain names, e-mail addresses and so on.

The political preference in these articulations was clear: primacy of state sovereignty and the need to correct digital divide should remain the definitive features of Internet governance, which needs to be managed through multilateral, participatory and transparent mechanisms that facilitate consultations among all stakeholders and develop appropriate legal framework to ensure security, freedom and accountability while at the same time helping the capacity of the disadvantaged developing countries. Many observers, especially from the Western quarters, are baffled that India, being a democratic and open society, does not support the multi-stakeholder approach to Internet governance, but tilts in favour of government-led multilateral mechanism within or outside the purview of the UN (Kaul 2014).

What is, however, notable is the lack of well thought out and consistent state policy on the issue, for the positions India has taken represent flips and flops on important occasions. At the 2012 IGF meet in Baku (Azerbaijan), the Indian communications minister indicated willingness to work with the Internet Corporation for Assigned Names and Numbers (ICANN), signalling a reversal of the earlier position of support to setting up a UN body for Internet governance. At the next year's meet in Bali, neither the ministerial level delegate attended nor did the officials present make any major statement. At the NETmundial meet at Sao Paulo in April 2014, Indian government deemed the Internet a shared resource and global commons, and looked forward to a transformation of the Internet into 'equinet' through universal access and affordable devices.[9] Upset about non-reflection of its views in the summit's final document—which put its weight behind the multi-stakeholder model 'with the full participation of governments, the private sector, civil society, the technical community, academia and the users in their respective roles and responsibilities'[10]—India joined China, Russia and Cuba to reject the outcome. While India's civil society groups do not fully share the official positions, there appears some symmetry in the view that access to the Internet and building

---

[9] Available at: http://mea.gov.in/Speeches-Statements.htm?dtl/23246/Statement+by+Mr+Vinay+Kwatra+Indian+representative+at+the+Global+Multi stakeholder+Meeting+on+the+Futu re+of+Internet+Governance+in+Sao+Paulo +April+2324+2014, accessed on 11 November 2014.

[10] Available at: http://netmundial.br/netmundial-multistakeholder-statement/, accessed on 5 July 2019.

equal opportunities for unconnected Indians must be a national and international priority. One analyst writes, India should aim to unbundle the contentious claims by making the widespread desire for 'inclusive multistakeholder participation in Internet management', a task of a more representative ITU to reconcile the interests of diverse stakeholder groups (Saran 2014).

Summing Up

Clearly, the complexities of contemporary world expose the inadequacies of the existing mechanisms and techniques to address what Kofi Annan once described as 'problems without passports'. Global governance represents the evolving and yet imperfect search to bring on board new players apart from states and IGOs from within and across countries. The multiplication of participants in the global governance has broadened the stakeholders beyond governments; it is doubtful whether the new technique is adequately suited to substitute the role of states and safeguard the interests of majority on the margins. This scenario offers both new opportunities and dilemmas to countries like India. On the one hand, it is expanding its engagement beyond traditional multilateral intergovernmental channels. On the other hand, it is facing the dilemmas of choosing between unreformed intergovernmental multilateralist and the untested multi-stakeholder pathways to govern global affairs. The issue area of Internet governance of late serves as an illustration to underline the clumsiness of India's policy responses. While seeking to play a greater role in the global Internet governance, India's minister told the ICANN Conference held at Hyderabad in 2016 (the first to be held after the US ceded its control over the corporation) that the language of the Internet cannot be English alone (Economic Times 2016). The coming years will guide course of action to shape the best possible and useful mechanism to govern Internet. The UN, though far from a perfect venue, seems best poised to oversee this transformation by negotiating an orderly transfer of power from ICANN and other organizations into a new intergovernmental multi-stakeholder treaty-based body (Drissel 2006: 118).

CHAPTER 13

Conclusion
Aligning Interests with Principles

The analyses in the preceding chapters bring out two striking features of India's 75-year-long engagement with the UN. First, the range of issue areas of interest to India is ever growing: from conventional armed conflicts to non-traditional threats to international security, nuclear disarmament, international peacekeeping, protection of human rights, action against global terror, sustainable development, climate action, regulation of digital technology and more. This has, of course, paralleled with the nature of new problems that erupted from time to time. Secondly and equally strikingly, the account of India's role in varied issue areas can be constructed on the core theme of its pronounced preference to pursue the country's vital security and economic interests while being pragmatic on a case-by-case basis in regard to adherence to basic principles of international relations. India strove to bring principles in sync with its politics at the UN all these decades. Notably, moreover, this feature is evident during the times of more or less all governments, not peculiar to a particular government. What follows is elaboration of this fundamental assessment.

I

During the first four and a half decades dominated by the systemic feature of the East–West Cold War, India's approach to the UN was essentially determined by the charismatic leadership of Jawaharlal Nehru and his familial successors. The widespread criticism that Nehru era represented emphasis on idealistic principles at the expense of the country's national interests is not entirely correct. The non-alignment policy that aimed to work for an effective role of the UN in securing international peace was driven by the need to create peaceful environment for India's economic advancement. Notably, the early trend of investing in the world body's objectivity and capability to resolve bilateral problems with Pakistan began to ebb in Nehru's times. The publicly belaboured retraction in 1957 from the unflinching commitment on conduct of internationally supervised plebiscite in Jammu and Kashmir occurred during Nehru's premiership after realizing that its strategy of aligning the international principles of high statesmanship with the national interests was not yielding expected results. The strident posture in the wake of liberation of Goa was another instance of assertion of interests over Charter principles. Similarly, India did not see any use in taking up the 1962 Chinese aggression to the UN. The much respected advocacy of the principles of non-use of force and uses of negotiations and moderation in Korea could be interpreted as India's assertion of its interests in the Asian continent. India could mobilize the Afro-Asian coalition to script the politics of anti-colonialism, anti-racism, economic development and nuclear disarmament by aligning the agenda with the UN principles. The work of Indira and Rajiv Gandhis who were dominant in the post-Nehru India's foreign policy administration till the end of 1980s too further strengthened and sharpened calibrated approach to the UN. Particularly, Indira Gandhi distinctly privileged bilateral channel for addressing issues with Pakistan or Bangladesh, while seeking to maximize use of the UN for widely shared interests involving issue areas of nuclear disarmament, Indian Ocean Peace Zone, fair terms of trade, and so on. Simultaneously, the selective use of the UN was evident in refusal after the 1971 Bangladesh war to allow recourse to the world organization by the South Asian neighbouring countries to raise bilateral problems. The hallmark of India's determination to keep security interests intact while invoking the principles of sovereign equality and non-discrimination is manifest in the fact that India resolutely refused to sign the NPT, by objecting tirelessly that the Treaty does not require time-bound obligations from the existing nuclear weapon powers to eliminate their nuclear arsenals while prohibiting others from acquiring such weapons.

The sudden end to the Cold War denied India the advantages it had previously. The emergence of the US-led unipolar world in the beginning of the 1990s heightened the dilemmas for India to be more pragmatic on war and peace questions. The 1990s also represented frequent domestic political realignments along with bold abandonment of licence-raj economic policies to come out of the most severe foreign exchange crisis. A politically and economically weak India acquiesced with the UNSC actions against a defeated Iraq in 1991, although they clearly violated the sovereignty principle, with a meek hope that it would not be a precedent. Similarly, India went along with UNGA's recommendation in favour of market-friendly economic policies to member states. The 1990s also witnessed India coming under pressure on account of Pakistan's attempts to internationalize the Jammu and Kashmir issue in the human rights bodies and the 1998 nuclear weapon tests. India's counter-terror strategy to blame Pakistan for cross-border terror did not receive sufficient support from the Western countries. However, what is remarkable is India's readiness to stand out in order to protect its vital security interests when required. India stoutly opposed (but without success) the indefinite extension of the NPT in 1995 and single-handedly blocked the CTBT—by citing the failure of those measures to meet the principles of equality and universality.

II

Whereas the last decade of the 20th century brought mixed experiences of pragmatism and persistence, India seemed to have bettered its political participation in the new century mainly because of its impressive economic performance and strides in space, missile and information technologies. On the one hand, Indian representatives preferred nationally owned peace process to end conflicts in Afghanistan and Syria. A touch of conservatism is evident in its singling out the actions of non-state actors (who unlike state actors remain outside the rubric of international norms) as a major menace to international security, threatening lives of innocent civilian population. And in the case of Afghanistan, India's concerns were underpinned by the serious security implications of the continuing conflict abetted by Pakistan's interference and support to Taliban and to the terror entities such as Al-Qaida. In response to an alarming rate of intrastate conflicts in Africa and elsewhere, India evinced interest in the reinvigorated peacekeeping by the UN and readily agreed to send fully formed military and police units to difficult missions, such as Democratic Republic of Congo and South Sudan. Interestingly, in a perfect intermix of interests with principles, India with nuclear weapons continued to commit itself for the cause of total and non-discriminatory nuclear disarmament. In another important feature of new India at the UN in the first two decades of the 21st century is the effort made to present the country as a mature and responsible power in addressing global problems—whether climate change, addressing the effects of globalization, protectionism in global trade or dip in development finance. The UN has long served the aims of India's development-centred economic diplomacy. Through the UN, India has pursued its central goals of framing an inclusive and equitable global economic agenda and creating consensus on specific action programmes. This is exemplified by India's sustained focus on the dwindling levels of development finance and its pursuit of human development goals to bring the benefits of globalization to all the people and nations. Various poverty alleviation programmes launched in the new century helped the country to showcase them for adoption by other countries. India was more satisfied with the post-2015 SDGs than the MDGs, because the latter were guided by technocratic solutions rather than intergovernmental agreement. In essence the post-2015 development agenda should be transformational rather than transactional in nature. Guided by this approach, India served as a member of the Open Working Group that finally framed SDGs comprising a set of 17 goals spread across social, economic, environmental dimensions of sustainable development with poverty eradication as a central goal. India has resorted to a mix of intricate tactics in order to extract from the advanced countries' desired contributions for the improvement of economies of poor countries. Besides, India's financial contributions to UN regular budget and voluntary contributions to various development and humanitarian agencies have appreciably gone up. Clearly, India emerges as a responsible economic power for sharing its financial resources for development and humanitarian work through the UN channels, while at the same time pursuing particularistic interests through smaller elite groups, such as BRICS (Brazil, Russia, India, China and South Africa) on multilateral economic issues. Of course, by being part of such powerful issue-based coalitions, India worked, in the eye of Western critics, more as a spoiler in global negotiations.

As an open society with flourishing democracy and constitutionally guaranteed civil, political, social and cultural rights, India's interest in international human rights standards is natural and its track record is critically watched. From a fleeting phase wherein India worked for an international mechanism to make human rights justiceable, India has quickly become statist in its discourse, especially since the 1960s. Since then India has consistently demonstrated a good deal of risk aversion by emphasizing the principles of non-interference by external agencies and interstate cooperation as the principal pillars of international human rights regime. In essence, it is these concerns that prompted India to express strong reservations on the question of humanitarian intervention and its successor concept, the RtoP. India's considered view was that the coercive nature of the new concept would imply military humanism and was most likely to be misused. On the positive side, India has been elected to the newly established Human Rights Council with big margins, reflecting a certain degree of standing the country enjoyed in the eye of other member countries. Critical comments made in the three UPR cycles relate to the issue of death penalty, status of vulnerable population, such as minorities, women and children, and in recent years the proposal for national register of citizens. There have been always divergent views within India on the country's human rights approach in the UN. A section holds the view that the record was tantamount to failure of diplomacy characterized by lack of adequate preparedness and evasive replies in Geneva. According to analysts, India's overall record was less forthcoming than Brazil but somewhat better than South Africa. Nonetheless, in the universal periodic reviews of particularly Asian countries, India is seen as a perennial fence-sitter and standing to oppose resolutions against specific countries. The contrarian school opines that India did not have to pay much attention to the criticism by foreign countries in the Human Rights Council; instead, it should demonstrate confidence in its capability to come up with its own solutions to the problems.

On a related, but very critical to India's development and human rights projects is the global governance of Internet. India's sovereignty-centric conservative positions on subjects, such as human rights, agriculture trade, climate change and nuclear test ban have attracted labels, such as the spoiler to the scheme of global governance. After one or two flip-flops, India has stuck to state-centric multilateral form of governance within the UN framework, rather than the countervailing model of multi-stakeholderism that dilutes the role of the UN and recognizes the role of private players and civil society. The political preference in these articulations was clear: primacy of state sovereignty and the need to correct digital divide should remain the definitive features of Internet governance while helping the capacity of the disadvantaged developing countries.

On the question of UN reforms, India's perspectives were both critical and constructive; it sought to test various proposals on the basis if they strengthened the functional autonomy and capacity of the UN. India took active interest in the efforts aimed at revitalization of the work of the General Assembly which, it was hoped, could trigger improvements in the other organs of the system. The intergovernmental character of the Assembly is so sacrosanct to India that it criticized the recommendations of the Eminent Persons Panel Report on Civil Society–United Nations Relations. India opposed opening up of the General Assembly deliberations to accredited non-governmental organizations, on the ground that civil society and NGOs lack the quality of democratic transparency and accountability. Surely India here is trying to safeguard its sovereign political and security interests by questioning the credentials of new players on the scene. As regards the Secretariat, India contended that only about 40 per cent of posts at the senior and policymaking levels were occupied by staff from developing countries, even though developing countries constituted the overwhelming majority of the organization's membership. Therefore, the urgent need to rationalize the selection process, especially as the mathematical formula for calculating desirable ranges of representation gave undue weight to the budget.

III

The political exercise in aligning principles and pragmatism is very much evident in India's experiences vis-à-vis UN peacekeeping activities. By and large, India held that the traditional principles of consent, non-use of force and non-interference in internal affairs should continue to be adhered to. In fact, India strongly held the view that the setbacks the UN peacekeeping received in Somalia, former Yugoslavia or elsewhere were due to deviation from those time-tested principles. India expressed unhappiness that in most instances the mandates were too ambiguously framed without wider consultations and without ensuring that the missions are afforded commensurate resources. The discussion on India's experiences in UN peacekeeping also brings out different phases, particularly the reasons for India's high-profile association in the past 30 years, that is, in the post-Cold War era. As the AU representative put it once in the Security Council thematic debate in 2011, India has become an 'exemplary reference point' in the area of peacekeeping. The principle of commitment to international peace and security was certainly one of the factors, but India was guided by policy considerations whether receiving country wanted its participation, existence of friendly relations with it, or if restoration of peace and stability in the troubled area helped the broader objectives of the country's foreign policy. A seasoned analyst sums up Indian approach as 'soft' peacekeeping, which stands in contrast to 'pull the trigger' approach. From a different perspective, India had viewed that its peacekeeping activism would fetch future political dividends, such as strengthening its claim for permanent seat in an enlarged Security Council or opening up of opportunities for economic linkages and investments in the countries of deployment. As a major contributor of military and police personnel, however, India complained about lack of timely consultations with the troop-contributing countries when mandates of missions are framed or modified.

As far as episodes of India–Pakistan armed conflict are concerned, the success of the UN in the initial years was limited only to inserting a ceasefire observer mission along the LoC (Ceasefire Line prior to 1971 war) in Jammu and Kashmir. Neither the attempts to mediate nor plans to hold a plebiscite in order to end the Kashmir dispute yielded results. While on the one hand, India–Pakistan armed conflicts represent a test case for the UN ability to resolve interstate territorial disputes, a discerning observer would also find a steady shift in India's outlook to the UN as a useful instrument to address its security needs and interests. From the stage of unrealistic hopes of a quick help from the UN, India steadily shifted to a stance of minimizing and then rejecting any third party role by the UN. Accordingly, India has been insisting that India–Pakistan dispute would be resolved peacefully through bilateral channels, not through the UN, although Pakistan seeks international involvement. Also, India demanded unsuccessfully that the UN observer mission to report LoC ceasefire violations should be taken off the field as the ground situation changed after the 1971 war. To buttress its long held position that legally Kashmir is its inalienable part, India rescinded the special status of Jammu and Kashmir under the Constitution in August 2019, partly conscious of the possible negative reception in some of the international circles.

This, however, does not constrain India from inviting the international community's attention against the terror attacks from outfits enjoying support of Pakistan to launch attacks in and outside Jammu and Kashmir. Though it took time to get required political reception, India's claim that the fight against terrorism was not India's alone, but it affected the core values of the international community effectively turned tables against Pakistan after 2001. India is among the earliest countries to portray terrorism as a serious threat to international peace and security and the imperative of acting against it unitedly. India's efforts to secure support in the UN to delegitimize Pakistan-based terror networks received only lukewarm response from the West until the September 2001 attacks by Al-Qaida against the United States. India unreservedly supported the strong measures the Security Council took to suppressterrorism by criminalizing sheltering, financing or armed support to terrorists. India took keen interest in work of the CTC and the 1267 Taliban/Al-Qaida Sanctions Committee, instituted by the Security Council. Very significantly, India brought about two notable shifts in its traditional positions. First, by unequivocally rejecting any distinction between terrorists and freedom fighters, India has moved away from its position in the 1970s to support armed struggles for liberation and self-determination. Equally notable is the demand India makes in favour of effective coercive measures against non-state actors indulging in terrorism, signifying adjustment of its traditionally cautious stand on rushing with sanctions against states. It is in this context that India's perseverant efforts to successfully get Masood Azhar, the chief of Pakistan-based Jaish-e-Mohammed (accused of masterminding major terror attacks against India) added to the UN Consolidated List for enforcing freezing of bank accounts in Pakistan in 2019 after China ended its opposition need to be applauded. While joining consensus on the 2006 GCTS, India described terrorists as real threat to human rights, as they unlike state actors are not bound by norms of international humanitarian and human rights laws. In a move to strengthen the normative framework for concerted action against terrorism, India proposed in 1996 a comprehensive convention, described as 'capstone of the structure of conventions' against terrorism, but it hit a roadblock owing to unreconciled differences on definition of a terrorist and scope of the convention's application.

IV

India clearly valued its experience as elected member of important organs, such as the Security Council. As a non-permanent member in the Council, India had served seven two-year terms during the period 1950–2012 during which distinct trends emerged in its participation in the deliberations and voting behaviour. During those years, major armed conflicts erupted in Korea, West Asia, central Europe, Africa and elsewhere. In their wake, India's stress on respect for sovereignty and advocacy of amicable, peaceful negotiations instead of use of force for resolving conflicts have been a constant feature. It highlighted the need to address problems faced by developing countries while complying with economic sanctions under Chapter VII. Also, India sought to forge unity among non-permanent members and supported consensus decisions in the Council.

India's contribution at the Security Council mirrors the larger picture of India's role at the UN, especially the General Assembly, encompassing a good mix of maturity, flexibility, moderation, pragmatism and propriety. The discretion in participation in meetings evidently varied from a low of 17–19 per cent in three years to a high of 47–49 per cent in four years in the UNSC. As a reflection of its maturity and propriety, India not merely abstained in the vote on the resolutions adopted on the question of Jammu and Kashmir dispute, but also ceded its turn to preside over the Council meetings in March 1951, because the Kashmir question came up for discussion. Moderation was manifest in the total absence of a negative vote, while abstentions remained few and far between. It is a little known fact that India never cast its negative vote on any text so far. Only rarely India abstained on a resolution—in all 14 times in a span of 14 years as elected member in the Council. The characteristics of flexibility and pragmatism were evident in plenty in terms of the willingness to work with others in helping the process of drafting or refining texts that had the potential of obtaining widest possible support. In any case, India let on numerous occasions its words of caution or reservations go on record without ambiguity or rancour. Again with a few deviations—warranted or otherwise—India espoused and applied the core principles of respect for sovereignty and territorial integrity, non-use of force and peaceful resolution of disputes as a preferred path. This experience would be a pointer to India's role in the Security Council as a permanent member in future, if and when it happens.

As part of the campaign for enlargement of the membership of the Security Council, India made vigorous efforts to buttress its candidature for a permanent seat, by suggesting that countries from the under- or unrepresented geographical regions should find a place based on the size of population, economic potential and contribution to international peace and security, by which India's claim could become self-evident. India is convinced that only enlargement in the existing categories would make the Council both legitimate and effective. Having formally staked claim for a permanent seat in 1994, India joined other aspirants to form 'Group of 4' (G-4), aligned with the African Union countries' demand for two permanent seats for that region and mobilized support from small developing countries. It was encouraged by the initiation of intergovernmental negotiations on the subject, but is dismayed by the disarray in the deliberations so far. Aside from the manipulations by the key permanent members, the stalemate is caused by lack of unity among the developing countries and opposition from countries of the Uniting for Consensus (Ufc) group for adding new permanent members. Most of these countries have apprehensions about the geopolitical impact on respective regions if the claimants succeed in becoming permanent members. Keeping their interests in mind, the UfC group has proposed having additional elected seats for terms longer than the existing non-permanent members without veto power. The question may remain in limbo for foreseeable future unless the United States and/or China realize India's usefulness to them in the management of global order, or India concedes the position of the UfC group in favour of creating a new category of elected members with renewable longer terms and without veto power. And both these options would privilege pragmatism, setting aside the principled preference for equal status between new and existing permanent members.

As indicated in the Introduction to the book, the liberal and constructivist theoretical perspectives do emerge as useful lenses to explain India's role at the UN. For instance, in relation to issue areas of international peacekeeping, development diplomacy and counterterrorism, constructivist paradigm establishes India's identity and interests being shaped in a continual fashion as a matured, responsible state actor. It explains that in the case of countering terrorism, India clearly played a key role in securing stigmatization of all kinds of terrorism, besides shifting from its previous position to distinguish between freedom fighters and terrorists. Likewise, in respect of economic development issues, India's role is successful in keeping collective focus on development imperatives of less and least developed (including small island countries) in the changing political ideological climate and at the same time, it acquired a new identity on the basis of growing economic profile. The liberal lens is applicable to understand India's attempts to use UN mechanisms in respect of international peacekeeping or even human rights performance to serve its specified interests.

In conclusion, India's policy and politics at the UN in the past 75 years signify an attempt not to view principles and interests in mutually exclusive terms, but to persistently better align principles to suit issue-related interests at a given moment with varying measure of success. Admittedly, India's effort may not be exceptional, but the country's experiences in this practice of parliamentary diplomacy may hold a few useful lessons to other countries as well.

Bibliography

Abbasi, Shahid K. 2017. Statement in the General Assembly, 72nd Regular Session, Plenary Verbatim Record of 14th Meeting, 21 September. Doc. A/72/PV.14.
Adiseshiah, Malcolm, ed. 1987. *Forty Years of Economic Development: UN Agencies and India*. New Delhi: Lancer International for India International Centre.
Aditya Vidyasagar, S. V. and Siddharth Tatiya. 2010. 'European Court of Human Rights and India: A Study Contrasting Approaches to Human Rights Issues'. *Asia-Pacific Journal of Human Rights and the Law*, 11(2): 31–51.
Advani, L. K. 2012. Statement at the Disarmament and International Security Committee of the General Assembly, 67th Regular Session, Plenary Record of 5th Meeting, 11 October. Doc. A/C.1/67/SR.5.
African Union. 2011. Statement at the Security Council, 66th Year, Provisional Verbatim Record of 6603rd Meeting Resumption 1, 26 August. Doc. S/PV.6603, Resumption 1.
Ahamed, Edappakath. 2008. Statement in the Security Council, 63rd Year, Provisional Verbatim Record of 6034th Meeting, 9 December. S/PV.6034.
Ahmed, Abrar. 1991. Statement at the General Assembly, 46th Regular Session, Economic and Financial Committee, Summary Record of 20th Meeting, 24 October. Doc. A/C.2/46/SR.20.
Akbaruddin, Syed. 2016a. Statement at the Security Council, 71st Year, Provisional Verbatim Record of 7606th Meeting, 19 January. Doc. S/PV.7606.
———. 2016b. Statement at the Security Council, 71st Year, Provisional Verbatim Record of 7658th Meeting, 28 March. Doc. S/PV.7658.
———. 2016c. Statement in the Security Council, 71st Year, Provisional Verbatim Record of 7670th Meeting, 14 April. Doc. S/PV.7670.
———. 2016d. Statement in the Security Council, 71st Year, Provisional Verbatim Record of 7690th Meeting, 11 May. Doc. S/PV.7690.
———. 2017. Statement in the General Assembly, 71st Regular Session, Plenary Verbatim Record of 93rd Meeting, Doc. A/71/PV.93, 28 July.
———. 2018a. Statement at the General Assembly, 72nd Regular Session, Plenary Verbatim Record of 99th Meeting, 25 June. Doc. A/72/PV.99.
———. 2018b. Statement at the Security Council, 73rd Year, Provisional Verbatim Record of 8407th Meeting, 20 November. Doc. S/PV.8407.

———. 2019a. Statement at the Informal Meeting of the General Assembly Plenary on Intergovernmental Negotiations on Security Council Reform, 29 January. Available at: https://www.pminewyork.gov.in/pdf/uploadpdf/statements__1790410061.pdf, accessed on 1 October 2019.
———. 2019b. Statement at the Informal Meeting at the General Assembly Plenary on Intergovernmental Negotiations on Security Council Reform, 25 February. Available at: https://www.pminewyork.gov.in/pdf/uploadpdf/statements__423385771.pdf, accessed on 1 October 2019.
———. 2019c. Statement on behalf of G4 at the Informal Meeting of the General Assembly on Intergovernmental Negotiations on Security Council Reform, 1 May. Available at: https://www.pminewyork.gov.in/pdf/uploadpdf/statements__907111598.pdf, accessed on 30 September 2019.
———. 2019d. Statement at the Security Council, 74th Year, Provisional Verbatim Record of 8612nd Meeting, 9 September. Doc. S/PV.8612.
Annan, Kofi. 2005. 'In Larger Freedom: Towards Security, Development and Human Rights for All'. Report of the Secretary General, 21 March. Doc. A/59/2005.
Aravind, Indulekha. 2017. 'So What Is India's Human Rights Record Really Like?', *ET Bureau*, 14 May. Available at: https://economictimes.indiatimes.com/news/politics-and-nation/so-what-is-indias-human-rights-record-really-like/articleshow/58662843.cms., accessed on 30 September 2019.
Arya, Vimarsh. 2019. Right of Reply Delivered under Agenda Item 2 at the 42nd Session of the Human Rights Council, 10 September. Available at: https://www.pmindiaun.gov.in/pages.php?id=2009, accessed on 16 September 2019.
Ausderan, Jacob. 2014. 'How Naming and Shaming Affects Human Rights Perceptions in the Shamed Country'. *Journal of Peace Research*, 51(1): 81–95.
Aziz, Sartaj. 1999. Statement at the General Assembly, 54th Regular Session, Plenary Verbatim Record of 9th Meeting, 22 September. Doc. A/54/PV. 9.
Bailey, Sydney and Sam Daws. 1998. *The Procedure of the UN Security Council*, 3rd ed. Oxford, Oxford University Press.
Bailey, Sydney. 1982. *How Wars End: The United Nations and Termination of Armed Conflicts*, Vol. 2. Oxford: Clarendon Press.
Bandyopadhyaya, Jayantanuja. 1980. *The Making of India's Foreign Policy: Determinants, Institutions, Processes and Personalities*. New Delhi: Allied Publishers.
Banerjee, Sanjoy. 2015. 'Human Rights Diplomacy and Performance of India since 2000'. In *Shifting Power and Human Rights Diplomacy – India*, edited by Doutje Lettinga and Lars van Troost, 27–33. Amsterdam: Amnesty International Netherlands.
Basu, Anil. 2006. Statement at the General Assembly Special Political Committee, 61st Regular Session, Summary Record of 15th Meeting, 23 October. Doc. A/C.4/61/SR.15.

Beg, Mehboob. 2010. Statement at the Budgetary and Administrative Committee of the General Assembly, 65th Regular Session, Summary Record of 9th Meeting, 7 December. Doc. A/C.5/65/SR.9.

Berdal, Mats. 1993. *Whither UN Peacekeeping?* (Adelphi Paper No.281). London: International Institute for Strategic Studies.

Berkes, Ross N. and Mohinder S. Bedi. 1958. *Diplomacy of India: Indian Foreign Policy in the United Nations*. Stanford: Stanford University Press.

Bhagat, Bali Ram. 1986. Statement in the Security Council, 41st Year, Provisional Verbatim Record of 2683rd Meeting, 24 April. Doc. S/PV.2683, 24 April.

Bhagavan, Manu. 2010. 'A New Hope: India, the United Nations and the Making of UDHR', *Modern Asian Studies*, 44(2): 311–348.

———. 2013. *The Peacemakers: India and the Quest for One World*. New Delhi: HarperCollins Publishers India.

Bhardwaj, Deeksha. 2018. 'String of UN red flags about human rights violations: Is India's Global diplomatic Clout fading?' *The Print*, 5 June. Available at: file:///C:/Users/DELL/Desktop/String%20of%20UN%20red%20flags%20about%20human%20rights%20violations%20-%20Is%20India's%20global%20diplomatic%20clout%20fading_.html, accessed on 1 October 2019.

Bhutto, Benazir. 1995. Address to the General Assembly, 50th Regular Session, Plenary Verbatim Record of 39th Meeting, 24 October. Doc. A/5 0/PV.39.

Bishnoi, Bhagwant. 2001. Statement on Agenda Item 99: Operational Activities for Development, October 25. Available at: https://www.pminewyork.org/adminpart/uploadpdf/1882735.pdf, accessed on 12 March 2012.

———. 2015. Statement at the Security Council, 70th Year, Provisional Verbatim Record of 7505th Meeting, 18 August. Doc. S/PV.7505.

Bose, Krishna. 2000. Statement at the Security Council, 55th Year, Provisional Verbatim Record of 4208th Meeting (Resumption 1), 24 October. Doc. S/PV. 4208 (Resumption 1).

Boulden, Jane and Thomas G. Weiss, eds. 2004. *Terrorism and the United Nations: Before and After September 11*. Bloomington, IN: Indiana University Press.

Boutros-Ghali, Boutros. 1992. *An Agenda for Peace: Preventive Diplomacy, Peacemaking and Peacekeeping*, New York, United Nations.

———. 1994. *An Agenda for Development (Report of the Secretary General)*, 11 November. Doc. A/49/665.

———. 1995. *An Agenda for Peace: Preventive Diplomacy, Peacemaking and Peacekeeping*, 2nd ed. New York: United Nations.

Brecher, Michael. 1953. 'Kashmir: A Case Study in the United Nations'. *Pacific Affairs*, 26(1): 195–207.

———. 1968. *India and World Politics: Krishna Menon's View of the World*. London: Oxford University Press.

Brines, Russell. 1968. *The India–Pakistan Conflict*. London: Pall Mall.

Bullion, Alan. 1997. 'India and United Nations Peacekeeping Operations'. *International Peacekeeping*, 4(1): 98–114.
———. 2001. 'India in Sierra Leone: A Case of Muscular Peacekeeping'. *International Peacekeeping*, 8(4): 77–91.
Canada. 2005. Statement at the General Assembly, 59th Regular Session, Plenary Verbatim Record of 115th Meeting, 26 July. Doc. A/59/PV.115.
Chandra, Satish and Aravind Gupta. 2014. 'India–Pakistan Human Rights Imbroglio at Geneva'. *Strategic Analysis*, 38(4): 528–547.
Chandumajra, Prem Singh. 1998. Statement at the General Assembly, Legal Affairs Committee, 53rd Regular Session, Summary Record of 11th Meeting, 22 October. Doc. A/C.6/53/SR.11.
Chaturvedi, S. C. 1997. Statement at the General Assembly Special Political Committee, 52nd Regular Sesssion, Summary Record of 14th Meeting, 10 November. Doc. A/C.4/52/SR.14.
Chaturvedi, Suresh. India, 1994. Statement at the General Assembly, 49th Regular Session, Plenary Verbatim Record of 29th Meeting, 13 October. Doc. A/49/PV.29.
Chidambaram, P. 2007. Statement at the High-level Event on Climate Change convened by the Secretary General: 'The Future in Our Hands: Addressing the Leadership Challenge of Climate Change' at the Thematic Plenary on 'The Challenge of Adaptation – From Vulnerability to Resilience', September 24. Available at: https://www.pminewyork.org/adminpart/uploadpdf/31242ind1341.pdf, accessed on 12 March 2017.
Chimni, B. S. 2003. 'Status of Refugees in India: Strategic Ambiguity'. In *Refugees and the State: Practice of Asylum and Care in India*, edited by Ranbir Samaddar, 443–471. New Delhi: SAGE Publications.
———. 2010. 'Mapping Indian Foreign Economic Policy'. *International Studies*, 47(2–4): 163–185.
Choedon, Yeshi. 2007. 'India and the Current Concerns of UN Peacekeeping: Issues and Prospects'. *India Quarterly*, 63(2): 150–184.
———. 2014. 'India's UN Peacekeeping Operations Involvement in Africa: Change in Nature of Participation and Driving Factors'. *International Studies*, 51(1–4): 16–34.
Choudhry, Shruti. 2013a. Statement at the Economic and Financial Committee of the General Assembly, 68th Regular Session, Summary Record of 18th Meeting, 3 December. Doc. A/C.2/68/SR.18.
———. 2013b. Statement at the Economic and Financial Committee of the General Assembly, 68th Regular Session, Summary Record of 20th Meeting, 17 December. Doc. A/C.2/68/SR.20
Chowdhury, B. G. 2012. Statement at the Economic and Financial Committee of the General Assembly, 67th Regular Session, Summary Record of 19th Meeting, 24 December. Doc. A/C.2/67/SR.19.
Commission on Global Governance. 1995. *Our Global Neighbourhood*. Oxford: Oxford University Press.

Dasgupta, Swapan. 2017. Statement at the Economic and Financial Committee of the General Assembly, 72nd Regular Session, Summary Record of 15th Meeting, 14 December. Doc. A/C.2/72/SR.15.

Dayal, Rajeshwar. 1976. *Mission for Hammarskjold: The Congo Crisis*. Delhi: Oxford University Press.

de Cuellar, Javier Perez. 1990. Report of the Secretary General on the Work of the Organization. New York, United Nations. Doc. A/45/1 (Supplement).

Deora, M. S. and R. Grover. 1991. *Documents on Kashmir Problem*, Vol. 1. New Delhi: Discovery Publishing House.

deReuck, Anthony. 1984. 'The Logic of Conflict: Its Origin, Development and Resolution'. In *Conflict in World Society: A New Perspective on International Relations*, edited by Michael Banks, 96–111. London: Harvester Press.

Devi. Ms. 1998. Statement at the Social, Humanitarian and Cultural Committee of the General Assembly, 53rd Regular Session, Summary Record of 26th Meeting, 27 October. Doc. A/C.3/53/SR.26.

Dingwerth, K., and P. Pattberg, 2009. 'Actors, Arenas, and Issues in Global Governance'. In *Global Governance*, edited by Jim Whitman. Basingstoke: Palgrave Macmillan.

Dixon, Owen. 1950. Report of the United Nations Representative on India and Pakistan, 15 September. Doc. S/1791.

Drissel, D. 2006. 'Internet governance in a Multipolar World: Challenging American Hegemony'. *Cambridge Review of International Affairs*, 19(1): 105–120.

Dubey, Muchkund. 2014. 'The Historic Importance of G-77'. *UN Chronicle*, 51(1): 23–26.

Duchatel, Mathieu. 2016. 'Terror Overseas: Understanding China's Evolving Counter Terror Strategy'. *Policy Brief*, October. London: European Council on Foreign Relations.

Economic Times. 2016. 'India Key Player in Internet Governance, Enabling Localization of Internet Is Essential: RS Prasad at ICANN57', 5 November. Available at: https://economictimes.indiatimes.com/tech/internet/india-key-player-in-internet-governance-enabling-localisation-of-internet-essential-rs-prasad-at-icann57/articleshow/55259738.cms?from=mdr, accessed on 18 September 2019.

———. 2019. "UN designates Jaish-e-Mohammed chief Masood Azhar as global terrorist", May 2. Available at: https://economictimes.indiatimes.com/news/international/world-news/masood-azhar-listed-as-global-terrorist-after-china-lifts-restrictions/articleshow/69131579.cms?from=mdr, accessed on 18 September 2019.

Faleiro, Eduardo. 1992. Statement at the General Assembly, 47th Regular Session, Plenary Verbatim Record of 13th Meeting, 25 September. Doc. A/ 47/PV.13.

Falk, R. 1995. *On Humane Governance: Towards a New Global Politics*. University Park, PA: Pennsylvania State University Press.

Ferdinand, Peter. 2014. 'Rising powers at the UN: An analysis of voting behavior of BRICS in the General Assembly'. *Third World Quarterly*, 35(3): 376–391.
Finkelstein, L. 1995. 'What Is Global Governance?' *Global Governance*, 1(3): 367–372.
———. 2009. 'Global Governance as Liberal Hegemony'. In *Global Governance*, edited by Jim Whitman, 105–122. Basingstoke: Palgrave Macmillan.
Gambhir, Eenam. 2016. Statement at the Disarmament and International Security Committee of the General Assembly, 71st Regular Session, Plenary Record of 24th Meeting, 31 October. A/C.1/71/PV.24.
———. 2017. Statement in the General Assembly, 72nd Regular Session, Plenary Verbatim Record of 14th Meeting, 21 September. Doc. A/72/PV.14.
Gandhi, Rajiv. 1985. Address to the UN General Assembly, 40th Regular Session, Plenary Verbatim Record 48th Meeting, 24 October. Doc.A/40/PV.48.
———. 1987. Address to the UN General Assembly, 42nd Regular Session, Plenary Verbatim Record of 41st Meeting, 20 October. Doc.A/42/PV.41.
———. 1988. Address to the 15th Special Session of the General Assembly, Plenary Verbatim Record of 14th Meeting, 15 June. Doc. A/S-15/PV.14.
Ganguly, Meenakshi. 2013. 'Can India Be an International Human Rights Leader?' *Open Global Rights*, 23 June. Available at: https://www.hrw.org/news/2013/06/21/can-india-be-international-human-rights-leader, accessed 5 February 2019.
Ganguly, Sumit. 2002. *Conflict Unending: India–Pakistan Tensions since 1947*. New Delhi: Oxford University Press.
GAOR. 1971. General Assembly 26th Regular Session, Resolution 2793 (XXVI), adopted at the 2003rd Plenary Meeting, 7 December. Doc. A/2973 (XXVI).
———. 1989. General Assembly, 44th Regular Session, Resolution 44/21 adopted at the 56th Plenary Meeting, 15 November. Doc. A/RES/44/21.
———. 1991a. General Assembly, 46th Regular Session, Resolution 46/86 adopted at the 74th Plenary Meeting, 16 December. Doc. A/RES/46/86.
———. 1991b. General Assembly, 46th Regular Session, Resolution 46/166 on 'Entrepreneurship', adopted at the 78th Plenary Meeting, 19 December. Doc. A/RES/46/166.
———. 1994. General Assembly, 49th Regular Session, Declaration on Measures to Eliminate International Terrorism, Resolution 49/60 adopted at the 84th Plenary Meeting, 9 December. Doc. A/RES/49/60.
———. 1995. General Assembly. 50th Regular Session. Resolution 50/65 adopted at the 90th Plenary Meeting, 12 December 1995. Doc. A/RES/50/65.
———. 1996. General Assembly, 51st Regular Session, Legal Committee. Draft international convention on the suppression of terrorism, annexed to the letter from the Permanent Representative of India to the Secretary General, 1 November. Doc. A/C.6/51/6.
———. 1998. General Assembly, 53rd Regular Session. Resolution 53/30 on the Question of equal representation on and increase in the membership of the Security Council and related matters, adopted at 66th Plenary Meeting, 23 November. Doc. A/RES/53/30.

———. 2000. General Assembly, 55th Regular Session, Legal Committee, Draft Comprehensive Convention on International Terrorism: Working document submitted by India, 28 August. Doc. A/C.6/55/1.

———. 2003. General Assembly, 58th Regular Session, Social, Humanitarian and Cultural Committee, Summary Record of 60th Meeting, 28 November. Doc. A/C.3/58/SR.60.

———. 2004a. General Assembly, 55th Regular Session. 'We the peoples: civil society, the United Nations and global governance' (Report of the Panel of Eminent Persons on United Nations-Civil Society Relations), annexed to the Note of the Secretary-General, 11 June. Doc. A/58/817.

———. 2004b. General Assembly, 59th Regular Session, A more secure world: our shared responsibility (Report of the High-level Panel on Threats, Challenges and Change), annexed to the Note by the Secretary-General, 2 December. Doc. A/59/565.

———. 2006a. General Assembly, 60th Regular Session, Plenary Verbatim Record of 72nd Meeting, 15 March. Doc. A/60/PV.72.

———. 2006b. General Assembly, 60th Regular Session. Global Counter Terrorism Strategy: Resolution 60/288 adopted at 99th Plenary Meeting, 8 September. Doc. A/RES/60/288.

———. 2006c. General Assembly, 61st Regular Session, Composition of the Secretariat, Report of the Secretary-General, 15 August. Doc. A/61/257.

———. 2014. General Assembly, 69th Session, Resolution on International Day of Yoga, adopted at 69th Plenary Meeting,11 December. Doc. A/RES/69/131.

———. 2015. General Assembly, 70th Regular Session, Resolution on 'Transforming our world: the 2030 Agenda for Sustainable Development', adopted at 4th Plenary Meeting, 25 September. Doc. A/RES/70/1.

———. 2019. General Assembly, 74th Regular Session, Financial Situation of the United Nations, Report of the Secretary-General, 14 October. Doc. A/74/501.

Gharekhan, Chinmaya, 1991a. Statement at the Security Council, 46th Year, Provisional Verbatim Record of 2977th Meeting (Part II, Closed, Resumption 1), 15 February, Doc. S/PV.2977 (Part II, Closed, Resumption 1).

———. 1991b. Statement at the Security Council, 46th Year, Provisional Verbatim Record of 2977th Meeting (Part II, Closed, Resumption 3), 23 February. Doc. S/PV.2977 (Part II, Closed, Resumption 3).

———. 1991c. Statement at the Security Council, 46th Year, Provisional Verbatim Record of 2978th Meeting, 3 March. Doc. S/PV.2978.

———. 1991d. Statement at the Security Council, 46th Year, Provisional Verbatim Record of 2981st Meeting, 3 April. Doc. S/PV.2981.

———. 1991e. Statement at the Security Council, 46th Year, Provisional Verbatim Record of 2982nd Meeting, 5 April. Doc. S/PV.2982.

———. 1992a. Statement at the Security Council, 47th Year, Provisional Verbatim Record of 3033rd Meeting, 21 January, Doc. S/PV.3033.

———. 1992b. Statement at the Security Council, 47th Year, Provisional Verbatim Record of 3059th Meeting, 11 March, Doc. S/PV.3059.
———. 1992c. Statement at the Security Council, 47th Year, Provisional Verbatim Record of 3060th Meeting, 17 March, Doc. S/PV.3060.
———. 1992d. Statement at the Security Council, 47th Year, Provisional Verbatim Record of 3063rd Meeting, 31 March, Doc. S/PV.3063.
———. 1992e. Statement at the Security Council, 47th Year, Provisional Verbatim Record of 3082nd Meeting, 30 May, Doc. S/PV.3082.
———. 1992f. Statement at the Security Council, 47th Year, Provisional Verbatim Record of 3106th Meeting, 13 August, Doc. S/PV.3106.
———. 1992g. Statement at the Security Council, 47th Year, Provisional Verbatim Record of 3116th Meeting, 19 September, Doc. S/PV.3116.
———. 1992h. Statement at the Security Council, 47th Year, Provisional Verbatim Record of 3122nd Meeting, 9 October, Doc. S/PV.3122.
———. 1992i. Statement at the Security Council, 47th Year, Provisional Verbatim Record of 3137th Meeting, 16 November. Doc. S/PV.3137.
———. 1992j. Statement at the Security Council, 47th Year, Provisional Verbatim Record of 3138th Meeting, 19 November, Doc. S/PV.3138.
———. 2006. *The Horshoe Table: An Inside View of the Security Council.* New Delhi: Dorling Kindersley.
Ghose, Arundhati. 1996. Statement at the General Assembly, 50st Regular Session, Plenary Verbatim Record of 125th Meeting, 10 September. Doc. A/50/PV.125.
Ghosh, Arunabha, Arundhati Ghose, Suman Bery, C. Uday Bhaskar, Tarun Das, Nitin Desai, Anwarul Hoda, Kiran Karnik, Srinivasapuram Krishnaswamy, Radha Kumar, Shyam Saran. 2011. *Understanding complexity, anticipating change: From interests to strategy on governance* (Report of the Working Group on India and Global Governance) December, New Delhi: Council on Energy Environment and Water.
Gill, Amandeep. 2012. Statement at the Disarmament and International Security Committee of the General Assembly, 67th Regular Session, Plenary Verbatim Record of 19th Meeting, 5 November. Doc. A/C.1/67/PV.19.
Gilpin, R. 2001. *Global Political Economy: Understanding the International Economic Order.* Princeton, NJ: Princeton University Press.
Goodrich, Leland, Edvard Hambro, and Anne Patricia Simons. 1969. *Charter of the United Nations: Commentary and Documents.* New York: Columbia University Press.
Gopal, Sarvepalli. 1979. *Jawaharlal Nehru: A Biography, 1947–1955.* Vol. 2. New Delhi: Oxford University Press.
Gopinathan, Achamkulangare. 2005. Statement at the Security Council, 60th Year, Provisional Verbatim Record of 5230th Meeting (Resumption 1), 21 July. Doc. S/PV.5230 (Resumption 1).
Gowan, Richard, and Sunil K. Singh. 2013. 'India and UN Peacekeeping: The Weight of History and Lack of Strategy'. In *Shaping the Emerging Order:*

India and the Multilateral Order, edited by WPS Sidhu, Bhanu Pratap Mehta and Bruce Jones, 177–195. Washington, DC: Brookings Institution Press.

Gujral, Inder K. 1990a. Statement at the General Assembly, 18th Special Session, Plenary Verbatim Record of 2nd Meeting, 2 May. Doc. A/S-18/PV.2.

———. 1990b. Statement at the General Assembly, 45th Regular Session, Plenary Verbatim Record of 13th Meeting, 28 September. Doc. A/45/PV.13.

———. 1994. Statement at the General Assembly, 49th Regular Session, Plenary Verbatim Record of 62nd Meeting, 21 November. Doc. A/49/PV.62.

———. 1996. Statement at the General Assembly, 51st Regular Session, Plenary Verbatim Record of 22nd Meeting, 4 October. Doc. A/51/PV.22.

———. 1997. Statement at the General Assembly, 52nd Regular Session, Plenary Verbatim Record of 9th Meeting, 24 September. Doc. A/52/PV.9.

Gupta, Alka. 1977. *India and UN Peacekeeping Activities: A Case Study of Korea, 1947–1953*. New Delhi: Radiant Publishers.

Gupta, Sisir. 1966. *Kashmir—A Study of India-Pakistan Relations*. Bombay: Asia Publishing House.

Haidar, Suhasini and Kallol Bhattacharjee. 2017. 'Rajiv Sacked Minister to Repair Damage to US Ties: CIA'. *The Hindu*, 29 January. Available at: https://www.thehindu.com/news/national/Rajiv-sacked-Minister-to-repair-damage-to-U.S.-ties-CIA/article17110486.ece, accessed on 5 July 2019.

Haidar, Suhasini. 2019. 'India Cuts Off UN Panel after J&K Report'. *The Hindu*, 21 May, p.1.

Haque, Md. Nadimul. 2013. Statement at the Economic and Financial Committee of the General Assembly, 68th Regular Session, Summary Record of 28th Meeting, 12 December. Doc. A/C.2/68/SR.28.

Haroon, Abdullah H. 2008. Statement at the Security Council, 63rd Year, Provisional Verbatim Record of 6034th Meeting, Resumption 1, 9 December. Doc. S/PV.6034 (Resumption 1).

Held, D., and A. McGrew. 2002. 'Introduction'. In *Governing Globalization: Power, Authority and Global Governance*, edited by David Held and Anthony McGrew, 1–21. Cambridge: Polity Press.

Heptullah, Najma. 1992a. Statement at the General Assembly, 47th Regular Session, Plenary Verbatim Record of 38th Meeting, 29 October. Doc. A/47/PV.38.

———. 1992b. Statement at the General Assembly, 47th Regular Session, Plenary Verbatim Record of 38th Meeting, 14 October. Doc. A/47/PV.38.

ICWA, 1957. *India and United Nations: Report of the Study Group of the Indian Council of World Affairs*. New York: Manhattan Publishing Co.

ILO. 2019. *World Employment and Social Outlook: Trends 2019*. Geneva: International Labour Organization.

India. 1993. Communication of 29 June to the Chair of the Open-Ended Working Group on the Question of Equitable Representation on and Increase in the Membership of the Security Council. Report of the Secretary General, 20 July. Doc. A/48/264, pp.47–49.

Italy. 1993. Communication of 30 June to the Chair of the Open-ended Working Group on the Question of Equitable Representation on and Increase in the Membership of the Security Council. Report of the Secretary General, 20 July. Doc. A/48/264.

Jagmohan. 2001. Statement at the 25th Special Session of the General Assembly, Verbatim Record of 2nd Plenary Meeting, 6 June. Doc. A/S-25/PV.2.

Jaipal, Rikhi. 1977a. Statement at the Security Council, 32nd year, Verbatim Record of 2010th Meeting, 26 May, Doc. S/PV.2010.

———. 1977b. Statement at the Security Council, 32nd year, Verbatim Record of 2035th Meeting, 21 October, Doc. S/PV.2035.

———. 1977c. Statement at the Security Council, 32nd year, Verbatim Record of 2043rd Meeting, 28 October, Doc. S/PV.2043.

———. 1978a. Statement at the Security Council, 33rd year, Verbatim Record of 2058th Meeting, 30 January, Doc. S/PV.2058.

———. 1978b. Statement at the Security Council, 33rd year, Verbatim Record of 2073rd Meeting, 18 March, Doc. S/PV.2073.

———. 1978c. Statement at the Security Council, 33rd year, Verbatim Record of 2079th Meeting, 31 May, Doc. S/PV.2079.

———. 1978d. Statement at the Security Council, 33rd year, Verbatim Record of 2081st Meeting, 16 June, Doc. S/PV.2081.

———. 1978e. Statement at the Security Council, 33rd year, Verbatim Record of 2106th Meeting, 16 June, Doc. S/PV. 2106.

———. 1978f. 'Consensus-Making in the Security Council'. *India and Foreign Review*, 15(4): 21–23.

———. 1981. Statement at the Special Political Committee of the General Assembly, 31st Regular Session, Summary Record of 35th Meeting, 14 December. Doc. A/C.4/31/SR.35.

———. 1986. 'The United Nations, Peace and Disarmament'. *Indian Journal of International Law*, 26: 42–52.

Jaiswal, R. K. 2013. Statement at the Economic and Financial Committee of the General Assembly, 67th Regular Session, Summary Record of 27th Meeting, 29 January. Doc. A/C.2/67/SR.27.

James, Alan. 1987. 'The United Nations, Peacekeeping and Non-alignment'. In *The Non-aligned and the United Nations*, edited by M. S. Rajan, V.S. Mani and C.S.R. Murthy, 93–109. Dobbs Ferry, NY: Oceana Publishers.

———. 1990. *Peacekeeping in International Politics*. London: Macmillan.

Jarring, Gunnar. 1957. Report on the India–Pakistan Question in Pursuance of the Resolution of the Security Council of 21 February 1957, 29 April. Doc. S/3821l

Javadekar, Prakash. 2014. Statement at the Secretary General's Climate Summit, 23 September. Available at https://www.pminewyork.gov.in/sta tementgeneral?id=eyJpdiI6ImNmajlTYW0zeFJDd3RIS3V4Wkc1OVE9 PSIsInZhbHVlIjoiNjdBaW1ZUEZsNzdcL1FLMFhmQUhGelE9PSIsIm 1hYyI6IjJhODQwM2E5OTU2MGYyYjg4NjQxMmYyYjc0ZjZlMzg5

OTNlOGExYmE1OTU3MmNkZTI3ZjQ1YjZhNWVmNmY3ZGYifQ==, accessed on 6 May 2017.

Jha, C. S. 1983. *From Bandung to Tashkent: Glimpses of India's Foreign Policy*. New Delhi: Sangam Books.

———. 1987. 'The Economic and Social Council and India'. In *Forty Years of Economic Development: UN Agencies and India*, edited by Malcolm S. Adiseshiah, 19–25. New Delhi: Lancer International for India International Center.

Jolly, Richard. 2007. 'Human Development'. In *Oxford Handbook on the United Nations*, Thomas G. Weiss and Sam Daws, 634–649. Oxford: Oxford University Press.

Jordaan, Eduard. 2015. 'Rising Powers and Human rights: IBSA Dialogue Forum at UNHRC'. *Journal of Human Rights*, 14(4): 463–485.

Joshi, Murli Manohar. 2000. Statement at the 23rd Special Session of the General Assembly, Verbatim Record of 2nd Plenary Meeting, 5 June. Doc. A/S-23/PV. 2.

Kahler, M. 2013. 'Rising Powers and Global Governance: Negotiating Change in a Resilient Status Quo'. *International Affairs*, 89(3): 711–729.

Kamal, Ahmad. 1998. Statement at the Security Council, 53rd Year, Provisional Verbatim Record of 3890th Meeting, 6 June. Doc. S/PV.389.

Kapoor, Pavan. 2012. Statement at the Security Council, 67th Year, Provisional Verbatim Record of 6886th Meeting, 12 December. Doc. S/PV.6886.

Karns, M. P. and Karen Mingst. 2010. *International Organizations: Politics and Processes of Global Governance*. Boulder, CO: Lynne Rienner.

Kaul, M. (2014). Global Internet Governance: India's Search for a New Paradigm (ORF Issue Brief No. 74). New Delhi: Observer Research Foundation.

Kaur, Preneet. 2013. Statement at the Security Council, 68th Year, Provisional Verbatim Record of 7047th Meeting, 22 October. Doc. S/PV.7047.

Keating, Colin. 2015. 'Power Dynamics between the Permanent and Elected Members'. In *The UN Security Council in the 21st Century*, edited by Sabastian von Einsiedel, David Malone and Bruno S. Ugarte, 139–156. Boulder, CO: Lynne Rienner.

Khan, Sir Mohammad Zafrulla. 1949. Statement at the General Assembly, 4th Regular Session, Plenary Summary Record of 227th Meeting, 24 September. Doc. A/PV.227.

Khan, Khurshid. 1985. Statement at the Security Council, 40th Year, Verbatim Record of 2608th Meeting, 26 September, Doc. S/PV.2608.

Khurshid, Salman. 1994. Statement at the General Assembly, 48th Regular Session, Plenary Verbatim Record of 96th Meeting, 23 June 1994. Doc. A/48/PV.96.

———. 2013. Statement at the Inaugural Meeting of High-Level Political Forum on Sustainable Development, 68th Session of General Assembly, 24 September. Available at https://www.pminewyork.gov.in/pdf/uploadpdf/56930pmi64.pdf, accessed on 5 May 2017.

Kochanek, Stanley A. 1980. 'India's Changing Role in the United Nations'. *Pacific Affairs*, 53(1): 43–68.

Kothari, Miloon. 2018. 'Remembering India's Contribution to the Universal Declaration of Human Rights'. *The Wire*, 20 December. Available at: https://thewire.in/rights/indias-important-contributions-to-the-universal-declaration-of-human-rights, accessed on 5 January 2019.

Krishna, S. M. 2010. Statement at the High-level Plenary Meeting of the General Assembly on Millennium Development Goals, Verbatim Record of 9th Meeting, 22 September. Doc. A/65/PV.9.

———. 2011. Statement at the Security Council, 66th Year, Provisional Verbatim Record of 6621st Meeting, 22 September. Doc. S/PV.6621.

———. 2012. Statement at the General Assembly, 67th Regular Session, Plenary Verbatim Record of 19th Meeting, 1 October. Doc. A/67/PV.19.

Krishnan, N. 1984a. Statement at the Security Council, 39th Year, Verbatim Record of 2532nd Meeting, 3 May, Doc. S/PV.2532.

———. 1984b. Statement at the Security Council, 39th Year, Verbatim Record of 2546th Meeting, 1 June, Doc. S/PV.2546.

———. 1985. Statement at the Security Council, 40th Year, Verbatim Record of 2610th Meeting, 2 October, Doc. S/PV.2610.

Krishnasamy, Kabilan. 2003. 'The Paradox of India's Peacekeeping'. *Contemporary South Asia*, 12(2): 263–280.

———. 2010. 'A Case for India's 'Leadership' in United Nations Peacekeeping'. *International Studies*, 47(2–4): 225–246.

Kruger, Lennard G. 2016. Internet Governance and the Domain Name System: issues for Congress, Report R42351, November 18. Washington, DC: Congressional Research Service.

Kumar, Ashwani. 2013. Statement at the Administrative and Budgetary Committee of the General Assembly, 68th Regular Session, Summary Record of 12th Meeting, 15 November. Doc. A/C.5/68/SR.12.

Kumar, Mahesh. 2018a. Statement at the Administrative and Budgetary Committee of the General Assembly, 73rd Regular Session, 10 October. Available at: https://www.pminewyork.gov.in/pdf/uploadpdf/statements__1651231494.pdf, accessed on 6 October 2019.

———. 2018b Statement at the UN Pledging Conference for Development Activities, 5 November. Available at: https://www.pminewyork.gov.in/pdf/uploadpdf/statements__379916259.pdf, accessed on 23 September 2019.

Kumar. Vinay. 2012. Statement at the Security Council, 67th Year, Provisional Verbatim Record of 6789th Meeting, 20 June. Doc. S/PV.6789.

Kutesa, Sam. 2015. Letter from the President of the General Assembly to all Permanent Representatives. 15 July. Available at https://www.pminewyork.gov.in/pdf/menu/PGA_Letter_Annexes.pdf, accessed on 29 September 2019.

Lakshmi, Rama. 2013. 'India Loses Key Ally over UN Resolution against Sri Lanka'. *Washington Post*, 19 March. Available at: https://www.washington

post.com/world/indias-government-loses-key-ally-over-un-resolution-against-sri-lanka/2013/03/19/08e988ae-9071-11e2-9173-7f87cda73b49_story.html, accessed on 18 May 2018.

Lal, Tanmaya. 2016. Statement at the Security Council, 71st Year, Provisional Verbatim Record of 7711th Meeting, 10 June. Doc. S/PV.7711.

———. 2018. Statement at the General Assembly, 72nd Regular Session, Plenary Verbatim Record of 101st Meeting, 26 June. Doc. A/72/PV.101.

Lall, Arthur. 1968. *UN and the Middle East Crisis, 1967*. New York: Columbia University Press.

Langmore, John and Ramesh Thakur. 2016. 'The Elected but Neglected Security Council Members'. *Washington Quarterly*, 39(2): 99–114.

Latham, R. 1999. 'Politics in a Floating World: Towards a Critique of Global Governance'. In *Approaches to Global Governance Theory*, edited by Martin Hewson and Timothy J. Sinclair, 23–53. Albany, NY: State University of New York Press.

Lettinga, Doutje and Lars van Troost, eds. 2015. *Shifting Power and Human Rights Diplomacy – India*. Amsterdam: Amnesty International Netherlands.

Lodhi, Maleeha. 2015. Statement at the Assembly's Legal Committee, 70th Regular Session, Summary Record of 4th Meeting, 23 October. Doc. A/C.6/70/SR.4.

———. 2017. Statement at the General Assembly, 72nd Regular Session, Plenary Verbatim Record of 22nd Meeting, 23 September. Doc. A/72/PV.22.

Luck, Edward. 2005. 'How Not to Reform the United Nations'. *Global Governance*, 11(4): 407–414.

Mahajan, Pramod. 2005. Statement at the General Assembly Special Political Committee, 60th Session, Summary Record of 15th Meeting, 24 October. Doc. A/C.4/60/SR.15.

Mahbubani, Kishore. 2015. 'Council Reform and the Emerging Powers', In *The UN Security Council in the 21st Century*, edited by Sebastian von Einsiedel, David Malone and Bruno S Ugarte.157–174. Boulder, CO: Lynne Rienner Publishers.

Malhotra, Ajai. 2005. Statement at the General Assembly, 60th Regular Session, Plenary Verbatim Record of 99th Meeting, 8 September. Doc. A/60/PV.99.

Mathur, Hari Mohan. 1995. 'India in the United Nations and the United Nations in India'. In *State, Society and the UN System: Changing Perspectives on Multilateralism*, edited by Keith Krause and W. Andy Knight, 61–97. New York: United Nations University Press.

MEA. 2019. *Annual Report, 2018–19*. New Delhi: Ministry of External Affairs.

Mehta, Swadesh. 1976. 'India, the United Nations, and World Peace'. In *India's Foreign Relations during the Nehru Era*, edited by M. S. Rajan, 255–318. Bombay: Asia Publishing House.

Meier, Claudia, and C. S. R. Murthy. 2011. *India's Growing Involvement in Humanitarian Assistance*. Berlin: Global Public Policy Institute.

Menon, Shivshankar. 1990. Statement at the Security Council, 45th Year, Provisional Verbatim Record of 2914th Meeting, 28 March. Doc. S/PV.2914.

———. 1991. Statement at the General Assembly, 46th Regular Session, Plenary Verbatim Record of 15th Meeting, 4 October, Doc. A/46/PV.15.

Menon, V. K. 1957. Statement at the Security Council, 12th Year, Provisional Verbatim Record of 763rd Meeting, 23 January. Doc. S/PV.763.

———. 1958. Statement at the General Assembly, 13th Regular Session, Plenary Verbatim Record of 774th Meeting, 7 October. Doc. A/PV.774.

Ministry of External Affairs. 2015. Statement by Prime Minister at the Summit on Peacekeeping in New York, 29 September. Available at: https://mea.gov.in/outoging-visit-detail.htm?25856/Statement+by+Prime+Minister+at+the+Summit+on+Peacekeeping+in+New+York, accessed on 12 September 2019.

Mishra, Abhishek. 2018. 'The Changing Nature of India's Lines of Credit to Africa', 25 May. Available at https://www.orfonline.org/expert-speak/changing-nature-india-lines-of-credit-africa/, accessed on 23 September 2019.

Mishra, B. C. 1968. Statement at the Security Council, 23rd Year, Verbatim Record of 1441st Meeting, 21 August, Doc. S/PV.1441.

Modi, Narendra. 2014. Statement at the General Assembly, 69th Regular Session, Plenary Verbatim Record of 15th Meeting, 27 September. Doc. A/69/PV.15.

———. 2015. Address at the UN Summit for Adoption of the post-2015 Development Agenda, 70th Regular Session of the General Assembly, Plenary Verbatim Record of 4th Meeting, 25 September. Doc. A/70/PV.4.

———. 2019. Statement at the General Assembly, 74th Regular Session, Plenary Verbatim Record of 9th Meeting, 27 September. Doc. A/74/PV.9.

Mohan, C. R. 2010. 'Rising India: Partner in Shaping the Global Commons?' *Washington Quarterly*, 33(3): 133–148.

Mueller, M., J. Mathiason and H. Klein. 2007. 'The Internet and Global Governance: Principles and Norms for a New Regime'. *Global Governance*, 13(2): 237–254.

Mukerji, Asoke. 2013. Statement at the Security Council, 68th Year, Provisional Verbatim Record of 7085th Meeting, 17 December. Doc. S/PV.7085.

———. 2014a. Statement in the General Assembly, 68th Regular Session, Plenary Verbatim Record of 94th Meeting, 12 June. Doc. A/68/PV.94.

———. 2014b. Statement in the Security Council, 69th Year, Provisional Verbatim Record of 7316th Meeting, 19 November. Doc. S/PV.7316.

———. 2014c. Statement at the General Assembly, 69th Regular Session, Plenary Verbatim Record of 69th Meeting, 11 December. Doc. A/69/PV.69.

———. 2015. Statement at the General Assembly, 69th Regular Session, Plenary Verbatim Record of 104th Meeting, 15 September, Doc. A/64/PV.104.

Mukherjee, Pranab. 1994. Statement at the General Assembly, 49th Regular Session, Plenary Verbatim Record of 14th Meeting, 3 October. Doc. A/49/PV.14.

———. 1995. Statement at the General Assembly, 50th Regular Session, Plenary Verbatim Record of 12th Meeting, 29 September. Doc. A/50/PV.12.

Mukherjee, Rohan and David M. Malone. 2011. 'From High Ground to High Table: The Evolution of Indian Multilateralism'. *Global Governance*, 17(3): 311–329.

Mukherjee, Rohan. 2015. 'Indian Multilateralism and the Global Human Rights Order'. In *Shifting Power and Human Rights Diplomacy – India*, edited by Doutje Lettinga and Lars van Troost, 47–54. Amsterdam: Amnesty International Netherlands.

Muller, Joachim. 2010. *Reforming the United Nations: The Challenge of Working Together*. Leiden: Martinus Nijhoff.

Murphy, C. N. (2000). 'Global governance: Poorly Done and Poorly Understood'. *International Affairs*, 76(4): 789–803.

Murthy, C. S. R. 1989. 'Britain and the Kashmir Question, 1947–1953: Assessing the British Policy in the United Nations'. *International Studies*, 26(2): 141–163.

———. 1992. 'United Nations Sanctions against Libya: A Perspective'. *Journal of West Asian Studies*, 8: 15–25.

———. 1993. *India's Diplomacy in the United Nations: Problems and Perspectives*. New Delhi: Lancers Books.

———. 1998a. 'India and U.N. Peace-keeping Operations: Issues in Policy and Participation'. *Man and Development*, 20(2): 172–183.

———. 1998b. 'Reforming the UN Security Council: An Asian View'. *South Asian Survey*, 5(1): 113–124.

———. 2001. 'United Nations Peacekeeping in Intrastate Conflicts: Emerging Trends'. *International Studies*, 38(3): 207–227.

———. 2002. 'Nehruvian Nationalism and the United Nations, In *Nehru's Worldview: Internatinalism vs. Nationalism*, edited by Taufiq A. Niami, 177–200, Aligarh: Aligarh Muslim University Centre for Nehru Studies.

———. 2007a. 'New Phase in UN Reforms: Establishment of the Peacebuilding Commission and the Human Rights Council'. *International Studies*, 44(1): 39–56.

———. 2007b. 'Unintended Consequences of Peace Operations for Troop Contributing Countries from South Asia'. In *Unintended Consequences of Peacekeeping Operations*, edited by Chiyuki Aoi, Cedric de Coning and Ramesh Thakur, 156–170. Tokyo: UN University Press.

———. 2007c. 'U.N. Counter-Terrorism Committee: An Institutional Analysis'. *Dialogue on Globalization* Briefing Paper No. 15. New York: Friedric Ebert Stiftung.

———. 2010. 'Assessing India at the United Nations in the Changing Context'. *International Studies*, 47(2–4): 205–223.

———. 2013. 'Non-aligned Movement Countries as Drivers of Change in International Organizations'. *Comparative* 23(4–5): 118–136.
———. and Gerrit Kurtz. 2016. 'International Responsibility as Solidarity: The Impact of the World Summit Negotiations on the RtoP Trajectory'. *Global Society*, 30(1): 38–53.
Nambiar, Satish. 2009. *For the Honour of India: A History of Indian Peacekeeping*. New Delhi: United Services Institution of India.
Nambiar, Vijay. 2002a. Statement at the Security Council, 57th Year, Provisional Verbatim Record of 4579th Meeting (Resumption 1), 19 July. Doc. S/PV.4579 (Resumption 1).
———. 2002b. Statement at the Security Council, 57th Year, Provisional Verbatim Record of 4623rd Meeting (Resumption 1), 11 October. Doc. S/PV.4623 (Resumption 1).
———. 2002c. Statement at the General Assembly, 57th Regular Session, Plenary Verbatim Record of 40th Meeting, 31 October. Doc. A/57/PV.40.
———. 2003a. Statement at the Security Council, 58th Year. Provisional Verbatim Record of 4824th Meeting (Resumption 1), 15 September. Doc. S/PV.4824 (Resumption 1).
———. 2003b. Statement at the General Assembly, 58th Regular Session, Plenary Verbatim Record of 24th Meeting, 6 October. Doc. A/58/PV.24.
———. 2003c. Statement at the General Assembly, 58th Regular Session, Plenary Verbatim Record of 45th Meeting, 28 October. Doc. A/58/PV.45.
———. 2003d. Statement at the Security Council, 58th Year, Provisional Verbatim Record of 4798th Meeting, 29 July. Doc. S/PV.4798.
———. 2003e. Statement at the Security Council, 58th Year, Provisional Verbatim Record of 4734th Meeting, Resumption 1, 4 April. Doc. S/PV.4734.
———. 2004a. Statement at the Security Council, 59th Year. Provisional Verbatim Record of 4898th Meeting (Resumption 1), 20 January. Doc. S/PV.4898 (Resumption 1).
———. 2004b. Statement at the Security Council, 59th Year, Provisional Verbatim Record of 4976th Meeting, 15 May. Doc. S/PV.4976.
Naranag, Amit. 2014. Statement at the Economic and Financial Committee of the General Assembly, 69th Regular Session, Summary Record of 18th Meeting, 8 December. Doc. A/C.2/69/SR.18.
Narayanan, K. R. 1985. Statement at the Security Council, 40th year, Provisional Verbatim Record of 2624th Meeting, 13 November. Doc. S/PV.2624 (Provisional).
Narlikar, A. 2011. 'Is India a Responsible Great Power?' *Third World Quarterly*, 32(9): 1607–1621.
———. 2013a. 'India Rising: Responsible to Whom?' *International Affairs*, 89(3): 595–614.
———. 2013b. 'Introduction: Negotiating the Rise of New Powers'. *International Affairs*, 89(3): 561–575.

Nath, Kamal. 1992. Statement at the General Assembly, 47th Regular Session, Plenary Verbatim Record of 53rd Meeting, 2 November. Doc. A/47/PV.53.

NDTV. 2019. 'Trump's Kashmir Mediation Offer in Kashmir 'Not on Table Any More': India's US envoy', 13 August. Available at: https://www.ndtv.com/india-news/trumps-mediation-offer-on-kashmir-not-on-table-anymore-indian-envoy-harsh-vardhan-shringla-2084305, accessed on 6-9-2019.

Nehru, Jawaharlal. 1948. Address to the UN General Assembly, Third Session, 3 November. Available at: https://www.pminewyork.gov.in/pdf/uploadpdf/34084lms4.pdf, accessed on 27 August 2019.

———. 1961. *India's Foreign Policy* (Selected Speeches from September 1946 to April 1961). New Delhi: Ministry of Information and Broadcasting.

Nicholas, H. G. 1975. *The United Nations as a Political Institution*, 5th ed. London: Oxford University Press.

O'Brien, Derek. 2013. Statement at the Economic and Financial Committee of the General Assembly, 67th Regular Session, Summary Record of 16th Meeting, 4 January. Doc. A/C.2/67/SR.16.

Oestreich, Joel E. 2014. 'United Nations and Rights Based Approach to Development in India'. *Global Governance*, 20(1): 77–94.

Pai, Nitin. 2013. 'India and International Norms: R2P, Genocide Prevention, Human Rights and Democracy'. In *Shaping the Emerging Order: India and the Multilateral Order*, edited by W. P. S. Sidhu, Pratap Bhanu Mehta and Bruce Jones, 303–318. Washington, DC: Brookings Institution Press.

Parakatil, Francis. 1975. *India and United Nations Peace-keeping Operations*. New Delhi: S. Chand & Co.

Parkar, Pratibha. 2013. Statement at the Disarmament and International Security Committee of the General Assembly, 68th Regular Session, Plenary Verbatim Record of 20th Meeting, 30 October. Doc. A/C.1/68/PV.20.

Parthasarathi, G. 1967a. Statement at the Security Council, 22nd Year, Verbatim Record of 1343rd Meeting, 29 May, Doc. S/PV.1343.

———. 1967b. Statement at the Security Council, 22nd Year, Verbatim Record of 1352nd Meeting, 9 June, Doc. S/PV.1352.

———. 1967c. Statement at the Security Council, 22nd Year, Verbatim Record of 1373rd Meeting, 9/10 November, Doc. S/PV.1373.

———. 1967d. Statement at the Security Council, 22nd Year, Verbatim Record of 1382nd Meeting, 22 November, Doc. S/PV.1382.

———. 1968. Statement at the Security Council, 23rd Year, Verbatim Record of 1428th Meeting, 29 May, Doc. S/PV.1428.

Paul, T. V., ed. 2005. *India–Pakistan Conflict: An Enduring Rivalry*. New York: Cambridge University Press.

Payne, A. 2010. 'How Many Gs Are There in 'Global Governance' after the Crisis? The Perspectives of the "Marginal Majority"'. *International Affairs*, 86(3): 729–740.

Perri 6. 2002. 'Global Digital Communications and the Prospects for Transnational Regulation'. In *Governing Globalization: Power, Authority and Global Governance*, edited by David Held and Anthony McGrew, 145–170. Cambridge: Polity Press.

Pillai, Priya. 2019. 'The View from the Outside: As a Democracy, India Must Have a Better Record of Upholding Human Rights'. *The Hindu*, 18 January, p.10.

Poku, Nana K., and Jim Whitman (2011). 'The Millennium Development Goals and Development after 2015'. *Third World Quarterly*, 32(1): 181–198.

Puri, H.S. 2009a. Statement at the Security Council, 64th year, Provisional Verbatim Record of 6153rd Meeting, Resumption 1, 29 June. Doc. S/PV.6153 (Resumption 1).

———. 2009b. Statement at the Security Council, 64th Year, Provisional Verbatim Record of 6224th Meeting (Resumption 1), 25 November. Doc. S/PV.6224 (Resumption 1).

———. 2010a. Statement at the General Assembly Informal (Closed) Meeting on Intergovernmental Negotiations on Security Council Reform, 7 July, Available at: https://www.pminewyork.gov.in/pdf/uploadpdf/68540ind1706.pdf, accessed on 29 September 2019.

———. 2010b. Statement at the Security Council, 65th Year, Provisional Verbatim Record of 6300th Meeting (Resumption 1), 22 April. Doc. S/PV.6300 (Resumption 1).

———. 2010c. Statement at the Security Council, 65th Year, Provisional Verbatim Record of 6351st Meeting, 30 June. Doc. S/PV.6351.

———. 2011a. Statement at the Security Council, 66th Year, Provisional Verbatim Record of 6491st Meeting, 26 February. Doc. S/PV.6491.

———. 2011b. Statement at the Security Council, 66th Year, Provisional Verbatim Record of 6503rd Meeting, 23 March. Doc. S/PV.6503.

———. 2011c. Statement at the Security Council, 66th Year, Provisional Verbatim Record of 6557th Meeting, 17 June. Doc. S/PV.6557.

———. 2011d. Statement at the Security Council, 66th Year, Provisional Verbatim Record of 6587th Meeting, 20 July. Doc. S/PV.6587.

———. 2011e. Statement at the Security Council, 66th Year, Provisional Verbatim Record of 6603rd Meeting, 26 August. Doc. S/PV.6603.

———. 2011f. Statement at the Security Council, 66th Year, Provisional Verbatim Record of 6625th Meeting, 29 September. Doc. S/PV.6625.

———. 2011g. Statement at the Security Council, 66th Year, Provisional Verbatim Record of 6627th Meeting, 4 October. Doc. S/PV.6627.

———. 2011h. Statement at the Security Council, 66th Year, Provisional Verbatim Record of 6658th Meeting, 14 November. Doc. S/PV.6658.

———. 2012a. Statement at the Security Council, 67th Year, Provisional Verbatim Record of 6705th Meeting, 19 January. Doc. S/PV.6705.

———. 2012b. Extempore Remarks at the Eighth Round of Intergovernmental Negotiations on Security Council Reform, 21 February. Availabale at:

https:// www.pminewyork.gov.in/pdf/uploadpdf/39676ind1994.pdf, accessed on 1 October 2019.

———. 2012c. Statement at the Eighth Round of Intergovernmental Negotiations on Security Council reform, 2 May. Available at: https://www.pminewyork. gov.in/pdf/uploadpdf/33889ind2021.pdf, accessed on 1 October 2019.

———. 2012d. Statement at the Security Council, 67th Year, Provisional Verbatim Record of 6756th Meeting, 21 April. Doc. S/PV.6756.

———. 2012e. Statement at the Security Council, 67th Year, Provisional Verbatim Record of 6765th Meeting, 4 May. Doc. S/PV.6765.

———. 2012f. Statement at the Security Council, 67th Year, Provisional Verbatim Record of 6810th Meeting, 19 July. Doc. S/PV.6810.

———. 2012g. Statement at the Security Council, 67th Year, Provisional Verbatim Record of 6878th Meeting, 4 December. S/PV.6878.

———. 2013. Statement in the Security Council, 68th Year, Provisional Verbatim Record of 6900th Meeting Resumption 1, 15 January. Doc. S/PV.6900 Resumption 1.

———. 2016. *Perilous Interventions: The Security Council and the Politics of Chaos*. New Delhi: HarperCollins India.

Puri, M. 2010. Statement at the Security Council, 65th Year, Provisional Verbatim Record of 6341st Meeting (Resumption 1), 16 June. Doc. S/PV6341 (Resumption 1).

———. 2011a. Statement at the Security Council, 66th Year, Provisional Verbatim Record of 6498th Meeting, 17 March. Doc. S/PV.6498.

———. 2011b. Statement at the Security Council, 66th Year, Provisional Verbatim Record of 6592nd Meeting, 27 July. Doc. S/PV.6592.

———. 2011c. Statement at the Security Council, 66th Year, Provisional Verbatim Record of 6690th Meeting, 19 December. Doc. S/PV.6690.

———. 2012a. Statement at the Security Council, 67th Year, Provisional Verbatim Record of 6760th Meeting, 25 April. Doc. S/PV.6760.

———. 2012b. Statement at the General Assembly, 66th Regular Session, Plenary Verbatim Record of 118th Meeting, 28 June. Doc. A/66/PV.118.

———. 2013a. Statement at the Security Council, 68th Year. Provisional Verbatim Record of 7035th Meeting, 19 September. Doc. S/PV.7035.

———. 2013b. Statement at the General Assembly, 68th Regular Session, Plenary Verbatim Record of 46th Meeting, 7 November, Doc. A/68/PV.46.

Purkayastha, P. and R. Bailey. 2014. 'Evolving a New Internet Governance paradigm'. *Economic & Political Weekly*, 49(2): 29–33.

Rabbani, Hina. 2013. Statement at the Security Council, 68th Year, Provisional Verbatim Record of 6900th Meeting, Resumption, 15 January. Doc. S/PV.6900 Resumption.

Rajan, M. S. 1973. 'India and the Making of the UN Charter'. *International Studies*, 12(3): 430–459.

Rajan, M. S., V.S. Mani and C.S.R. Murthy, ed. 1987. *The Non-aligned and the United Nations*. Dobbs Ferry, NY: Oceana Publishers.

Ramesh, J. 2014. 'India's call at Cancun conclave'. *The Hindu.* 30 June. Available at: http://www.thehindu.com/todays-paper/tp-opinion/indias-call-at-cancun-conclave/article6161282.ece, accessed on 15 September 2014.

Rana, Swadesh. 1970. 'Changing Indian Diplomacy at the United Nations'. *International Organization*, 24(1): 43–73.

Rangachari, T. C. A. 2001. 'Statement' Presented at the United Nations Pledging Conference for Development Activities, November 7. Available at: https://www.pminewyork.org/adminpart/uploadpdf/9166456.pdf, accessed on 5 March 2017.

Rao, M. Koteswara. 2015. Statement at the Assembly's Legal Committee, 70th Regular Session, Summary Record of 4th Meeting, 23 October. Doc. A/C.6/70/SR.4.

Rao, Narasimha. 1992. Address at the Security Council, 47th Year, Provisional Verbatim Record of 3046th Meeting, 31 January. Doc. S/PV.3046.

———. 1995. Address at the General Assembly, 50th Regular Session, Plenary Verbatim Record of 40th Meeting, 24 October. Doc. A/50/PV.40.

Rau, Benegal N. 1950a. Statement at the Security Council, 5th Year, Verbatim Record of 474th Meeting, 27 June. Doc. S/PV.474.

———. 1950b. Statement at the Security Council, 5th Year, Verbatim Record of 487th Meeting, 14 August. Doc. S/PV.487.

Ravi, Vayalar. 2004. Statement at the UN General Assembly, 59th Regular Session, Economic and Financial Committee, Summary Record of 26th Meeting, 4 November. Doc. A/C.2/59/SR.26.

Ray, Anupam. 2010. Statement at the Security Council, 65th Year, Provisional Verbatim Record of 6374th Meeting, 25 August. Doc. S/PV.6374.

Reddy, Jaipal. 2002. Statement at the Economic and Financial Committee of the General Assembly, 57th Regular Session, Summary Record of 20th Meeting, 29 November. Doc. A/C.2/57/SR.20.

Reinicke, W. 1998. *Global Public Policy: Governing without Government?* Washington, DC: Brookings.

Rosenau, J. 1990. *Turbulence in World Politics: A Theory of Change and Continuity.* Princeton, NJ: Princeton University Press.

———. 1992. 'Governance, Order, and Change in World Politics'. In *Governance without Government: Order and Change in World Politics*, edited by James N. Rosenau and Ernst-Otto Czempiel, 1–29. Cambridge: Cambridge University Press.

———. 2000. 'Governance in a Globalizing World'. In *Global Transformations Reader*, edited by David Held and Anthony McGrew, 223–233. Cambridge: Polity.

Saksena, K. P. 1974. *The United Nations and Collective Security: A Historical Analysis.* New Delhi: D.K. Publishing House.

———. 1977. 'Not by Design: Evolution of UN Peacekeeping Operations and Its Implications for the Future'. *International Studies*, 16(4): 459–481.

———. 1978. 'India and Diplomacy in the United Nations'. *International Studies*, 17(3–4): 799–826.

———. 1981. 'Non-alignment and the United Nations'. *International Studies*, 20(1–2): 81–102.

———. 1991. 'Human Rights and Right to Development'. *International Studies*, 28(1): 41–53.

———. 1995. 'India's Fifty Years at the United Nations: A Critique'. *International Studies*. 32(4): 375–397.

San Marino. 1994. Statement at the General Assembly, 49th Regular Session, Plenary Verbatim Record of 31st Meeting, 14 October. Doc. A/49/PV.31.

Sandhu, Taranjit S. 2009. Statement at the Security Council, 64th Year, Provisional Verbatim Record of 6075th Meeting, 23 January. Doc. S/PV.6075.

Saran, Samir. 2014. 'The ITU and Unbundling Internet Governance: The Indian Perspective'. Council on Foreign Relations Digital and Cyberspace Program. Available at: https://www.cfr.org/report/itu-and-unbundling-internet-governance, accessed 18 September 2019.

Schabas, William A. 2007. 'Preventing the "Odious Scourge": The United Nations and Prevention of Genocide'. *International Journal on Minority and Group Rights*, 14(2–3): 379–397.

Schaffer, T. 2009. 'The United States, India, and Global Governance: Can They Work together?' *Washington Quarterly*, 32(3): 71–87.

SCOR. 1950a. Security Council, 5th Year, Resolution 82, adopted at 473th Meeting, 25 June. Doc. S/RES/82 (1950)

———. 1950b. Security Council, 5th Year, Resolution 83, adopted at 474th Meeting, 27 June. Doc. S/RES/83 (1950).

———. 1957a. Security Council, 12th Year, Resolution 122 (1957), adopted at 765th meeting, 24 January. Doc. S/RES/122 (1957).

———. 1957b. Security Council. 12th Year, Verbatim Record of 773rd Meeting, 20 February. Doc. S/PV.773.

———. 1965a. Security Council, 20th Year, Resolution 209, adopted at 1237th Meeting, 4 September, Doc. S/RES/209(1965).

———. 1965b. Security Council, 20th Year, Resolution 211, adopted at 1242nd Meeting, 20 September. Doc. S/RES/211 (1965).

———. 1971. Security Council, 26th Year, Resolution 307, adopted at 1621st Meeting, 21 December. Doc. S/RES/307 (1971).

———. 1990. Security Council, 45th Year, Resolution 678, adopted at 2963rd Meeting, 29 November. Doc. S/RES/678 (1990).

———. 1991. Security Council, 46th Year, Resolution 687, adopted at 2981st Meeting, 3 April. Doc. S/RES/688 (1991).

———. 1992a. Security Council, 47th Year, Resolution 731, adopted at 3033rd Meeting, 21 January. Doc. S/RES/731 (1992).

———. 1992b. Security Council, 47th Year, Resolution 757, adopted at 3082nd Meeting, 30 May. Doc. S/RES/757 (1992).

———. 1998. Security Council, 53rd Year, Resolution 1172, adopted at 3890th Meeting, 6 June. Doc. S/RES/1172 (1998).

———. 1999a. Security Council, 54th Year, Resolution 1267, adopted at 4051st Meeting, 15 October. Doc. S/RES/1267 (1999).
——— 1999b. Security Council, 54th Year, Resolution 1269, adopted at 4053rd Meeting, 19 October. Doc. S/RES/1269 (1999).
———. 2001. Security Council, 56th Year, Resolution 1373, adopted at 4385th Meeting, 28 September. Doc. S/RES/1373 (2001).
———. 2004a. Security Council, 59th Year, Resolution 1540 adopted at 4956th Meeting, 28 April. Doc. S/RES/1540 (2004).
———. 2004b. Security Council, 59th Year, Resolution 1566, adopted at 5053rd Meeting, 8 October. Doc. S/RES/1566 (2004).
———. 2011a. Security Council, 66th Year, Resolution 1973 (2011), adopted at 6498th Meeting, 17 March. Doc. S/RES/1973 (2011.
———. 2011b. Security Council, 66th Year, A concept note on peacekeeping: taking stock and preparing for the future, annexed to the letter from the Permanent Representative of India to the Secretary-General, 5 August. Doc. S/2011/496.
———. 2014. Security Council, 69th Year, Resolution 2178 (2014). adopted at 7272nd Meeting, 24 September. Doc. S/RES/2178.
———. 2017. Security Council, 72nd Year, Resolution 2396 (2017), adopted at 8148th Meeting, 21 December. Doc. S/RES/2396.
Secretary-General. 1965. Report of the Secretary General, 16 September. Doc. S/6683.
Security Council (1992). Statement by the President on behalf of All Members at the Level of Heads of State/Government, 47th Year, Provisional Verbatim Record of 3046th Meeting, 31 January. Doc. S/PV.3046.
———. 1998a. Statement by the President, 14 May. Doc. S/PRST/1998/12.
———. 1998b. Statement by the President, 20 May. Doc. S/PRST/1998/17.
——— 2006. Statement by the President, 12 July, Doc. S/PRST/2006/30.
———. 2008. Statement by the President, 9 December. Doc. S/PRST/2008/45.
———. 2011. Statement by the President, 3 August. Doc. S/PRST/2011/16.
Sen, Nirupam. 2004a. 'Statement.' presented at the 28th Annual Meeting of the Foreign Ministers of the G77, 30 September. Available at: https://www.pminewyork.org/adminpart/uploadpdf/41709ind986.pdf, accessed on 11 January 2016.
———. 2004b. Statement at the Security Council, 59th Year, Provisional Verbatim Record of 5066th Meeting, 28 October. Doc. S/PV.5066.
———. 2004c. Statement at the Security Council, 59th Year, Provisional Verbatim Record of 5031st Meeting, 13 September. Doc. S/PV.5031.
———. 2004d. Statement at the Security Council, 59th Year, Provisional Verbatim Record of 5059th Meeting, 19 October. Doc. S/PV.5059.
———. 2005a. Statement at the General Assembly, 59th Regular Session, Plenary Verbatim Record of 90th Meeting. 8 April. Doc. A/59/PV.90.
———. 2005b. Statement at the Informal Thematic Consultations on Responsibility to Protect, 20 April. Available at: https://www.pminewyork.gov.in/pdf/uploadpdf/74929ind1085.pdf, accessed on 14 October 2019.

———. 2005c. Statement at the General Assembly, 60th Regular Session, Plenary Verbatim Record of 66th Meeting, 20 December. Doc. A/60/PV.66.

———. 2005d. Statement at the Security Council, 60th Year, Provisional Verbatim Record of 5293rd Meeting, 26 October. Doc. S/PV.5293.

———. 2006a. Statement at the General Assembly. 60th Regular Session, Plenary Verbatim Record of 72nd Meeting, 15 March. Doc. A/60/PV.72.

———. 2006b. Statement at the General Assembly, 61st Regular Session, Plenary Verbatim Record of 24th Meeting, 2 October. Doc. A/61/PV.24.

———. 2006c. Statement at the General Assembly, 61st Regular Session, Plenary Verbatim Record of 56th Meeting, 20 November. Doc. A/61/PV.56.

———. 2007a. Statement at the Security Council. 62nd Year, Provisional Verbatim Record of 5663rd Meeting (Resumption 1), 17 April. Doc. S/PV.5663 (Resumption 1).

———. 2007b. Statement at the General Assembly's Legal Committee, 62nd Regular Session, Summary record of 4th Meeting, 6 November. Doc.A/C.6/62/SR.4.

———. 2008a. Statement at the Security Council, 63rd Year, Provisional Verbatim Record of 5895th Meeting (Resumption 1), 20 May. Doc. S/PV.5895 (Resumption 1).

———. 2008b. Statement at the General Assembly, 62nd Regular Statement, Plenary Verbatim Record of 119th Meeting, 14 September. Doc. A/62/PV.119.

———. 2008c. Statement at the Security Council, 63rd Year, Provisional Verbatim Record of 5855th Meeting, 19 March. Doc. S/PV.5855.

———. 2008d. Statement at the Security Council, 63rd Year, Provisional Verbatim Record of 5886th Meeting, 6 May. Doc. S/PV.5886.

———. 2018. Statement at the General Assembly, 73rd Regular Session, Plenary Verbatim Record of 14th Meeting, 29 September. Doc. A/73/PV.14.

Sen, Samar. 1971. Statement at the Security Council, 26th Year, Provisional Verbatim Record of 1606th Meeting, 4 December. Doc. S/PV.1606.

———. 1972a, Statement at the Security Council, 27th Year, Verbatim Record of 1637th Meeting, 3 February, Doc. S/PV.1637.

———. 1972b, Statement at the Security Council, 27th Year, Verbatim Record of 1666th Meeting, 29 September, Doc. S/PV.1666.

———. 1973a. Statement at the Security Council, 28th Year, Verbatim Record of 1709th Meeting, 18 April, Doc. S/PV.1709.

———. 1973b. Statement at the Security Council, 28th Year, Verbatim Record of 1734th Meeting, 25 July, Doc. S/PV.1734.

———. 1973c. Statement at the Security Council, 28th Year, Verbatim Record of 1747th Meeting, 21/22 October, Doc. S/PV.1747.

———. 1973d. Statement at the Security Council, 28th Year, Verbatim Record of 1759th Meeting, 14 December, Doc. S/PV.1759.

Shah, Prakash. 1995. Statement at the Security Council, 50th Year, Provisional Verbatim Record of 3611th Meeting, 20 December. Doc. S/PV.3611.

———. 1996. Statement at the Security Council, 51st Year, Provisional Verbatim Record of 3650th Meeting, 9 April. Doc. S/PV.3650.

———. 1997. 'International Human Rights: A Perspective from India'. *Fordham Journal of International Law*, 21(1): 24–44.

Sharma, Kamalesh. 1988. Statement at the General Assembly Special Political Committee, 43rd Session, Summary Record of 12th Meeting, 26 October. Doc. A/C.4/43/SR.12.

———. 1997. Statement at the General Assembly, 52nd Regular Session, Plenary Verbatim Record of 62nd Meeting, 4 December. Doc. A/52/PV.62.

———. 1998. Statement at the Security Council, 53rd Year, Provisional Verbatim Record of 3864th Meeting, 29 March. Doc. S/PV.3864.

———. 1999. Statement at the Security Council, 54th Year, Provisional Verbatim Record of 3989th Meeting, 26 March. Doc. S/PV.3989.

———. 2000a. Statement at the Security Council, 55th Year, Provisional Verbatim Record of 4139th Meeting, 11 May, Doc. S/PV.4139.

———. 2000b. Statement at the General Assembly, 55th Regular Session, Plenary Verbatim Record of 30th Meeting, 27 September. Doc. A/55/PV.30.

———. 2000c. Statement at the General Assembly, 55th Regular Session, Plenary Verbatim Record of 64th Meeting, 16 November. Doc. A/55/PV.64.

———. 2000d. Statement at the General Assembly Special Political Committee, 55th session, Summary Record of 21st Meeting, 9 November. Doc. A/C.4/55/SR.21.

———. 2001a. Statement at the Security Council, 56th Year, Provisional Verbatim Record of 4414th Meeting (Resumption 1), 13 November. Doc. S/PV. 4414 (Resumption 1).

———. 2001b. Statement at the Security Council, 56th Year, Provisional Verbatim Record, 4259th Meeting (Resumption 1), 19 January. Doc. S/PV.4259 (Resumption 1).

———. 2001c. Statement at the General Assembly, 56th Regular Session, Plenary Verbatim Record of 16th Meeting, 3 October. Doc. A/56/PV.16.

———. 2001d. Statement at the General Assembly, 56th Regular Session, Plenary Verbatim Record of 5th Meeting, 20 September. Doc. A/56/PV.5.

———. 2002. Statement at the Security Council, 57th Year, Provisional Verbatim Record of 4453rd Meeting, 28 January. Doc. S/PV.4453.

———. 2004. Statement at the General Assembly, 59th Regular Session, Plenary Verbatim Record of 19th Meeting, 4 October. Doc. A/59/PV.19.

———. 2017. Statement at the Economic and Financial Committee of the General Assembly, 72nd Regular Session, Summary Record of 8th Meeting, 2 November. Doc. A/C.2/72/SR.8.

Shucksmith, Christy and Nigel White. 2015. 'United Nations Military Observer Group in India and Pakistan (UNMOGIP)'. In *The Oxford Handbook of United Nations Peacekeeping Operations*, edited by Joechim Koops Thierry

Tardy, Norrie MacQueen and Paul D. Williams, 133–143. Oxford: Oxford University Press.
Sidhu, Wahe Pal Singh, Pratap Bhanu Mehta and Bruce Jones, eds. 2013. *Shaping the Emerging Order: India and the Multilateral Order*. Washington, DC: Brookings Institution Press.
Singh, J. 2000. Statement at the General Assembly, 55th Regular Session, Plenary Verbatim Record of 23rd Meeting, September 19. Doc. A/55/PV.23.
Singh, M. 2004. Statement at the 59th Regular Session of the General Assembly, Plenary Verbatim Record of 7th Meeting, 23 September. Doc. A/59/PV.7.
———. 2005. Address at the High-Level Plenary Meeting of the General Assembly, 60th Regular Session, Verbatim Record of 5th Meeting, 15 September. Doc. A/60/PV.5.
———. 2013. Statement at the General Assembly, 68th Regular Session, Plenary Verbatim Record of 18th Meeting, 28 September. Doc. A/68/PV.18.
Singh, N. 2005. Statement at the General Assembly, 60th Regular Session, Plenary Verbatim Record of 14th Meeting, 19 September, Doc. A/60/PV.14.
Singh, Narinder. 2017. 'The United Nations' Efforts at Combating International Terrorism'. Policy Brief Series No. 81. Brussels: FICHL.
Singh, S. (Sujatha). 2013. Statement at the Special Event to Follow-up efforts Made toward Achieving the Millennium Development Goals, 25 September. Available at https://www.pminewyork.org/adminpart/uploadpdf/38891pmi65.pdf, accessed on 5 March 2017.
Sinha, Ashish. 2016. Statement at the Economic and Financial Committee of the General Assembly, 71st Regular Session, Summary Record of 9th Meeting, 27 October. Doc. A/C.2/71/SR.9.
———. 2017. Statement at the Economic and Financial Committee of the General Assembly, 72nd Regular Session, Summary Record of 8th Meeting, 2 November. Doc. A/C.2/72/SR.8.
Sinha K. 1990. Statement at the General Assembly Special Political Committee, 45th Regular Session, Summary Record of 27th Meeting, 28 November. Doc. A/C.4/45/SR.27.
Sinha, Yashwant. 2003. Statement at the 27th Annual Meeting of the Ministers of Foreign Affairs of the G77, 25 September. Available at https://www.pminewyork.gov.in/pdf/uploadpdf/8979078.pdf, accessed on 5 May 2017.
Sitapati, Vinay. 2015. *Half Lion: How PV Narasimha Rao Transformed India*. Delhi: Penguin Viking.
Solanki, M. S. 1991a. Statement at the Security Council, 46th Year, Provisional Verbatim Record of 3009th Meeting, 25 September. Doc. S/PV.3009.
———. 1991b. Statement at the General Assembly, 46th Regular Session, Plenary Verbatim Record of 11th Meeting, 26 September. Doc. A/46/PV.11.
Sreenivasan, T.P. 1993. Statement at the General Assembly, 48th Regular Session, Verbatim Record of 85th Plenary Meeting, 20 December. Doc. A/50/PV.85.

———. 1995a. Statement at the Security Council, 47th Year, Provisional Verbatim Record of 3492nd Meeting (Resumption 1), 18 January. Doc. S/PV.3492 (Resumption 1).

———. 1995b. Statement at the Security Council, 50th Year, Provisional Verbatim Record of 3499th Meeting, 8 February, Doc. S/PV.3499.

———. 1998. Statement at the General Assembly, 53rd Regular Session, Plenary Verbatim Record of 67th Meeting, 23 November. Doc. A/53/PV.67.

Srivastava, M. 2013. Internet Base in India Crosses 200 Million Mark. *Livemint*, 13 November. Available from http://www.livemint.com/Consumer/9p WsphmYL2YjdisfO7bGLM/Internet-base-in-India-crosses-200-million-mark.html, accessed on 9 November 2014.

Stephen, Mathew David. 2015. 'India, Emerging Powers and Global Human Rights: Yes, but ....' In *Shifting Power and Human Rights Diplomacy—India*, edited by Doutje Lettinga and Lars van Troost, 55–63. Amsterdam: Amnesty International Netherlands.

Surie, Nalin. 1995. Statement at the General Assembly, 50th Regular Session, Plenary Verbatim Record of 9th Meeting, 27 September. Doc. A/50/PV.9.

Swaraj, Sushma. 2017. Statement at the General Assembly, 72nd Regular Session, Plenary Verbatim Record of 19th Meeting, 23 September. Doc. A/72/PV.19.

———. 2018. Statement at the General Assembly, 73rd Regular Session, Plenary Verbatim Record of 14th meeting, 29 September. Doc. A/73/PV.14.

Swart, Lydia, 2013. 'Reform of the Security Council, 2007–13'. In *Governing and Managing Change at the United Nations: Security Council Reform from 1945 to September* 2013, edited by Lydia Swart and Jonas von Freiesleben, 23–59. New York: Center for UN Reform Education.

Swart, Lydia, and Jonas von Freiesleben, eds. 2013. *Governing and Managing Change at the United Nations: Security Council Reform from 1945 to September 2013*. New York: Center for UN Reform Education.

Tawale, S. N. 1975. *India's Economic Diplomacy at the United Nations*. Meerut: Meenakshi Prakashan.

Thakur, R., and Thomas Weiss. 2010. *The UN and Global Governance: An Unfinished Journey*. Bloomington, IN: Indiana University Press.

Thant, U. 1978. *View from the UN*. London: David and Charles.

Tharoor, Shashi. 2010. Statement at the General Assembly Special Political Committee, 65th Session, Summary Record of 16th Meeting, 26 October. Doc. A/C.4/65/SR.16.

The Wire. 2019. 'Six Charts to Make Sense of India's Budget for Foreign Policy.' Available at: https://thewire.in/diplomacy/budget-mea-foreign-policy-charts, accessed on 7 September 2019.

UNCIP. 1948. Resolution for Ceasefire Order and Truce Agreement, 13 August. Doc. S/995.

———. 1949. Second Interim Report of the Rapporteur, 10 January. Doc. S/1196.

UNCTAD. 2014. *World Economic Situation and Prospects 2014*. New York: United Nations. Available at: http://unctad.org/en/PublicationsLibrary/wesp2014_en.pdf, accessed on 11 January 2016.

UNHRC. 2011. Human Rights Council, 17th Session, Resolution 17/8 on Proclamation of 19th August as the International Day of Remembrance of and Tribute to the Victims of Terrorism, adopted at 33rd Meeting, 16 June. Doc. A/HRC/17/8.

United Nations. 1993. Report of the Secretary General to the General Assembly on the Work of the Organization, New York. Doc. A/48/1 (Supplement).

———. 1996. *Blue Helmets: A Review of the United Nations Peacekeeping*, 3rd ed. New York: Department of Public Information.

———. 1998. *50 Years of UN Peacekeeping*. New York: Department of Public Information.

———. 2000a. Report of the Panel on United Nations Peace Operations. Doc. A/55/305.

———. 2000b. 'We the Peoples: The Role of the United Nations in the 21st Century.' Report of the Secretary General. Doc. A/54/2000.

———. 2000c. 'United Nations Millennium Declaration.' Resolution adopted by the General Assembly, 8 September. Doc. A/RES/55/2.

———. 2015. *The Millennium Development Goals Report*, 2015. New York: Department of Economic and Social Affairs.

———. 2019. Operational Activities for Development of the United Nations system: Report of the Secretary-General, 22 April. Doc. A/74/73/Add.2.

———. 2020. *World Economic Situation and Prospects, 2020*. New York: Department of Economic and Social Affairs.

United States. 1994. Statement at the General Assembly, 49th Regular Session, Plenary Verbatim Record of 30th Meeting, 13 October. Doc. A/49/PV.30002E

Vajpayee, A. B. 2000. Statement at the General Assembly Millennium Summit, 55th Regular Session, Plenary Verbatim Record of 7th Meeting, 8 September. Doc. A/55/PV.7.

———. 2003. Statement at the General Assembly, 58th Regular Session, Plenary Verbatim Record of 11th Meeting, 25 September. Doc. A/58/PV.11.

Venkat, Vidya. 2015. 'India in no position to meet SDGs'. *The Hindu*, September 10. Available at: https://www.thehindu.com/news/national/india-in-no-position-to-meet-sdgs/article7635948.ece, accessed on 12 October 2018.

Vijapur, Abdulrahim P. 2010. *Human Rights in International Relations*. New Delhi: Manak Publications.

Vijapur, Abdulrahim P., and K. Savitri. 2006. 'The International Covenants on Human Rights: An Overview'. *India Quarterly*, 62(2): 1–37.

Vijayaraghavan, A. 2007. Statement at the Administrative and Budgetary Committee of the General Assembly, 61st Regular Session, Summary Record of 14th Meeting, 8 January. Doc. A/C.5/61/SR.14.

Von Einsiedel, Sabastian, David Malone and Bruno S. Ugarte, eds. 2015. *The UN Security Council in the 21st Century*, 139–156. Boulder, CO: Lynne Rienner.
Von Freiesleben, Jonas. 2013. 'Reform of the Security Council, 1945–2008'. In *Governing and Managing Change at the United Nations: Security Council Reform from 1945 to September 2013*, edited by Lydia Swart and Jonas von Freiesleben, 1–22. New York: Center for UN Reform Education.
Waz, J., and P. Weiser. 2012. 'Internet Governance: The Role of Multistakeholder Organizations'. *Journal on Telecommunications & High Technology Law*, 10(2): 331–349.
Weiss, T. 2000. 'Governance, Good Governance and Global Governance: Conceptual and Actual Challenges'. *Third World Quarterly*, 21(5): 795–814.
Whitman, Jim, ed. 2009. *Global Governance*. Basingstoke: Palgrave Macmillan.
World Bank. 2012. *Global Development Finance*. Washington, DC: World Bank.
Yadav, Manish K. 2014. 'Global War on Terror a Clear and Present Danger, India's Stand on It in the United Nations and Other Forums with a South Asian Perspective'. *International Journal of Social Science Review*, 2(1): 74–85.
Yearbook of International Organizations (1981–2019). Leiden: Brill, for Union of International Associations, Especially Volume 5 on Statistics.
Young, O. R. 1999. *Governance in World Affairs*. Ithaca, NY: Cornell University Press.
Ziai, Aram. 2011. 'The Millennium Development Goals: Back to the Future?' *Third World Quarterly*, 32(1): 27–43.

About the Author

C. S. R. Murthy is Professor at School of International Studies, JNU, Delhi. He has a total teaching experience of 35 years. He was Chairperson of the Centre for International Politics, Organization and Disarmament for three terms, besides serving as Director of Human Rights Studies Programme during 2013–15 at JNU. He was Book Review Editor (2000–2003) and then the Chief Editor for *International Studies* (2004–2007). Professor Murthy was visiting fellow/professor at Keele (UK), Columbia (USA) Universities, Sciences Pro (France) and Friedrich Ebert Foundation (Germany). He has authored *India's Diplomacy in the United Nations: Problems and Perspectives* (1993) and edited three volumes on *Nonaligned and the United Nations* (1987), *India in Tomorrow's United Nations* (1995) and *Five Decades of Cooperation between India and UNESCO* (1997). He has contributed nearly 60 chapters in edited books and research articles in journals such as *Conflict, Security and Development*; *Comparative Contemporary Review of the Middle East*; *Global Society*; *India Quarterly*; *International Studies*; *South Asian Survey* and so on. Further, Professor Murthy served as co-convenor for two annual all-India international and area studies conventions held in Delhi during 2013–2019.

Index

Abdullah, Farooq, 213
Afghanistan, India's interest in security and prosperity, of, 101
Air India Flight Kanishk, terror attack, 167
Airy idolization, 9
Al-Qaida
  Afghanistan's security and stabilization, 52
  and Islamic State, financial sanctions, 104, 185, 187
  Pakistan's interference and, 252
  terror camps, and, 168
  terrorism, and, 184
  against United States, 169, 256
Annan, Kofi, 194, 213, 229, 241
Annual Reports of Ministry of External Affairs, 190
Ansari, Hamid, 213
Arab–Israel conflict
  India and Pakistan conflict, and, 143–144
  India's participation in, 26
  resolution of, 100, 110
Assam National Register of Citizens process, 231
Association of Southeast Asian Nations (ASEAN), 238

Bhagwati, P. N., 210
Bosnia–Herzegovina, conflict in, 32
  military intervention, Council authorizing, 101–102
  peacekeeping troops, by India, 106
Bottom-up Internet governance, 243
Boutros-Ghali, Boutros, 158, 213

Brazil, Russia, India, China and South Africa (BRICS), elite group, 253
Bretton Woods Institutions, 189–190
Brookings Institution, 239

Cambodia conflict, 27–28
Carter administration, 102
Climate change, in India, 61–62
  Habitat Agenda, 62–63
  non-conventional threats, as, 109
  renewable energy, and, 62
  2015 Paris Agreement on, 62
Cold War peacekeeping
  non-participation and participation in
  Congo operation, 126
  India's contribution, 125–126
  India's non-participation, 126–127
  military observer missions, 125
Commission on Global Governance, 235
Commonwealth of Independent States (CIS), 142
Comprehensive Test Ban Treaty (CTBT), 152
Congo operation, 122
  India's contribution in, 126
Consumer Unity and Trust Society, 237
Contemporary development discourse and diplomacy of India at UN, 189
developed countries, faulting policies of

global trade regime, 199
OECD DAC countries, aid
  flows from, 197–198
South–South cooperation, by
  India, 200
economic diplomacy
  challenges, 191
  dynamics of, 190
  features of, 190
  liberalization, and, 190
  rural farming, crisis in, 190
MDGs and Post-2015 Agenda,
  194
  challenges for, 194
  development agenda, 196
  domestic socioeconomic welfare
    schemes, by India, 195
  economic crisis in 2008, and,
    195
  global capital unsettled
    economies, 195
  human development and, 194
  unemployment levels, 195
  women and children, health
    issues affecting, 194
reworking group strategy
  canny negotiator, 206
  environmentalism, and, 205
  global economic wellbeing, 205
  per capita GHG emissions, 205
  role of UN organs, revitalization
    of, 203–204
UN development activities,
  growing profile as resource
  provider to
  aid provider, profile as, 203
  assessed contributions, 200
  disaster relief funds, 203
  grants and loans to foreign
    countries, 203
  multilateralism, 201
  regular budget, contribution to,
    201
  voluntary contributions, 202

UN instrumentality, and India's
  role, 191
  approach to problems, 192
  economic flows among member
    countries, 192–193
  funding for, 193–194
  NAM, Group of 77 (G77) and
    UNCTAD, formation of,
    192
  policy initiative, 192
  support for larger goals of, 192
Contemporary peacekeeping
  India's contribution in
  Cambodia operation, in,
    128–129
  ceasefire line, and Pakistan, 133
  and Indian police, 128–130
  missions in India, 132–133
  non-contribution, 131–132
  pre-deployment training, 128
  statistics and, 130
  Nobel Peace Prize, 127
  time-tested technique and, 127
Convention on Rights of Persons
  with Disability, 210
Copenhagen Summit on Climate
  Change, 204
Counter Terrorism Committee
  (CTC), 104
Counter-Terrorism Implementation
  Task Force (CTITF), 170
Cyprus, territorial integrity and, 97

Declaration on Measures to
  Eliminate International
  Terrorism, 167
1986 Declaration on the Right to
  Development, 212
de Cuellar, Javier Perez, 115
Desai, Nitin, 241
Digital India Programme, 241
Dixon, Owen, 157
Doha Development Round
  negotiations, 238

Ebola emergency in African
    countries, 201
Economic Community of West
    African Countries
    (ECOWAS), 142
Entrepreneurship and market-
    oriented approach, 42

Foreign policy of India, 45–46
Forest Rights Act, 214

Gandhi, Mahatma, 7
Ganguly, Meenakshi, 230
General Agreement on Tariffs and
    Trade (GATT), 43
Global counter terrorism strategy, 168
    caveats and consensus
    comprehensive approach, 179
    Global Counter-Terrorism
        Strategy resolution, 180
    Global Strategy, 179
    human rights in, 179–180
    Islam and Islamic beliefs, 179
    moderate views, 178–179
    root causes of terrorism, 179
    state-sponsored terrorism, 179
Global Governance and India
    contending models
    bottom-up approach to, 243
    characteristics of, 240
    concern areas, 242
    economic and social benefits, 244
    global regime, 242
    issues associated with, 241
    mechanism for, 244
    multi-stakeholder model,
        242–243
    outline of its views, on, 245
    power and predicament, 241
    global policymaking forums, in,
        237–238
    India's policy approaches, 239
    international relations, ordering
        principle in, 237

key partners, bilateral relations
    with, 239
multilateral diplomacy, 239
Globalization and development, and
    India, 58
    food reserves, and, 60
    post-2015 development agenda,
        60–61
    UN, role in, 59–60
Goa liberation, 250
Gopinathan, A., 220
Graham, Frank, 157
Group of four (G4), 49–50, 82
Gujral, I.K., 24–27, 35, 42, 44
Guterres, Antonio, 170

Hammarskjold, Dag, 121–123
High Commissioner's report on
    human rights in Kashmir,
    220
High-Level Panel on Threats,
    Challenges and Change,
    168
Highly Indebted Poor Countries
    (HIPC) Initiative, 200
Human rights
    civil war situations in Africa, 108
    global security, threats to, India's
        concern on
    Indian Prime Minister's view
        on, 108
    terrorism and proliferation of
        WMDs, 108
    terrorist-criminal drug-
        trafficking nexus, 107
Human Rights Committee, 210
    anti-India resolution, by
        Pakistan, 212–213
Human Rights Council (See
    Human Rights Council)
    establishment, India's views on, 67
India and core human rights
    instruments, status on, 211
India's record at UN

actionable and justiceable at international level, 209
domestic legislation and implementation, normative instruments for, 207
short-lived internationalism, 208–209
statism, sustained shift towards, 209–214
issues, 39–40
Human Rights Council
establishment, India's views on, 67
India's participation, in, 214–215
critical assessment, 230–231
friendly and like-minded countries, teaming up with, 228–230
human rights as foreign policy tool, politicization of, concern over, 220–221
organizational concerns, 221–223
Pakistan's propaganda on Kashmir, countering, 219–221
resolution, 217
right to development, continuing focus on, 218
UPR cycles, managing feedback in, 223–227
violations, and, 216

IGF meet, 247
Indian Ocean Rim Countries (IORC), 238
India–Pakistan conflict. *See also* Jammu and Kashmir, question
UN involvement, 143, 144, 148
action–reaction process, 145
armed conflict, 256
British-declassified documents, 159
cessation of hostilities, 153–154
Charter framework, 148
Charter mandate, 148
China's role in, 147–148
Communist influence and China, 147
decision-making dynamics of, 146
deep-rooted causes, 150
diplomatic conduct, patterns of, 145
end of Cold War, and, 147
field observation, 154–156
high profile legal battle, 146
imposing sanctions, unlikelihood of, 161–162
assessment, 162–164
India's concerns and sentiments, 145
India's 'hegemonic' tendencies, 145
initiatives in, 147
international conflicts, and, 148
issues in, 146
Junagadh, accession of, 150
Kashmir question, 147–148
Kulbhushan Jadhav, 146
LoC ceasefire violations, 256
Mumbai terror attacks, 152
non-condemnation, 151–152
nuclear tests, 152
organizing armed intrusions, 151
pacify on priority, 149–151
Pakistan-based terror networks, 256
Pakistan-sponsored intrusion into Kargil, 151
Pakistan views, 144–145
previous resolutions adopted, 150
resolution, roadblocks to mediation, 156–159
plebiscite, 159–161
situation across LoC, 155
Soviet mediation, and, 158

Soviet Union and United States,
    initiatives in, 147
    time-tested and well-established
      practice, 149–150
    zero-sum equations between, 146
India–UN Development Partnership
    Fund, 201
Indira Gandhi's tenure
    Bangladesh, emergence of, 16–17
    foreign capitals, visits to, 17
    nuclear weapons, and, 15–16
    Pakistan
      East Pakistan, liberation of,
        16–17
      relationship with, 15–16
    Soviet support to India, 17–18
International Commission of Jurists,
    213
International Committee of Red
    Cross (ICRC), 213
International Convention against
    Torture, 210
International Covenant on Civil and
    Political Rights (ICCPR),
    210
International Covenant on Economic,
    Social and Cultural Rights
    (ICESCR), 210
International Monetary Fund (IMF),
    193
International Telecommunication
    Regulations (ITRs), 244
International Telecommunication
    Union (ITU), 240, 243
Internet Corporation for Assigned
    Names and Numbers
    (ICANN), 240, 247
Iraq and Kuwait, boundary line
    between, after Gulf War,
    96–97
Iraq–Iran war and Namibia's
    transition, 18
Iraq–Kuwait conflict, 28–29, 103
Ireland-sponsored resolution, 216

Jammu and Kashmir, question, 11–12
    communal violence after partition,
      150
    human rights, and, 219–220
    military confrontation, 150
    Pakistan
      cross-border terror, 251
      human rights violations in,
        claims about, 222
      internationalize, attempts to, 251
      intervention in, 221
      propaganda on, 219–221
    tribal invasion of, 151
Jarring, Gunnar, 157
Jetley, Vijay, 139

Kargil war, 133
Khan, Ayub, 150
Khurshid, Salman, 213
Kishwar, Madhu, 230
Korea War, and India's role in, 99–100

Lakhdar Brahimi Panel, 122
Lankesh, Gauri, 231
Libya case, resolution 731
Little Assembly, 109

Mahatma Gandhi National Rural
    Employment Guarantee
    Act, 214
Market-plus model of development,
    42
Marrakesh agreements, 42–43
McNaughton, A. G. L., 157
Mehta, Hansa, 209
Menon, Krishna, 14, 98, 126, 160
Millennium Summit, 189, 199
Mishra, Brajesh, 213
Modi, Narendra, 135, 158, 186, 196
Mogadishu
    ethnic conflict in, 102
Mudaliar, Ramaswamy, Sir, 191–192
Multilateral Governance of Internet,
    India's approach, 232

global governance and order,
theoretical approaches to,
233–235
IGOs and INGOs, number of,
236
as process, 235–237
Mumbai terror attacks, 152
Munich, terrorist attack in, 108

Nair, Ravi, 230
National human right institutions
(NHRIs), 216
National Human Rights Commission,
40, 213
Nehru and India
death and domestic problems,
127
familial successors, and, 250
Indira and Rajiv Gandhi's, work
of, 250
Jammu and Kashmir question,
11–12
Nehruvian ideas and inclinations,
8–9
post-Nehru India's foreign policy
administration, 250
Neutral Nations Repatriation
Commission, 10–11, 99
Nimitz, Chester, 160
Non-Aligned Movement (NAM), 24
and G-77, 190
Non-permanent member in Council,
India's experience in, 89
abstentions in, 94
approach to UN, participation, 91
conflict situations, 91–92
consensus and partnership, accent
on, 110–113
decision-making, 90
diverse perspectives on
military action, authorizations
for, 101–102
new threats, concerns on,
107–109

overreach to impinge on, role of
other organs, opposition to,
109–110
peacekeeping, need and risks
of, realistic appraisal of,
104–107
transparency in sanctions,
unintended suffering,
102–104
features of, participation, 95
foreign policy principles and goals
force use, opposition to, 97–99
peaceful resolution, advocacy of,
99–101
sovereignty and territorial
integrity, 96–97
non-discrimination among, 92
participation, 92
resolutions, 92
voting, and, 92
Nuclear Non-Proliferation Treaty
(NPT), 15–16
Nuclear policy, in India
nuclear disarmament, 57–58
WMDs, acquiring, 57

Office of High Commissioner for
Human Rights (OHCHR),
219
Open Working Group, 196
Organization of American States
(OAS), 142
Organization of Economic
Cooperation and
Development, 240

Pakistan's Peshawar, terror attacks
against school children in,
177
Palestine, and India's support,
100–101
Pan Am aircraft over Lockerbie
bombing, 167
Pandit, Vijaya Lakshmi, 10, 73

Partial Test Ban Treaty, 10
Peace-Building Commission, 66–67
Peacekeeping operations, 4, 15, 18, 28, 32, 35–36, 255. *See also* Cold War peacekeeping
   financing crisis, 137–138
   India's contribution
     Cold War context, and, 124
     emergence, and, 121
     foreign policy, and, 120
     guiding principles, 122
     Indian army, and, 138–139
     international peace, 120
     joint working group, with US, 140
     non-aligned mode, 124
     non-partisan credentials, 123
     regionalization of, 124
     renewal and change, 135–137
     statistics of, 116–117
     UNEF, establishment of, 121
     world affairs, and, 120–121
   India's participation in, 117–119
   India's support to
     Bosnia–Herzegovina, 106
     Cambodia and Democratic Congo, 107
     Gulf War against Iraq, 106
     Liberia and Somalia, 107
     mandate renewal, 105
     multidimensional association of India, with UN on, 105
     South Sudan and Sudan, 106–107
     views, by India, 106
     Yugoslavia, 106
   India's stand on UNEF, 104–105
   Western media, negative stories about, 139
Pearson, Lester, 126
Permanent Mission of India (PMI) to UN, 208
Post-2015 Development Agenda, 196
Post-Cold War years, peace and security, and UN, 35–37, 255
Prevention, Prohibition and Redressal of Sexual Harassment of Women at Workplace Act, 214
Protection of Human Rights Act, 214

Race-based politics, 7–8
Rajiv Gandhi's tenure
   Afghan situation, 18
   environment protection, 18–19
   INF Treaty, 19
   Khalistan extremists, 18–19
   nuclear disarmament, 19
   US attack on Libya, view on, 19–20
Rao, Narasimha, 24–25, 32, 34, 42, 45, 91–92
Rau, B. N., 98
Refugee Convention, 209
Responsibility to Protect (RtoP), concept, 55
Rights of Persons with Disabilities Act, 214
Right to Education Act, 214
Right to Information Act, 214
Rio Summit, 43
Rwanda and Srebrenisca, genocide in, 55
Rwanda Mission, 138

San Francisco Conference, 7
Saxena, N.C., 196
Security concerns of India
   Afghanistan, conflict in, and, 51–52
   arms and light weapons, 56–57
   development-related issues, 57
   humanitarian intervention, concept of, 55
   Middle East, political stability in, 53
   Palestine, and, 52–53
   peacekeeping missions and, 55

regional and international, 51
RtoP, 55–56
Syria and Yemen, civil wars in, and,
    53–54
terrorism, and, 54
Security Council, 69
  Article 23 of Charter, 70–71
  Counterterrorism Committee,
    engaging with, 180–183
  credibility and legitimacy, 73
  India's candidature, for, 73
    articulation, 78–79
    aspiration, 82–84
    economic rise, 77
    G4 initiative, 85–86
    like-minded countries, and,
      81–82
    nuclear weapon and missile tests,
      76–77
    permanent five (P5), and, 85
    permanent seat, claim for, 74–76
    positions, adjustments of, 80
    UfC countries and, 84
    veto power, and, 80–81
  international peace and security,
    71–72
  responsible and reliable partner,
    India as, 77
  membership, 70
  permanent, lack of unity among,
    73
  non-permanent membership,
    70–71
  performance, 73
  purpose of, 70
  Security Council Resolution 1325,
    54–55, 72
  text-based negotiations, 87
  'veto' power, 72–73
Sen, Nirupam, 165
Shanghai Cooperation Organization
    (SCO), 238
Sibal, Kanwal, 230
Sierra Leone mission, 139–141

Singh, Arun, 220–221
Singh, Manmohan, 195, 213
Sinha, Yashwant, 194
Somalia
  ethnic conflict in, 102
  military intervention, Council
    authorizing, 101–102
South Africa
  mandatory ban on sale of arms
    against, 102
  military adventurism, 98–99
South–South cooperation, 200
South West Africa People's
    Organisation (SWAPO),
    98–99
Special Procedures, 222
Sri Lanka, in rehabilitation,
    resettlement and
    reconstruction projects,
    India's role, 229
Suez crisis, 11
Syria
  national reconciliation and end to
    violence, India's role in, 101
  Yemen, civil wars in, and, 53–54,
    111–112

Taliban, 168
Taliban/Al-Qaida Sanctions
    Committee, 256
Tashkent agreement, 158
Technical Cooperation Voluntary
    Fund, 201
Terrorism
  comprehensive convention,
    prioritization of
    multiple and growing
    manifestations, 171
  Global counterterrorism strategy,
    Global counterterrorism
    strategy
  India's battle against, 165–166
  political delegitimization, national
    instrument as

India's approach, 176
India's counter terror approach, 175
  scale of suffering, 176–177
  September 2001 attacks, after, 175
  terrorist groups responsible, banning and tough sanctions against, 177
  tragic and indiscriminate killings, 177
  Russian Federation, convention proposed, 168
sanctions
  transparent and effective implementation, pleading for, 184–186
Secretary-General, recommendation by, 168
Security Council Counter Terrorism Committee, engaging with, 180
  areas of concern, by India, 181–182
  coordination and information exchanges, 182
  emerging threats, tackling, 181
  national anti-terrorist legislation, 182
  Resolutions 1373 and 1566, 183
  Security Council Resolution 1373, 181
  subsidiary bodies, 182–183
  victim of terrorist attacks, 183
  zero-tolerance approach, 183
UN action against, 167–171
  administrative structure, 170
  counter terrorism, aspect of, 170
  Hafiz Muhammad Saeed, notorious activities, 178
  India and Pakistan diplomats, counter comments, 178
  India's revised draft counter-terror convention, 172–173

omnibus resolution, 169
Osama bin Laden, Pakistan sheltered, 178
path-breaking measures, 169
terror attacks on 11 September 2001, by Al-Qaida, 169–172
terrorists and terror camps, sheltering of, 168
troubling manifestation, 169
Thant, U., 150
Third World solidarity, 24
Trump, Donald, 158
Tunis Agenda, 241

Union of International Associations, 238
United Arab Republic
  India's support to, to withdrawal of UNEF, 104–105
United Nations Force in Cyprus (UNFICYP), 105–106
United Nations (UN)
  Afro-Asian opinion, 11
  Bosnia-Herzegovina, conflict in, 32
  Cold War era, in
    India's role in, 11
  India's economic diplomacy at (*See* Contemporary development discourse and diplomacy of India at UN)
  India's participation in, 8
    Arab-Israeli problem, 26
    Cambodia conflict, 27–28
    country's political leaders, and, 48–49
    development system, and, 63
    ECOSOC's mandate, 65
    India-Pakistan military escalation, 13
    Indira Gandhi's role, 15–16
    Iraq-Kuwait conflict, 28–29
    Jammu and Kashmir question, 11–12

Menon's role, 14
Nehru's role, 10
non-aligned approach, 11
peace making and peacekeeping, 35–36, 41
post-Cold War era, 23–25
pro-Kuwait US-led coalition, 30–31
reform of UN, 66
Security Council reform process, 49–50
Yugoslavia, aerial bombing, and, 33
International Development Association, 10
international peace and security, 9–10
Iraq–Iran war and Namibia's transition, 18
marginalization of UN, 44
nuclear arms race, India's views in, 10
post-Cold War years, peace and security, and, 35–37
Prime Ministers and India's policy, and, 6–7
socio-economic development, of underdeveloped countries, 43
UN Charter, 7–8
UN Commission on Human Rights (UNCHR), 40
UN Commission on India and Pakistan (UNCIP), 156
UN Committee for Internet-Related Policies (UN-CIRP), 244
UN Conference on Trade and Development (UNCTAD), 42
UN Development Programme (UNDP), 10
UN Economic Development Administration, proposal, 10

UN Emergency Force (UNEF), 11
UN India–Pakistan Observer Mission (UNIPOM), 133–134, 154
UN Interim Force in Lebanon (UNIFIL), 106
UN Military Observer Group in India and Pakistan (UNMOGIP), 132
UN Office for South–South Cooperation, 201
UN Truce Supervision Organization (UNTSO), 125
United States and Soviet Union rivalry between
  India's approach to, 6–8
Uniting for Consensus' (UfC) group, 84
Uniting for Peace, 109
Universal Declaration of Human Rights (UDHR), 208
Universal Periodic Review (UPR), 215
Unlawful Activities Prevention Act 1968, 166
Uruguay Round trade negotiations, 42–43

Vajpayee, Atal Bihari, government, 213
  security and disarmament-related issue, 38–39
  Security Council, and, 76

Weapons of mass destruction (WMDs), 19, 57, 107–108, 166, 184
Western Sahara situation, 161
World Bank, 193
World Conference on Human Rights in Vienna, 213
World Conference on International Telecommunications (WCIT), 244

World Intellectual Property
    Organization, 240
World Summit, 189, 214
World Summit on the Information
    Society (WSIS), 243
World Trade Organization (WTO),
    43, 199, 236, 238–239
WTO Doha Development Agenda,
    199

Young, Andrew, 102
Yugoslavia, 255
    aerial bombing, and UN, 33
    India support, with
        India support to,
    UNPROFOR in,
        establishment of,
        106
    sanctions on, 103